COGNITIVE CONTROL THERAPY
WITH CHILDREN AND ADOLESCENTS

Pergamon Titles of Related Interest

Dangel/Polster TEACHING CHILD MANAGEMENT SKILLS
Feindler/Ecton ADOLESCENT ANGER CONTROL:
Cognitive-Behavioral Techniques
Gelfand/Hartmann CHILD BEHAVIOR ANALYSIS AND THERAPY,
Second Edition
Morris/Kratochwill THE PRACTICE OF CHILD THERAPY
Morris/Kratochwill TREATING CHILDREN'S FEARS AND PHOBIAS:
A Behavioral Approach
Schwartz/Johnson PSYCHOPATHOLOGY OF CHILDHOOD:
A Clinical-Experimental Approach, Second Edition
Varni CLINICAL BEHAVIORAL PEDIATRICS:
An Interdisciplinary Biobehavioral Approach

Related Journals *

CHILD ABUSE & NEGLECT
CLINICAL PSYCHOLOGY REVIEW
JOURNAL OF CHILD PSYCHOLOGY AND PSYCHIATRY
JOURNAL OF SCHOOL PSYCHOLOGY

*Free sample copies available upon request

PSYCHOLOGY PRACTITIONER GUIDEBOOKS

EDITORS

Arnold P. Goldstein, Syracuse University
Leonard Krasner, SUNY at Stony Brook
Sol. L. Garfield, Washington University

COGNITIVE CONTROL THERAPY WITH CHILDREN AND ADOLESCENTS

SEBASTIANO SANTOSTEFANO

Hall-Mercer Children's Center of McLean Hospital
and Harvard Medical School

PERGAMON PRESS

New York   Oxford   Toronto   Sydney   Paris   Frankfurt

Pergamon Press Offices:

U.S.A.   Pergamon Press Inc., Maxwell House, Fairview Park, Elmsford, New York 10523, U.S.A.

U.K.   Pergamon Press Ltd., Headington Hill Hall, Oxford OX3 0BW, England

CANADA   Pergamon Press Canada Ltd., Suite 104, 150 Consumers Road, Willowdale, Ontario M2J 1P9, Canada

AUSTRALIA   Pergamon Press (Aust.) Pty. Ltd., P.O. Box 544, Potts Point, NSW 2011, Australia

FRANCE   Pergamon Press SARL, 24 rue des Ecoles, 75240 Paris, Cedex 05, France

FEDERAL REPUBLIC   Pergamon Press GmbH, Hammerweg 6,
OF GERMANY   D-6242 Kronberg-Taunus, Federal Republic of Germany

Copyright © 1985 Pergamon Press Inc.

Library of Congress Cataloging in Publication Data

Santostefano, Sebastiano, 1929–

  Cognitive control therapy with children and adolescents.

  (Psychology practitioner guidebooks)
  1. Learning disabilities. 2. Cognitive therapy.
3. Child psychotherapy. 4. Adolescent psychotherapy.
I. Title. II. Series. [DNLM: 1. Cognition – in
adolescence. 2. Cognition – in infancy & childhood.
3. Psychotherapy – in adolescence. 4. Psychotherapy –
in infancy & childhood. WS 350.2 S237c]
RJ506.L4S26 1985   618.92'89   84-26647
ISBN 0-08-031581-X
ISBN 0-08-031580-1 (pbk.)

Printed in Great Britain by A. Wheaton & Co. Ltd., Exeter

To Susan, our cave, and its treasures: Cristiano, Jessica,
Stephanie, Natalie, and Damon

Contents

List of Figures

List of Tables

Preface

This book describes a cognitively oriented, psychodynamic method of psychotherapy, called cognitive control therapy (CCT), designed to treat children and adolescents who suffer from both learning disabilities and serious behavior disorders. Since first reported (Santostefano, 1967, 1969a, 1969b), and detailed 10 years later (Santostefano, 1978), CCT has been evolving in my clinical practice and that of colleagues, and like most therapeutic innovations, has been undergoing continuous change, shaped by therapeutic necessity, clinical experiences, and research findings.

Because this update of CCT is being presented in the midst of a cognitive revolution and a rash of different types of cognitive therapies, and because I hope to interest psychotherapists from various persuasions, I would like to provide a broad historical context within which the reader could consider cognitive psychotherapies and CCT in particular.

It is hard to imagine that there was once a time when cognition was essentially ignored by psychologists conducting research and treating patients. But, this was the case in the decades prior to the middle 1950s. Why was there little interest in cognition during this period? One reason, noted at the time by Fritz Heider was the rise of behaviorism with its "glorification of the skin" (Gruber, Hammond, & Jesser, 1957, p. 203). Another was the preoccupation by psychoanalysis with unconscious motivation, feelings, and psychic conflict.

The Department of Psychology of the University of Colorado convened a symposium on May 12, 1955 and invited leading psychologists of the day to discuss cognition because, the sponsors believed, "For a long time psychology in America has slighted what may be considered to be its ultimate purpose, the scientific understanding of man's cognitive behavior," (Gruber, Hammond, & Jesser, 1957, p. v). The sponsors also hoped that the published discussions would stimulate theoretical developments and observations and return cognition to its rightful position as a major lens through which psychology studied and treated human beings.

Several motifs emerged from the presentations and debates: (a) cognition is at the center of a person's adaptations to environments; (b) the en-

vironments to which a person adapts are essentially cognitive representations, or symbols; and (c) underlying cognitive structures are codes that
make representations possible; that is, cognitive structures determine
what pictures, so to speak, a person takes of a specific environment and
the actions a person engages.

Looking back, it appears that the Colorado symposium, now viewed as
one of the critical moments in recent psychological history, accomplished
its goal. The publication of its proceedings (Gruber, Hammond, & Jesser,
1957) proved to be one of the major forces that sparked the cognitive revolution, which rapidly spread during the 1960s and 1970s and continues
today.

As the cognitive revolution unfolded, two camps emerged. One, influenced by psychoanalytic theory, flourished under the label of ''the new
look in perception,'' emphasizing the need to correlate cognition, motivation, and personality functioning. The other, influenced by Piagetian
psychology, and soon after by learning and behavior theories, studied cognition as a domain separate from needs and personality, especially its unconscious aspects. From the 1950s, these two approaches followed quite
separate courses in spite of the fact that they shared a basic point of view:
that cognition plays a pivotal role in adaptation.

Beginning in the 1970s, the momentum of cognitive research in the psychodynamic camp declined sharply (Erdelyi, 1974; Santostefano & Reider,
1984) with interest turning to topics such as object-relations theory, self
psychology, and borderline states. In contrast, the momentum of cognitive
research intensified in the Piagetian and behaviorist camp. Further, it was
during this period of time that cognitive research began to influence the
way professionals viewed and practiced psychotherapy. As a result, relatively few proposals have been made of cognitively-oriented psychodynamic therapy (e.g., Feather & Rhoades, 1972; Wachtel, 1977; Wiener,
1968) while numerous proposals have been offered of cognitively-oriented
behavior therapies (references are cited in the main text).

In both camps, the proposals maintain the point of view that cognition
plays a central role in the formation of psychopathology, and each emphasizes the need to modify how a person thinks rather than what a person
thinks. In this sense, both camps embrace one of the motifs of the Colorado symposium, namely, that cognition is at the center of a person's adaptation to environments. However, beyond this common position, there
is a fundamental difference. Psychodynamic-cognitive therapies have included the other motifs of the Colorado symposium: that underlying, *unconscious* cognitive structures, which code and represent experiences and
which are an integral part of the personality functioning, should be the
targets of intervention, preferably within a transference process. Behavioral-cognitive therapies emphasize identifying and replacing a patient's
conscious maladaptive beliefs and self-statements.

More important than this difference is the fact that many behavioral-cognitive therapies ignore, or in some cases explicitly oppose, the methods and concepts of psychodynamic psychotherapy. In my view, it is regretable that the two camps are isolated to such a degree, when so much can be gained if therapists take fibers from each position and experiment with weaving entirely new fabrics to guide the practice of psychotherapy. This point is underscored by Marmor and Woods (1980) in a recent volume devoted to the interface between psychodynamic and behavioral therapies, ''It is clearly just as insufficient for dynamic psychotherapists to ignore the rich literature in behavioral learning as for the behavioral therapist to ignore the manner by which unconscious processes and conflicts shape learning'' (p. xii).

It is on this note that I turn the reader's attention to CCT. Although CCT originated and has been growing within the new look approach to cognition, its rationale and techniques represent an integration of aspects of psychodynamic psychology and behavioral psychology as well as developmental psychology.

If viewed through the psychodynamic lens, CCT emphasizes that: (a) cognition is a set of nonverbal and verbal conscious and unconscious strategies that copy and flexibly coordinate the requirements of information both from changing external environments and from changing internal worlds and fantasies, emotions, and representations of past experiences, conceptualized as personal metaphors; (b) whenever cognition maintains an inflexible coordination between these two worlds of information, maladaptations result; (c) before changing a person's conscious beliefs and self-statements, it is necessary first to change deeper, nonverbal cognitive structures, which produce cognitive rigidity; (d) restructuring cognitive strategies is best accomplished within a transference process (i.e., when the child repeats in the office the same maladaptive cognitive-behavioral-emotional strategies and pathological personal metaphors that impede successful learning and adapting in everyday environments); (e) whenever possible the child is taught to know about knowing—that is, to become conscious of his/her unique cognitive equipment and the way this equipment operates.

If viewed through the cognitive-behavioral lens, CCT emphasizes: (a) the importance of specifying cognitive target behaviors and fitting interventions to these behaviors; (b) the need to include behavioral events in the treatment process in addition to wishes, fantasies, and feelings; (c) the need to relate thoughts to actions and actions to thought; and (d) the value of directing therapy.

If viewed through the developmental lens, CCT emphasizes that: (a) some cognitive-personality dysfunctions originate during the first three years of life, before language is fully developed, and therefore the child is deficient in symbolic functioning and ill-equipped to put into the words the manner in which she conducts her life; (b) cognitive-behavioral structures differentiate as they assimilate and accommodate to new and more complex information, and therefore cognitive therapy should emphasize a sequence of tasks and experiences which are carefully graded in complexity.

CCT integrates these three points of view into one set of techniques, which is used in an initial phase of highly directed therapy, and during which unconscious and conscious cognitive structures are rehabilitated. CCT also integrates these three points of view into another set of techniques, which is used in a later phase of nondirected therapy, during which the child applies newly acquired cognitive tools to reform personal pathological metaphors and beliefs.

The dynamically-oriented therapist, accustomed to a nondirected format, may be turned away by the highly structured, directed phase of CCT. On the other hand, behaviorally-oriented therapists, accustomed to directed therapy methods, but less familiar with addressing fantasy, process, and transference may be turned away by the nondirected phase of CCT or by the emphasis given symbolic functioning and transference. I recognize that therapists from either persuasion must examine this book initially through their respective, preexisting "categories" and beliefs about cognitive therapy. Borrowing from George Kelly, I can only hope that readers from both camps do not suffer from "hardening of the categories" and will attempt to perceive and assimilate the particular combination of psychodynamic, behavioral, and developmental concepts and methods used in CCT.

In one sense then, when considering CCT or other cognitive therapy proposals, the reader is obliged, I believe, to work on restructuring his or her own cognition and points of view about the topic. In an effort to help the reader with this task of "self cognitive therapy" I provide in the first chapter an outline of basic issues, articulated by reviewers in the field of cognitive therapy, in terms of which any cognitive approach to psychotherapy could be considered. These same issues and others are used in the last chapter to guide the reader in critiquing CCT and comparing CCT with other methods.

I assume it is not necessary to persuade behavioral practitioners to consider cognitive approaches to psychotherapy. However, psychodynamic practitioners may require persuasion since the cognitive revolution has not yet affected the practice of psychoanalysis or of psychodynamic psychotherapy to any appreciable degree. To this end, I would like to point out that long before the Colorado symposium, a prominent psychoanalyst, Thomas French (1933), discussed how psychoanalysis and the concepts of Pavlov could enrich each other. Following the Colorado symposium, the surge of cognitive research included investigations and discussions of psychoanalytic concepts in terms of Piagetian psychology (e.g., Anthony, 1956; Decarie, 1965; Wolff, 1960) as well as George Klein's seminal studies (Klein, 1951; Santostefano, 1977b) which set the foundation for a psychodynamic theory of cognition that was elaborated and extended by my own work (Santostefano, 1978) and is discussed in this book. At the same time, psychodynamic practitioners were urged not to ignore developments in cognitive psychology (e.g., Arieti, 1970; Benjamin, 1961) and to consider how these developments could influence clinical practice (Holt, 1964). While these promptings have led several prominent psychoanalysts to point out that technique in child psychoanalysis and psychotherapy should be modified to take into account a child's cognitive dysfunctions (e.g., A. Freud, 1965; Rees, 1978; Ritvo, 1978), descriptions of techniques for the practice of psychodynamic-cognitive psychotherapy have been limited to the treatment of adults (e.g., Marmor & Woods, 1980; Wachtel, 1977). I would like CCT, which has been shaped by my experiences with practicing child psychotherapy, child psychoanalysis and cognitive therapy, to stand among these contributions as one possible method designed especially for children and adolescents.

In closing I wish to express my deepest appreciation to Dr. Albert Cotugno, my colleague of many years, and to Dr. Robert Azrak and Dr. Keith Cohen, who, while sustaining a commitment to exploring the effectiveness of CCT, address the broader challenge of weaving a new therapeutic fabric with fibers from psychodynamic psychotherapy, cognitive-behavioral therapy, and child development. I am also grateful to Ms. Grace Berestecki for her dedicated administrative and secretarial assistance and to Ms. Ann McCarthy and Ms. Cora Levick who patiently and conscientiously typed several versions of the manuscript. And special thanks to Dr. Silvio Onesti, Director, Hall-Mercer Children's Center, who has consistently supported cognitive control therapy as one of the treatment modalities made available at the Center as well as my interest in refining the method. Finally, a very special acknowledgement: my wife, Susan, has not only supported me throughout this and related projects, but of equal importance has creatively contributed to discussions of the need to understand children in terms of a cognitive-psychodynamic perspective from the same type of data base used by the earliest developmental psychologists and psychotherapists—astute naturalistic observations of our own children and those of others functioning in home settings, schools, playgrounds, and neighborhoods.

Chapter 1
Introduction

The method of cognitive control therapy (CCT) is designed to treat children and adolescents whose cognitive dysfunctions are a major source of school failure and maladaptive functioning and who seem not to benefit from traditional play and verbal psychotherapy. It is assumed that psychotherapy is a process of learning, and to benefit from this process, a person should have available cognitive structures necessary for efficient learning. But, children for whom CCT is intended do not have these requisite cognitive structures. They need first to learn how to learn before they are able to learn about themselves.

To illustrate this point, and to set the stage for the concepts and techniques that make up CCT, we begin by comparing children during moments of psychotherapy. In each comparison, one child shows cognitive capacities required by the process of psychodynamic verbal and play therapy, and another shows deficiencies in these requisite capacities.

THE FIRST CLINICAL COMPARISON

Case A. John, a 15-year-old, flops into the chair he usually uses. Suddenly he pops up, sits in another chair further away from the therapist and chuckles, "That (the chair he vacated) is hard on my back today." His right hand clenches his left, he glares at the therapist, looks away, and sighs, "Since we met last . . . " He pauses, handles an ashtray on the table next to him, glares at it, and seems to be miles away. Shifting restlessly in his chair, he turns his attention to the bookshelves and wonders how many books each holds, and then recalls with pleasure a vacation the family took this time last year. The books and vacation fade away as he comments, "Yesterday I was late for school. My father blasted me and made me put tools back in the garage. I felt like s_____ . I can't seem to do anything right . . . " His attention shifts to a homework assignment. He ignores this thought, fingers the ashtray again, moves it toward the therapist and says with an edge of anger, "Your ashtray is cracked like my father." Then he laughs anxiously.

During these moments, John regulated his body motility (e.g., he moved further away from the therapist; he shifted about in his chair; he sat still), and he visually and tactually scanned and copied information from his external environment (e.g., books, ashtray) and from his internal environment (e.g., a happy memory of a family vacation; anxiety over a homework assignment). As he coordinated information from these two environments, he organized a theme, very likely without awareness, that contained the following ingredients: the office chair is hard on his back; an incident in which his father blasted him causing him to feel a failure and rejected; a cracked ashtray symbolizing father and therapist and associated with anger and anxiety. This theme, offered to the therapist for examination as a source for learning (he pushed the ashtray toward the therapist), resulted from cognitive structures which (a) copy and select information from the environment and the personal world of thoughts, fantasies, and emotions; (b) coordinate and integrate these two pieces of information, transforming them into symbols that represent and express one of his conflicts, e.g., authority is on his back, is cracked (flawed), and makes him feel impotent and angry; (c) enable John, while dealing with the issue, to pretend that the therapist is father and at the same time a source of assistance. During these moments, then, John's cognition was operating efficiently and serving the process and goals of psychotherapy.

Case B. Tom, also 15 years old, sits relatively still, stares at the floor, and initiates no conversation, behaviors typical of him since the start of treatment six sessions ago. The therapist acknowledges Tom's difficulty with being in treatment and sharing his concerns. Tom continues looking at the floor, carefully adjusts the creases of his trousers with thumb and forefinger of each hand, slowly picks at a piece of lint on his jersey, and stares out the window. After a long pause, he comments that he is bored, and then directs intense annoyance and anger at the therapist. He points out that he is missing a special TV program because of this appointment. The therapist acknowledges the inconvenience, empathizes with Tom's disappointment, and notes that he is trying to help Tom learn why he is failing school and has a difficult time relating to classmates. Tom glares at the therapist, looks away, and after a long pause says, "There are just a lot of things racing through my mind." The therapist urges him to "Catch one of those things and share it." Another long pause and Tom notes with irritation that he, " . . . can't; they just go too fast; and, if I could, why should I share it?" At this point he unties and carefully ties his shoelaces and then carefully repositions a Kleenex box on the table.

Tom's behavior suggests several cognitive dysfunctions which are viewed as a major source of his academic and social failures. He was unable or unwilling to produce information about his external environment and his personal world. He also seemed unable to balance and coordinate external and internal stimulation, at one moment withdrawn and apparently preoccupied with private thoughts, and at another bound to external, isolated stimuli (e.g., creases of his trousers, lint on his shirt). As a result, he did not transform information into symbols that express his private experiences and concerns. While behaviors such as aligning the Kleenex box symbolized his need to keep things in order, such symbolic behaviors did not serve the process of learning in therapy. Rather, they served to control and restrict any input from the relationship, the situation, as well as from his private fantasies.

THE SECOND CLINICAL COMPARISON

The following examples of younger children engaged in play therapy illustrate the same issues.

Case A. The parents of Mary, an 8-year-old, have separated and Mary and mother have moved from their home to an apartment. Moments after entering the playroom, Mary places a girl hand-puppet on the table and then other doll figures, at first randomly, then gradually forming a ring around the girl puppet. She interrupts this activity and discusses a school concert to be given for parents by the fourth and fifth grade glee club. She returns to the table and continues carefully locating other doll figures around the girl puppet. She comments, "This is her house, and she has a lot of aunts and uncles and cousins." She interrupts this activity again now to make an "exact" drawing of her home, taking much care to locate the correct number of windows, and so on. Satisfied that she has made a good reproduction of her house, she asks the therapist to draw "a mother" in the front yard while she draws "a father," commenting, "It's really a happy place." She continues locating more doll figures on the table, saying, "All of these are her (hand-puppet) mother and father," and then with a burst of laughter, "That's impossible!"

Case B. Sally, a 10-year-old, sits passively before a game of checkers, an activity she initiated each meeting since therapy started. When she did not engage the therapist in checkers, she seemed submerged in "private play," dreamily manipulating materials and ignoring the therapist's suggestion that he be invited into the play. As with past checker games, the therapist patiently waits for Sally to initiate conversation, however banal, and hopes for conversation and play related to her occasional, unprovoked angry outbursts at home and her refusal to attend school. The therapist also makes statements in an effort to construct a therapeutic process (e.g., "Maybe it's hard to talk about what worries you, like school, because the thoughts scare you.") and suggests they play a game with puppets. After a long silence, Sally carefully moves a checker on the board and calmly says, "Your move."

Case C. Harry, an 8-year-old, charges into the playroom and darts from toy to toy engaging each for seconds (e.g., he thrusts his hand into a puppet and waves it about vigorously; he sets a doll figure on a truck, racing it along the floor). He punctuates this frantic behavior with comments that seem to bear no relation to the activity at hand, e.g., "My father is the greatest!" (the therapist is aware that Harry's father is an alcoholic and sometimes behaves abusively); "My teacher sucks! She said I stepped on chalk and squashed it, but Johnny did." As the session progresses, Harry's behavior escalates from restless, diffuse play to impulsive, destructive actions (e.g., he nearly tips over a lamp, he tugs at the curtain, and he pulls the therapist's necktie). As with previous sessions, the therapist intervenes by attempting to channel Harry's aggression into an organized game (shooting darts at a target), bringing attention to his difficulties, "You act like this in school, and it gets you in trouble," and setting standards, "You can't hurt anything here." But, again, the therapist is forced to restrain Harry when he pounds his fist against the window, trying to lift it so he can throw out a toy.

In Case A, Mary's cognition selectively produced information from the external and internal worlds and shifted flexibly between pretend playing (locating many relatives and then many parents around a girl doll), drawing an exact copy of her house, and remembering a real-life event (a concert for parents). As cognition coordinated information from her external and internal worlds, a theme was constructed which would serve her learning about one source of her conflicts, namely, the way in which she has construed and managed the separation of her parents and disruption of her home life (e.g., instead of being separated and lost as a couple, her parents are very available, surrounding her in multiple numbers; and, instead of losing her happy home, it is present in all its detail.)

In contrast, Sally did not or could not share observations of current events or engage in pretend play that expressed how she experienced her current situation, especially her difficulty attending school. She maintained control over the therapist and over her fantasies by limiting her interactions to repetitive checker games. Harry, although very active, capable of engaging play material and offering comments and complaints, was, nonetheless, unable to produce and coordinate information from reality and fantasy and sustain pretending in a way that enabled the therapist to help him understand and work through his aggressiveness and school difficulties.

THE APPROACH OF CCT

CCT maintains that it is not effective to engage children such as Tom, Sally, or Harry, described above, in a process which requires them to learn about themselves by scanning, selecting, and talking about private thoughts, fantasies, and emotions, either literally or symbolically, or which requires them to express themselves in pretend play, since the cognitive structures required by these processes are dysfunctional. They become stuck in therapy because their cognitive deficits remain unmodified, and therefore they perpetuate in therapy the flight and fight behaviors that cause them difficulty at home and school.

These children must first develop new, or rehabilitated, cognitive structures. To accomplish this, CCT asks a child to deal with a series of structured cognitive tasks which, in a stepwise fashion, attempt to improve the way in which a *particular* cognitive function copies information, then considers that information from different points of view, and then participates in transforming that information (i.e., pretending the information is something else).

For children whose cognition avoids fantasies (outer-oriented children), the tasks initially consist of neutral, "conflict free" information and gradually contain stimulation that arouses emotions and fantasies. For children whose cognition avoids reality in favor of fantasy (inner-oriented children), the tasks initially incorporate elements from the child's fantasies and gradually become more neutral. For children with impulse disorders, the tasks integrate aggressive actions and fantasies within the requirements of the task, cultivating cognitive control over action.

In all cases, the tasks are designed to rehabilitate selected cognitive structures so that they become efficient in copying and coordinating the requirements of reality, fantasy, and affects and in guiding actions taken. In addition, the tasks provide an arena within which the child is trained to observe and become aware of his/her unique approaches to learning and adapting. When dealing with the tasks, the child relives and reveals the unconscious cognitive maneuvers and associated emotions of boredom, anger, anxiety, which the child uses to cope and learn. During these moments, the therapist teaches the child, bit by bit, to examine these maneuvers, to learn how they mediate between the demands of reality and fantasy and how they influence the way in which the child acts in and experiences the environment, and to use this knowledge to develop new actions that are more adaptive.

The child not only develops new cognitive structures that make available new information but is also able to use his/her thinking in a qualitatively different way, more efficiently adapting to and coordinating the requirements of reality and fantasy in the service of learning and adapting. When the child has cultivated these cognitive tools, CCT shifts from a format of directed tasks to a format resembling traditional nondirected verbal and play therapy. In this more nondirected format CCT emphasizes a process within which the child is free to initiate, repeat, and restructure key pathological metaphors that are major souces of maladaption and inefficient learning.

With the approach of CCT before us, emphasizing the need to rehabilitate cognitive structures that produce and coordinate information from reality and fantasy, it is necessary to consider in more detail what is meant by cognition and cognitive structures in therapy.

WHAT IS COGNITION
IN THERAPY?

CCT is being presented at a time when a "cognitive revolution" is occurring within psychology, resulting in numerous cognitive treatment methods and points of views (e.g., Arnkoff & Glass, 1982; Kendall & Hollon, 1979; Mahoney, 1977). Whenever such a revolution occurs clinicians often experience confusion as they set out to decide which methods to use in certain circumstances. Therefore, I would like to address this confusion from several angles, to aid the reader in navigating through this cognitive revolution and in relating the CCT approach to others.

All cognitive approaches to therapy maintain that cognitive processes play a central role in psychological functioning and development, and accordingly, in the formation of psychopathology and maladaptations. However, beyond this agreement, widely different behaviors are proposed as the cognitions to be treated and changed in therapy. One volume (Emery, Hollon, & Bedrosian, 1981), for example, refers to "sleeping cognitions" (p. 288); "dream content (cognition)" (p. 231); cognition as "helplessness . . . anxiety" (p. 231), as "discussing perceptions of an event" (p. 57); as "a person's tendency to drift from topic to topic" (p. 88) and as "distortions" concerning physical appearances (p. 71). Some (e.g., Cacioppo & Petty, 1981) propose a broad definition of cognitive behaviors to be addressed in therapy ("Those thoughts that pass through a person's mind," p. 310) while others (Bedrosian & Beck, 1980) propose a more circumscribed one ("dysfunctional ideation" p. 128).

While a wide variety of cognitive behaviors have been proposed as the target for therapy, Arnkoff & Glass (1982) point out in their critique that there is an "overwhelmingly narrow focus in the literature on self-statements and beliefs" (p. 9). (See also, Goldfried, 1980; Kendall & Hollon, 1979; Mahoney & Arnkoff, 1978). Belief systems (and thought patterns) are the rational and irrational rules and thoughts a person holds which influence the way he/she conducts life (e.g., I'm not very good at what I try). Self-statements refer to the thoughts a person says to herself while dealing with situations or performing a task. Other behaviors, which are dominant in current cognitive assessment and therapy methods, include: attributional styles—the inferences a person draws across different situations to explain why a particular event occurred (e.g., John was picked for the baseball team because "taller people are better"); role-taking (or perspective-taking)—the degree to which a person assumes the point of view (thoughts, perceptions, and emotions) of another person; and cognitive problem solving—whether and how a person thinks of alternative solutions to a problem (e.g., Joe wants to play with a toy that Harry has; think of different ways he could get it).

In their critique, Arnkoff and Glass also articulate several problems that arise from the emphasis given self-statements and beliefs by many current approaches to cognitive therapy. Highlighting a few of these is another useful way to introduce the reader further to CCT within the current cognitive revolution.

1. A belief or self-statement such as, "I am a failure," may have several meanings and several different statements may convey a single meaning (e.g., "I hate life; I like the color gray."). Arnkoff and Glass suggest that what a person says may be the "tip of an iceberg," and therefore there is a need to consider "surface and deep" cognitive structures in order to learn the meaning underlying a particular verbalized statement. (See also Sollod & Wachtel, 1980.)

2. The cognitive therapy literature tends to dichotomize self-statements and beliefs as irrational versus rational, unrealistic versus realistic, and task irrelevant versus task relevant. Not only are these bipolar distinctions used interchangably, but according to Arnkoff and Glass, underlying these classifications is also the inherent assumption that it is better to be rational, realistic, and task relevant, than it is to be irrational, unrealistic, and task irrelevant. Because of this assumption, self-statement therapies set out to help the client identify the "bad thoughts" and replace them with "good ones." Arnkoff and Glass propose that an "irrational" thought could sometimes be adaptive, while a rational thought, maladaptive, depending upon the meaning of the thought to the individual and the function it serves.

3. Some experiences may be less amenable to self-report because of their inaccessibility to language. A belief could have been formed, Arnkoff and Glass note, prior to the full development of language.

Each of these issues should be familiar to therapists from a psychodynamic-developmental persuasion. The issue of deeper structures underlying conscious beliefs and self-statements relates to the concept of multiple determinism—that a belief may be determined by different behavioral structures which may be conscious or unconscious and expressed by alternative modes and modalities (e.g., in thought/language and fantasy, or in action). The concept that a rational thought may be maladaptive, and an irrational thought adaptive, depending upon the function each serves, is related to the notion of regression. That is, returning to a developmentally early form of behaving, can under certain circumstances, serve successful adaptation. And, the concept that an experience may be formed prior to the full development of language, and therefore less amenable to self-statements, is a familiar one, expecially to child clinicians who observe the difficulty many emotionally-disturbed children have verbalizing. Some clinicians take the postion that the child's problem is not her current inability to express experiences in verbal terms. Rather, the child may need to use other behavioral modes (e.g., actions, fantasies) which were dominant when the particular experience was encoded. In a therapy process that emphasizes self-statements, the child is required to express presymbolic experiences in verbal-symbolic terms.

This sketch of the current cognitive revolution, with its emphasis on self-statements and beliefs as the cognitions to be changed, and the limitations brought by this emphasis, provides a bridge to the population of children and adolescents for whom CCT is intended.

FOR WHOM IS CCT INTENDED? COGNITIVE DYSFUNCTIONS PRIOR TO THE FULL DEVELOPMENT OF LANGUAGE

Over the past two decades an increasing number of children and adolescents have been identified as needing assistance because they experience severe difficulty both in learning and adapting, despite their adequate intelligence. In terms of cognitive difficulties, observations have included: short attention span, distractibility, inability to organize and stick with a task, excessive daydreaming, anxiety or depression while learning and working in the classroom, and poor retention of details. In terms of difficulty with coping at home and school, observations have included: shy, withdrawn, lost in fantasy, frequently bored or sleepy, excessive moving about, easily frustrated, low self-esteem, and outbursts of physical and verbal aggression.

Labels such as perceptual handicap, minimal brain dysfunction, hyperkinetic, developmental deviation, and tension discharge disorder have been used in the past to diagnose these children. While these labels acknowledged that neurotic conflicts are not the main source of the difficulties these children experience, they failed to be useful in guiding innovations in treatment. Psychodynamically oriented therapists tended to try to aid these children with nondirected play therapy, while behaviorally oriented clinicians used various forms of perceptual training.

Recently a new diagnostic category, "Attention Deficit Disorder," has been proposed by the American Psychiatric Association in its revision of the Diagnostic Statistical Manual (DSM III) to formulate the difficulties of these children. Attention Deficit Disorder is defined by various forms of inattentive as well as aggressive, hyperactive, and impulsive behaviors.

These behaviors are also implicated in many other clinical syndromes (e.g., conduct disorders, developmental disorders, oppositional disorders, overanxious disorders, and schizophrenia). In defining Attention Deficit Disorder, the manual states, ''The essential features are signs of *developmentally* inappropriate inattention'' and the *onset* is ''typically by the *age of 3 years*.'' [italics added] In other words, the disorder begins before language is fully developed.

The significance of this new category is that, for the first time, many children who need assistance are treated by integrating, rather than by segregating, cognition and personality, by emphasizing a developmental view, and by proposing that the origin of their pathology predates the full development of verbal-symbolic functioning. The formulation of attention deficit disorder, then, challenges clinicians to make operational what is ''developmentally inappropriate inattention,'' to determine which cognitive-personality processes become derailed by the age of three, resulting in pathological functioning, and to design treatment methods that address preverbal as well as verbal cognitive structures. The development of CCT over the past 20 years can be viewed as one response to this challenge. While intended primarily for the broad population of children noted above, the approach, with modification, is also appropriate with children who are mentally retarded, autistic, or psychotic, as well as with severe neurotic disorders within which cognitive dysfunctions dominate.

THE POINT OF VIEW OF CCT

From our sketch of issues raised by prevailing approaches to cognitive therapy and from our discussion of the method of CCT and the populations for which it is intended, we can now turn full circle and revisit the anecdotes presented at the start of this introduction. Tom, who was failing all of his subjects and incompetent at peer relations, could not verbalize in therapy and showed that he coped and learned by shifting between very active private fantasies and thoughts and concrete, isolated details in his environment (lint on his shirt), each domain of information segregated from the other. Sally, who resisted attending school and occasionally became physically and verbally aggressive, coped and learned by responding primarily to the requirements of her fantasies while tenaciously limiting interventions by playing checker games. Harry, who presented an aggressive disorder and school failure, revealed fragments of pretending from his fantasy life and produced some self-statements and beliefs, both of which failed to establish a therapeutic process within which he could learn about himself and ways of regulating the steady stream of aggression that invaded his functioning at home and school.

Each of these children suffers from attention deficit disorder. More importantly, according to CCT, the cognitive and personality difficulties these children show are two sides of the same coin. Not only do they lack the cognitive control necessary to copy, coordinate, and integrate information from reality and fantasy, they also are unable to use this information when learning and adapting. And, their deeper nonverbal, cognitive structures are deficient as well as structures concerned with expressing beliefs and self-statements. Therefore, therapy should be directed at rehabilitiating cognitive structures, within personality, at all levels. To accomplish this we need a model of cognition which consists of:

1. A developmental-interaction view of an individual as an active organism who creates his/her own knowledge (i.e., imposes symbols on things and events, giving them meaning; takes actions according to this meaning; assimilates the outcomes of these actions, which, in turn, modify the original symbols; uses the modified symbol to construe new things and events, etc.).
2. Cognition as a range of structures from surface, verbal ones to deeper, nonverbal ones; these structures are mobile so that a person may behave in logical and illogical ways from one moment to the next in the same situation or from one situation to another. The person's adaptive intention influences how cognition shifts within this range.
3. The notion that the purposes cognitive structures serve change throughout development in concert with changes in personality, while the structures remain the same.
4. The structures and functions of cognition in the first three years of life, especially symbolizing/pretending, which are critical for future development and adaptational skill.
5. The relations between cognition, on the one hand, and affect, fantasy, reality, and action, on the other.
6. How the meanings given experiences undergo change and the purpose of these changes for successful psychological development and adaptation.

The next two chapters address these needs. Chapter 2 presents a model based on research findings of cognition in personality and adaptation. Chapter 3 translates this model into a set of principles that guide the approach and techniques of CCT detailed in Chapters 4 to 10.

To make optimal use of the techniques described in this book, the reader should have some knowledge of the theory and rationale presented. Of course, at the same time, familiarity with the techniques is necessary to make optimal use of the theory and rationale. Therefore, the reader is encouraged to review one discussion, and then another, and to return to each, recycling the total presentation in order to ascertain how theory and technique are combined in conducting CCT and whether and how CCT could serve the reader in treating children or innovating other techniques more suited for a particular child.

Chapter 2
Cognition in Personality and Adaptation

This chapter describes a theory which places cognition within personality functioning and adaptation and addresses the several needs listed at the close of Chapter 1. In brief, this theory brings together a person's cognition, her inner world, and the environment in which she is functioning. Cognition is defined as a particular set of mobile cognitive functions. A person's inner world is defined as continually changing metaphors which condense and represent key past experiences while at the same time prescribing the way current stimulation is to be experienced and handled. The environment is defined as stimulation that continually changes and requires particular responses. The cognitive functions coordinate the requirements of reality with those of metaphor, and the coordination achieved guides the actions a person takes in the service of learning and adaptation.

First, a note about the historical roots of the theory presented here. Probably due to the influence of Freud and Piaget, studies of cognition changed emphasis after 1940 from "formal" to "functional" approaches (Bruner & Postman, 1948). Formal approaches explained cognition as determined by physical properties of stimuli. Functional approaches emphasized the ways in which cognitive behaviors serve an individual's personality needs and adaptation to changing environments. The scientific ethos which emerged in the behavioral sciences at this time embraced the "organismic model" of human behavior (Reese & Overton, 1970), which viewed the individual as inherently and spontaneously active—approaching, avoiding, modifying, and giving meaning to stimuli in the service of adaptation and learning. This shift in emphasis gave rise to what came to be known as the "New Look" in perception (Bruner & Klein, 1960), a look that clinicians initially embraced eagerly.

What was it that was new? An attempt was being made to correlate cognition, affects, and personality. One of the New Look approaches was that of cognitive controls, a concept initially formulated by George Klein (1949, 1951, 1954) when he observed that adults consistently use particular cognitive-ego strategies to approach, avoid, compare, and cluster information. Klein proposed that in managing information with these strategies, individuals coordinate information from external reality and from emotions, fantasies, and motives so as to remain in adaptive control of information. Hence the term "cognitive controls."

Taking Klein's formulation as a starting point, the author conducted a program of research over the past two decades to study cognitive control functioning in normal and pathological children, as well as in adults. This program has focused on operationalizing and assessing the development of cognitive controls within personality development, the relations between cognitive controls, emotions, and fantasy, and the role cognitive controls play in learning and coping with usual and unusual environments. The findings, reported elsewhere (Santostefano, 1978; 1984; in press a; in press b; Santostefano & Rieder, 1984) have been used to elaborate and refine cognitive control theory and to shape continually the techniques and concepts of CCT.

THE CONCEPT OF
COGNITIVE CONTROLS

As noted in the first chapter, children for whom CCT is intended do not have the cognitive structures required for efficient learning. Piaget provides a brief but effective definition of learning in cognitive terms. "To know (to learn) . . . is to . . . reproduce the object (information) dynamically; but to reproduce, it is necessary to know how to produce (copy the information) . . . " (Piaget, 1977, p. 30). Copying and producing information, then, is a critical first step in learning. Recall the children described in Chapter 1 who were learning efficiently in therapy. John, for example, produced an ashtray, the number of books in the office, and a memory of a family trip. Mary produced the concert to be held for parents and a picture of her house. What cognitive mechanisms are involved in this process? And, how do the statements a person makes fit with these mechanisms? (Recall that John expressed the belief, "I can't seem to do anything right.") And, once information is copied, how is it reproduced dynamically? (Recall that John reproduced his father as "cracked," and Mary produced her separated parents as multiple, never-ending persons.) With these questions as guides, cognitive controls are defined in more detail.

Cognitive Controls: Definition and Process

When children and adults deal with various tasks, how many distinctively different processes account for the ways information is gathered and produced? Of the several cognitive controls identified to date, five have withstood the test of numerous experiments. Each of these controls follows a developmental course, from cognitive behaviors characterizing the young child to those characterizing the adolescent and adult, and the five controls form a developmental hierarchy (see Figure 2.1).

Body-ego–tempo regulation, the first cognitive control, concerns the manner in which an individual uses images/symbols to represent and regulate the body and body motility. The young child registers vague body percepts represented in global images. In addition, body motility is regulated poorly. When asked to move fast and slow, the child produces about the same tempo and represents these with global images (e.g., a turtle walking, a rocket blasting off). With age, perceptions and representations of the body gradually become more detailed and differentiated (e.g., while balancing on one leg, the child imagines a gymnast performing on parallel bars), and many tempos are refined and regulated, each distinguished from the other.

Focal attention concerns the manner in which a person surveys a field of information. The young child typically scans information slowly and directs attention to only narrow segments of the available field. With age, the child scans more actively and sweeps attention across larger segments.

Field articulation defines the manner in which an individual deals with a field of information which contains elements that are both relevant and irrelevant to the task at hand. The young child attends to relevant and irrelevant information almost equally. With age, the child gradually directs attention toward what is relevant while withholding attention from what is irrelevant to the task at hand.[1]

Leveling-sharpening concerns the manner in which an individual constructs images of information that change or remain stable over time and then compares these with present perceptions. The young child typically constructs fuzzy images of past information and fuses these with present perceptions so that subtle changes are not recognized. With age, the child constructs sharper, more differentiated images and distinguishes these from present perceptions so that subtle similarities and differences between past and present information are noticed.

Equivalence range concerns the way information is grouped and categorized in terms of a concept or belief. The young child groups information in terms of a few narrow and concrete categories (e.g., "These go together because they are all round," "These are all happy."). With age, the child constructs increasingly more broad categories, which are conceptualized in terms of more abstract concepts (e.g., "These are tools," "These kids all break rules in school but not at home.").

[1]The cognitive control principle of field articulation is related to, but not synonymous with, Witkin's cognitive style of the same name (see Santostefano, 1978).

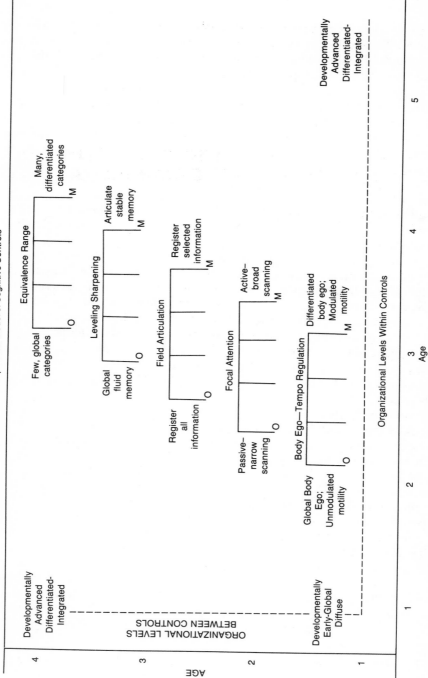

FIGURE 2.1. Santostefano's Developmental Model of Cognitive Controls

Key: O = Onset; M = Maturity;

From the definition of each control mechanism, we consider several concepts that add to our understanding of how these mechanisms produce information and serve learning and adaptation.

The Emergence of Cognitive Controls and the Relationships Among Them

These five cognitive controls become fully structured by the third year of life.[2] Moreover, the *process* of each remains the same throughout development, but the *organization* changes. For example, information is surveyed with the focal attention process whether the scanner is 3 or 13 years old. It is the organization of scanning that distinguishes these two individuals. The 3-year-old scans with narrow-passive visual sweeps, a less differentiated organization, while the 13-year-old scans with broad-active visual sweeps, a more differentiated organization. Growth in a behavioral structure from less to more differentiated forms is conceptualized in terms of the principle of "directiveness of behavior," which characterizes normal development. The growth of each of the other cognitive controls is viewed in similar terms from less differentiated to more differentiated organizations.

This principle permits us to view cognitive controls as interdependent and "nested one within the other," a view which has special relevance when diagnosing and treating cognitive control dysfunctions. When functioning adequately, the process of one control is viewed as relying upon, subsuming, and integrating the processes of other controls lower in the hierarchy. Consider the field articulation control as an illustration. The distinguishing feature of the process of this control is that a field of information is articulated into relevant and irrelevant parts and attention is sustained on what is relevant while withheld from what is irrelevant. But, if this process is to operate efficiently, it is necessary that two other controls, lower in the hierarchy, also operate efficiently. Body motility must be subordinated and regulated (body ego—tempo regulation cognitive control) and the field of information must be scanned actively and broadly (focal attention cognitive control).

Similarly, the equivalence range control relies upon all of the others in its operating. Consider as an example a child who is asked to look over and group various objects that share something in common. The child groups a bottle of white glue, a hammer, and a roll of Scotch Tape because

[2]While the author's own research shows that cognitive controls can be measured reliably from the age of 30 months, observations made of infants can be interpreted as indicating the operation of cognitive controls from the first days of life (see Kogan, 1976; Santostefano, 1978; Winner, Wapner, Cicone, & Gardner, 1979).

they are "things to fix with." While performing, the child regulated motility, scanned the available objects, articulated the attributes of each, compared perceptions of objects on the table with images of similar objects
and experiences with them, and then united a particular cluster of objects in terms of a functional attribute they share (fixing). In constructing this group, it should be noted other attributes of these objects were
subordinated as irrelevant to the category under construction (e.g., the
glue bottle was white plastic, the Scotch Tape holder red metal). In the
anecdote described in Chapter 1, when John offered that the therapist's
ashtray and his father "were both cracked," and when he expressed the
self-statement, "I can't seem to do anything right," he constructed categories having scanned, articulated, and related a wide array of information.

Cognitive Controls as Nonverbal and Verbal Activity: Deep and Surface Structures

We noted in Chapter 1 that other cognitive therapies emphasize verbal
behaviors (e.g., beliefs, self-statements) as cognitions. The description of
cognitive controls presented this far should make clear that words, thoughts,
and beliefs are part of the process of only *one* cognitive control, namely,
equivalence range. The preceding discussion also emphasizes that constructing a label, belief, self-statement, or an inference as to how something was caused, relies upon, and is nested within, deeper processes
unique to each of the other four cognitive controls conceptualized as
nonverbal, sensorimotor, and cognitive activity (i.e., regulating body schema
and tempos, scanning, articulating information in terms of relevance, and
comparing present information with images of past experiences). As will
be discussed later, the notion that labeling relies upon deeper, nonverbal cognitive structures suggests that, when indicated, therapy should first
rehabilitate deeper structures on which statements rely before treating beliefs as such.

Are Different Levels of Cognitive Controls "Good" or "Bad"?

One of the most common errors made by professionals when considering levels of behavioral structures is that one level is taken to denote
"good" and another "bad." The reader was acquainted in Chapter 1 with
Arnkoff and Glass's criticism of cognitive therapies that view logical beliefs
as good and illogical beliefs as bad.

One cognitive control is conceptualized as higher, or lower, in a hierarchy, and one level of a control (e.g., narrow scanning) is defined as developmentally less mature than another level (e.g., broad scanning). These structures describe levels of development and do not indicate the adaptive value of a particular cognitive process. Functioning with the focal attention process is not automatically "bad," while sharpening information good. Discussed in more detail later, any cognitive control, and any structural level within a control, can be adaptive or maladaptive depending upon the age and developmental status of the child, the environmental conditions and expectations, and the requirements of the child's fantasies and emotions.

Adaptive Intention and Cognitive Control Functioning

Since all controls are available, what determines which control, or level within a control, dominates a person's functioning at the moment? Particular structures become operative depending upon an individual's "adaptive intention"; that is, the fit a person intends to negotiate between the demands of the environment and those of his/her motives, affects, and fantasies.

For example, a teacher sends a child to the supply closet to obtain a particular workbook, "like this one." Guided by this intention, the child actively compares perceptions of the attributes (e.g., color, size, lettering) of many workbooks with an image of the book the teacher held up and quickly selects the correct one. Another child, guided at the moment by the intention to deal with the requirements of fantasies, compares a fuzzy image of the workbook the teacher displayed with inefficient perceptions of the workbooks in the closet and returns with the wrong one.

Cognitive Controls and the Issue of Conscious/Unconscious

An individual may or may not be conscious of his intention to cope with some task or situation. And, a person may be aware of a particular intention when another, unconscious intention, may in fact be guiding cognitive activity. The adaptive intention and cognitive control functioning in most situations are usually unconscious until experiences such as those made available in therapy bring them into awareness. For example, a child waiting to undergo surgery may be conscious of the intention to cope with the situation and his/her anxiety and fear, but unaware of the intention to level information in the external environment while attending to private thoughts and fantasies (see Chapter 11).

Cognitive Controls and Mechanisms of Defense

Cognitive controls are viewed as ego mechanisms that are separate from, but function in concert with, mechanisms of defense. The effective functioning of mechanisms of defense requires the effective functioning of cognitive controls and vice versa. Each has a defensive purpose. Mechanisms of defense are organized to deal with the clash between drives and reality limitations. Cognitive controls are organized to deal with the clash between the demands of internal and external information. Each has an adaptive purpose. Mechanisms of defense disguise and displace needs and drives. Cognitive controls seek and avoid information in order to maintain a pace of stimulation that serves learning and adaptation.

When working in concert with mechanisms of defense, cognitive controls recruit particular information contributing to the direction behavioral expressions of drives take, either toward or away from certain objects and events. Cognitive controls also provide information about objects and events in the environment to which behavioral expressions of drives must accommodate.

Cognitive Controls in Normal Development and Adaptation

With the preceding discussions as a frame, we can now center more closely on cognitive control development and set the stage for a view of cognition within personality functioning and adaptation. In the view of adaptation maintained here, the individual and the environment are seen as interacting and negotiating with each attempting to influence the other until an accommodation is reached between their respective demands and expectations. In this process, the individual actively avoids or remains autonomous from some stimuli in the environment while also engaging other stimuli and seeking change and novelty. The environment presents particular stimuli and demands, but also adjusts to unique features of the individual such as his developmental capabilities. The adaptive process explains how cognitive controls are structured over a relatively long time, as the child reciprocates with environments, and how cognitive controls are restructured temporarily in response to short-term changes in the environment.

Long-Term Adaptation and the Structuring of Cognitive Controls. In the course of development, the individual phases in and presents to the environment an evolving series of average and expectable behavioral structures (e.g., cognitive, motoric, and affective) that more or less match the environment's expectations, opportunities, and limitations. The environment, in turn, presents the individual with a continuous series of average and ex-pectable organizations of stimulation that more or less fits the sensing and responding equipment of the individual. Since stimulation impinges on a person who has already adapted to what has taken place before, this stimulation activates cognitive structures already available to the individual and which are suited (preadapted) to accommodate to and assimilate the information.

In this give and take between individual and environment, cognitive controls become shaped to fit the complexity and pace of stimulation characteristic of the individual's usual environments and to satisfy the individual's need for repetition of stimulation as well as for novelty and change. From this view, cognitive controls structured to manage stimulation unique to a small inner-city apartment and street life, for example, would be different than those structured to manage the stimulation of a surburban community.

Short-Term Adaptation and the Mobility of Cognitive Controls. The environment could shift, more or less abruptly, from usual to unusual stimulation. Examples would be: mother's depression leading to change in the pace and complexity of stimulation she provides; hospitalization of a child for several months; moving to a very different community, type of housing, or school. In dealing with these marked environmental changes, cognitive controls regress to earlier levels of organization or new levels evolve that depart significantly from modes previously employed, a process referred to as *cognitive control mobility.*

Individuals differ in the flexibility with which cognitive controls shift to handle short-term changes in the environment because of factors such as constitutional make-up (e.g., temperament, activity level), frequency, types and timing of unusual environmental changes the person has experienced in the past, and personality dynamics that the person is negotiating at the time the environmental change occurs. In short-term adaptation, then, cognitive controls reorganize in a direction (regressive or progressive) that fit with the opportunities and limitations of the unusual situation and enable the person to regulate and express affects and fantasies aroused by the situation in ways that serve adaptation and learning.

Relating Long- and Short-Term Cognitive Control Adaptation. It follows from the previous discussions that the cognitive control functioning of an individual is represented both by a single level of a particular cognitive control process and by a range of levels within that process. The single level defines a relatively stable cognitive structure the individual uses to deal with many usual environments and which is modified slowly by the process of long-term adaptation. The range of levels defines a series of organizations within a cognitive control through which cognitive functioning temporarily moves (either regressively or progressively) as the person deals with short-term, unusual environments. When the environment returns to its usual status, the new organization is relinquished and cognitive activity returns to the structure the person uses in long-term adaptation.

To illustrate, consider a hypothetical situation involving an adolescent boy who has been brought into an emergency room and the surgeon attending him. When at home and school the adolescent usually directs attention actively both to external information and to private thoughts. As he is brought into the emergency room, however, he scans narrow pieces of the environment (e.g., pictures on the wall) while directing attention more at private thoughts and fantasies (e.g., he should have returned the blade guard on the mower; it serves him right since he failed his history exam, etc.). This change in the orientation of cognitive controls toward inner information is regressive but serves to insulate the adolescent from an unusual situation over which he has little control, and to make available his inner world and opportunities to work on meanings assigned to the accident.

For the surgeon, the emergency room is a usual environment. Approaching the boy, the surgeon actively scans relevant external information (e.g., the boy's skin color, emotional state, location and type of wound), withholds attention from irrelevant internal stimulation (e.g., an earlier disagreement with a supervisor) while at the same time coordinating this information with perceptions of thoughts and memories that concern training in, and past experience with, injuries like the one before him. The surgeon's cognitive control of information is the outcome of long-term adaptation in many emergency rooms.

In discussing cognitive controls, reference is made repeatedly to stimulation from the "inner world." At this point we define what is meant by this concept which forms the second part of the theory proposed here.

METAPHOR: A CONCEPTUALIZATION OF THE INNER WORLD

Metaphor in the Psychological Literature

Before conceptualizing metaphor[3] as a dynamic system that makes up a person's inner world, we should first remind ourselves of the usual view of metaphor held in the psychological literature. Metaphor, along with

---

[3]The formulation of metaphor developed here relies upon Mounoud's (1982) model of revolutionary periods in development, writings on metaphor (e.g., Ortony, 1979, and Piaget, 1977) conceptualization of the process equilibration and equilibrium states.

its close relatives, simile and analogy, involves the transfer of meaning; something is described in terms of properties that belong to something else. To illustrate consider the following anecdote.

Spotting a jogger, a 3-year-old boy immediately leaned his body forward and with exuberant, "Choo-Choo!" vigorously thrust his right arm forward and back. Moments later he appeared to pretend being a train engine. He loaded blocks onto a toy wagon, grabbed the string attached to it, lowered his head and marched forward forcefully and rhythmically, pulling the wagon behind him.

This anecdote provides an example of a linguistic metaphor. In exclaiming, "Choo-Choo!" the toddler is essentially saying, "The man is a powerful train engine." At an older age this same child could provide examples of a simile and an analogy with the respective statements, "That man is running like a powerful engine," and "That man runs as if he is a powerful engine."

How is meaning transferred from one thing to something else? First a referent and its substitute are classified together and compared on the basis of a shared attribute. In our example, the attribute of power is the basis of comparison between the referent (jogger) and its substitute (train engine). Once constructed, a metaphor achieves a new meaning that goes beyond the objects compared and substituted and that synthesizes present and past experiences with them. In our example, the jogger is assigned a new meaning by the toddler that transcends particular properties of both the jogger and a train engine and within which are both no longer what they once were.

What functions are served by metaphor? While the view persists that metaphors are ornamental, decorative speech, Ortony (1975) proposed that metaphors are necessary and serve several important functions (e.g., they condense many facts, depict events which by their nature are not describable, reconstruct experiences, and are vivid, lying much closer to personal experiences).

The purpose served by metaphor relates to a key problem articulated by reviewers (e.g., Billow, 1977; Ortony, Reynolds, & Arter, 1978) who point out that most workers assume a word, or sentence, is the exclusive locus of a metaphor, that metaphor construction also involves pretending and imaging, and that a broader definition should be adopted. In the previous anecdote, the toddler was surely imaging a train engine as he verbalized, "Choo-Choo." But, what should we make of the fact that he also postured and moved his body in a particular way? And, how should we understand that later he pretended and played being a train engine, dragging his wagon filled with blocks? And, how and why was this particular pattern of behavior prescribed? These questions lead us to the issue of a person's inner world.

Metaphor as a Person's Inner World

The reformulation of metaphor proposed responds to these promptings by expanding the definition to include, in addition to words, play action, imaging, emotions and cognition (Santostefano, 1977, 1978). In this way metaphor construction and the purpose of metaphor is given a more central role in personality development.

Acting, imaging (fantasizing), and verbalizing are conceptualized as alternative coding systems (modes of symbolic representation) as well as alternative modes of behaving. A physical object could be represented by a verbal label, an image, or an action, and a person can engage or respond to a physical object by verbalizing, imaging, or acting. For example, a child could represent a wooden block as a bomb by racing behind a barrier to protect himself from it, by imaging a bomb exploding, or by verbalizing, "It's a bomb!" Similarly, the child could engage the block by tossing it, as if a bomb, at a friend's fort, by sitting and imaging the block hurling toward the fort, or by verbalizing, "I'll throw this bomb at you!"

A Definition of Metaphor. Phenomenologically, a metaphor is a persistent, habitual organization (pattern) of one or more of the following interrelated behaviors: images, symbols, words, emotions, postures, and physical actions. This pattern of behavior condenses, conserves, and represents issues and past experiences fundamental to a person's negotiating key developmental issues vis-a-vis the self, other persons, objects, and situations. Examples of these issues are: attachment–trust–love; loss–detachment; separation–individuation; controlling–being controlled; dependence–independence; initiating–reciprocating; assertiveness–aggression. In addition to representing past experiences, metaphors, at the same time, construe present situations and prescribe particular actions and emotions to handle them.

Metaphors should be distinguished from the similar but more molecular process of symbol construction. In opening her mouth when a matchbox was opened, an infant represents the action of the box with an action of the body. In contrast, a 20-month-old authored and repeated over many weeks a particular "game," a pattern of behaviors. He sat on his father's lap and asked father to button his shirt around his (the boy's) body; then asking that the shirt be unbuttoned, slid off father's lap, and darted off, with father looking for him. Here a metaphor is at work negotiating the key developmental issue of attachment (being enveloped by father's shirt and at one with father's body) and separation (running off with father looking for him).

The Origin and Development of Metaphor. The first metaphors are constructed in the first year of life with roots primarily in body and sensory representations (Mounoud, 1982); a proposition that has received support from laboratory findings (Winner, Wapner, Cicone, & Gardner, 1979). These metaphors, coupled with cognitive structures, determine the infant's negotiations with caretakers.

One principle defines how an existing metaphor is reformed and another how new metaphors are constructed. Revolving continuously, and standing ready to assimilate each available situation, existing metaphors construe stimuli and prescribe actions in response to a range of available situations. In this process, during normal development, metaphors accommodate to particular experiences/environments with which the child engages and become ready to construe more complex stimuli and to require more complex calls for action. In abnormal development, metaphors do not accommodate to unique ingredients of experiences and remain fixed. As metaphors are repeatedly imposed on situations, the environment plays a specific role in restructuring them.

The following illustrates how the same metaphor can be imposed repeatedly on different situations but not accommodate to the experiences. A 10-year-old revealed in treatment that she construed a number of situations in terms of a metaphor of herself as an empty basket which others pass by, refusing to place something in it. When this metaphor was imposed on the following situations the child behaved with the same action (running off) and emotion (crying)—in a restaurant with her family, she happened to be waited on last; in the classroom she was standing second to last in line waiting to receive worksheets from the teacher; and, at a birthday party she happened to receive a balloon containing less air than most.

New metaphors are constructed as they take on a new organization with the emergence of new coding systems and new modes of behaving (e.g., in Piagetian theory from sensorimotor schema to imaging to verbal modes of behaving; and, in psychoanalytic theory from oral to anal to genital sources of excitation which code experiences). Here, experience plays a lesser role relative to maturational influence. Although metaphors structured by new coding systems subordinate and integrate earlier ones, the latter can be reactivated and determine behavior (regression).

The following illustrates how the same event could be experienced through early metaphors which construe diadic encounters in terms of nurture and control, as well as through a later metaphor which construes triangular relationships in terms of genital coding. In treatment a child revealed that while listening to mother read her a story, she construed the experience at one moment as mother giving her as much milk as her baby brother received; at another time she construed the experience as mother controlling her since she had to go to bed after the story was read; and, at another, she construed mother as jealous, reading to her as a way

CCTC-B*

of keeping her away from daddy's lap and the "special time" she spends with him.[4]

Metaphor as Representations and Plans of Action: A Progression of Ego Modes. In representing experiences and prescribing behaviors through metaphors, all three coding systems and modes of behaving are potentially available. However, younger children are more likely to represent events with the action mode. With development the action mode is subordinated by and integrated within the fantasy mode, and then both fantasy and action are integrated within the language mode. This progression is conceived as an ontogenetic shift from concrete processes (direct-immediate) to abstract (indirect-delayed). The action mode is most concrete and involves physically manipulating an object here and now. The fantasy mode is less concrete (direct) since images are manipulated rather than the object itself, both in the here and now and beyond in space and time, and since delay of action is required at least for the duration of the fantasy. The language mode is most indirect and delayed representing the greatest distance from the referents and action.

The same progression governs changes in metaphors within each mode. Initially, actions are immediate and tied to a narrow set of goals (e.g., a 4-year-old reveals a consistent pattern of behavior, striking his infant brother with his hand and striking his brother's crib and high chair with a toy hammer). With development, actions become tied to a wider range of goal objects and are more delayed (e.g., a 6-year-old topples various animal dolls belonging to his infant brother, obstructs the progress of an ant by laying a series of sticks in its path, and "decorates" his brother's crib with water colors). Similarly, fantasies are initially more concrete (e.g., a boy imagines his baby brother being attacked by a giant warrior) and gradually become more indirect and delayed (the boy imagines winning a bicycle race against a younger neighbor). Words also shift from concrete to more abstract forms (e.g., from "I'll smash you!" to "I'll win the game.").

By shifting from concrete to abstract, both within modes and from one mode to the next, the child gradually develops the capacity to employ alternative behaviors to achieve the same goal and to use alternative goals to satisfy the same behavior. The capacity for increasing delay and for multiple alternatives results in a range of representations and plans of action from highly personal to socially shared ones, permitting adaptive, flexible responses to changing opportunities (e.g., the second grader in the play-

[4]The metaphors stated by these three experiences are respectively: reading is milk; reading is you make me do with my body what you want my body to do; and reading is you keep me from the man I love because you want him for yourself.

ground tackles a classmate in a game of King of the Mountain, and in the classroom he tackles math problems to get the best grade).

Restructuring Metaphor: Internalizing Behaviors of Idealized Models. The content and timing of the behavior of idealized models are critical ingredients in restructuring metaphors. When the child's action mode dominates, the actions of idealized adults and peers are centered and become especially potent, when assimilated, in differentiating the range of action responses available (from concrete to abstract). As one example, an aggressive boy revealed in treatment that his metaphors about assertion and aggression included memories/representations, constructed when three years old, of father suddenly hurling a car wrench across the driveway, and of chasing his mother with a kitchen knife.

In like manner, when the fantasy mode spirals as dominant in the child's functioning, the fantasies expressed by models, when internalized, become especially potent in restructuring the child's fantasy metaphors; and, when the language mode dominates, verbalizations by models play a more critical role in the restructuring of language metaphors.

The Issues of Present–Past; Conscious–Unconscious; and Dreams. Metaphors may or may not be at work when an individual is experiencing stimuli or reliving the past. For example, if a child describes a trip the family took last summer, revealing details that form a photocopy of the event, no metaphor is at work. But, if the same child describes the trip while again knocking hand puppets together, a metaphor of family conflict is construing the event.

Similarly, a dream is not automatically a metaphor. A child could describe a dream (e.g., a tall building) as she would a picture and not show evidence that a metaphor is construing the information. In contrast, while describing the dream, the same child could stack and topple blocks, suggesting one meaning imposed on the dream.

Metaphors are not synonymous with unconscious. A person can be aware or unaware of a metaphor at work. While modeling clay, an encopretic boy did not reveal he was conscious of the possible meaning of his activity. Then, at one point, he oozed the clay between his fingers, grinned, and said, "A BM," suggesting he was becoming aware of his equation between clay and feces. Still later he angrily hurled pieces of clay at the wall. While aware that clay now equaled bullets, he was not yet conscious of the possible equation in his metaphor between defecation and destruction.

The Issue of Pathological Metaphors. A metaphor is pathological whenever its representation and associated calls for action: (a) result in behaviors that are highly idiosyncratic, inappropriate for, and/or rejected by the environment, producing anxiety, guilt, and conflict with significant others; (b) have failed over an extended period of time to accommodate to available experiences which contain ingredients (especially from models) suitable for restructuring; and (c) do not fit with developmental expectations. For example, if a 3-year-old repeatedly covers the bathroom wall with water colors, this behavior would not be viewed necessarily as prescribed by a pathological metaphor but would be if displayed by a 10-year-old. In terms of context, if a 10-year-old repeatedly smears paint on the walls of his bedroom and his parents accept this behavior, the metaphor prescribing this behavior in the home would not be pathological, but it would be if he behaved this way in school.

The Definition of Metaphor Revisited. The several issues discussed elaborate the definition of metaphor proposed at the start: (a) when the child constructs metaphors (patterns of actions/images/words/emotions) to represent experiences, a developmental sequence is followed from centering and assimilating action then fantasy then language ingredients of events; (b) the same developmental sequence defines the behaviors and emotions displayed by idealized adults which, when assimilated by the child, are especially potent in restructuring the child's existing metaphors; (c) the behaviors and associated emotions which metaphors prescribe to deal with a situation could be primarily actions, fantasies, language, or some combination of the three; (d) in development the child constructs a wide range of metaphors (from highly personal to conventional ones) which flexibly accommodate to opportunities and limitations in the environment; (e) in abnormal development metaphors remain fixed failing to assimilate and accommodate to available, relevant experiences; (f) a child could become aware of the meaning of a metaphor and the behaviors it prescribes.

CONTEXTS AND THE
EXTERNAL ENVIRONMENT

We have considered cognition as changing in response to changing environments and metaphors as interpreting events and prescribing behaviors to deal with them. We are now prepared to consider the stimuli/situation a person is handling, the third part of the theory being described. In recent years the environment as a variable has become the subject of vigorous theorizing and research (e.g., Magnusson, 1981; Zimmerman, 1983, pp. 2–17). Several issues from this domain of inquiry are noted here because they have special bearing on the theory proposed to guide CCT.

First the psychology of situations has emphasized the contextual dependency of behavior. Events and stimuli are experienced not as "discrete things out there" but as a unified whole, including the meaning a person gives them and what the person intends to do with them. A person's behavior is determined, then, as much by the context as the context, in turn, is determined by the person's fantasies and behaviors. This interaction is a reciprocal process with each system attempting to influence the other. The influence exerted by the context includes variables such as the degree to which a person has control over the stimulation and the degree to which the stimulation is unusual.

These variables in turn relate to whether and to what degree a situation will be construed by metaphors. The more a situation is unusual for a person, and/or limits the person in actively engaging the information, the more likely the situation will be interpreted in terms of the requirements of highly personal metaphors rather than socially shared ones. While individuals differ in the way a situation is interpreted, persons raised in the same environment and/or who share key personal variables are likely to share a representation of some situation. And, individuals may be conscious or unaware of the elements in a situation they are subjecting to some interpretation.

Situational psychology connects particularly to the issue of emotions and affects in terms of the stress a situation creates. While environments unusual for a person typically create stress, stress as such is not an inherent characteristic of situations but is determined by the way a person evaluates the demands of the situation and his/her ability to handle them successfully. Based on these evaluations the individual experiences the situation as requiring particular actions. Finally, situations are defined as ranging from molar ones (e.g., home; classroom; hospital setting; playground; dentist office) to molecular ones (e.g., a geometric design; a toy gun).

A MODEL OF COGNITION IN
PERSONALITY AND ADAPTATION

We are now in the position to integrate the concepts of cognitive controls, metaphor, and context to form a model which conceptualizes cognitive functioning within personality functioning and adaptation. As diagramed in Figure 2.2, the five cognitive controls are viewed as dealing simultaneously with the prescriptions and calls for action from metaphors and from stimuli/context. When coordinating and integrating these prescriptions, cognitive controls accommodate by restructuring regressively or progressively (e.g., shift in organization from leveling to increased sharpening). Once some degree of coordination is achieved, the person responds with a thought, belief, spoken statement, fantasy, physical action, or some com-

FIGURE 2.2. Model of Cognitive Controls, Metaphors, and Context in Personality Functioning

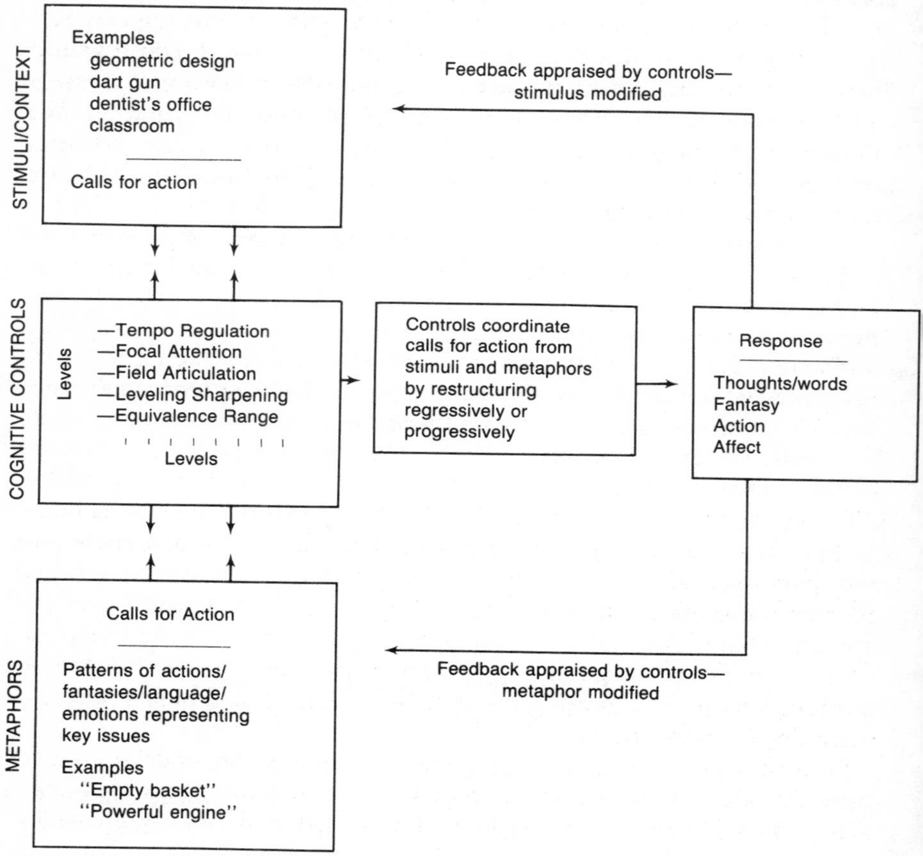

STIMULI/CONTEXT

Examples
  geometric design
  dart gun
  dentist's office
  classroom

Calls for action

Feedback appraised by controls—
stimulus modified

COGNITIVE CONTROLS

Levels
  —Tempo Regulation
  —Focal Attention
  —Field Articulation
  —Leveling Sharpening
  —Equivalence Range

  Levels

Controls coordinate
calls for action from
stimuli and metaphors
by restructuring
regressively or
progressively

Response

Thoughts/words
Fantasy
Action
Affect

METAPHORS

Calls for Action

Patterns of actions/
fantasies/language/
emotions representing
key issues

Examples
  "Empty basket"
  "Powerful engine"

Feedback appraised by controls—
metaphor modified

bination, and the response includes emotion. After a response is rendered, cognitive controls perceive and assimilate the outcome of the response within the context at hand. This feedback contributes to changes in the metaphor and its prescription and/or in the make-up of the stimulus/situation.

Examining an anecdote should help illustrate the model. A 6-year-old girl bounded happily through a neighborhood park, her father trailing a few steps behind. Passing a gentleman who greeted her warmly, she told him with excitement that they were on their way to fly a kite, quickly adding, "This is my bird kite that Uncle Charlie gave me. It can fly super high." At the same time her body leaped repeatedly, taking the form of a kite bobbing gracefully in mid-air. She abruptly said "Let's go Dad. This time the kite will go even higher." As they continued walking she happily recalled their flying a kite at the beach, and the "fantastic" kite exhibit they visited at the museum.

Chance would have it that when they set out that same afternoon again to fly kites, she passed another gentleman who also seemed magnetized by her exuberance and who greeted her warmly. The girl paused. Now her body slouched as if by heavy burdens. As she studied this man with a searching look, tears filled her eyes. She hurried on, failing to return his greeting. Her father asked her why she had begun to cry all of a sudden. Her response came in disjointed mumbles, "His blue eyes . . . white . . . really skinny . . . Uncle Charlie." But she made clear the issue was closed and asked to go home.

Of course, the father puzzled. Uncle Charlie, a favorite of hers, had died just about a year ago, after a long bout of cancer. The broad smile and the sparkling blue eyes of the second man she encountered were at odds, the father thought, with his pale, thin appearance, and Charlie did have sparkling blue eyes. But if this explained why she became sad when encountering the second gentleman, why is it that she remained happy that morning when encountering the first gentleman to whom she had also mentioned Uncle Charlie?

Reconstruction of these two experiences in terms of the model presented provides one answer and illustrates cognitive functioning within personality and adaptation.[5] When dealing with the first man, her cognitive controls perceived stimuli and prescriptions he presented: his physical appearance, warm greeting, and request, "What are you doing?" At the same time she perceived and assimilated stimuli and prescriptions from a personal metaphor which construed the man and the situation of the

---

[5]Illustrations from the treatment situation of the role metaphors play in shaping a child's experiences are discussed in Chapter 10.

moment in a particular way. The metaphor concerned ambition/achievement/pride, which included condensations of past experiences with Uncle Charlie symbolized by the kite he had given her. The metaphor could be inferred, without much risk, from her body repeatedly leaping and arching, her exuberance, and her spontaneous comments about the height her "super" kite achieved and the "fantastic" museum exhibit. Coordinating these two prescriptions, she responded with, "This time the kite will fly higher," and engaged in flying her kite. We can presume she assimilated this experience into a continually revolving metaphor of ambition/pride because of other situations she construed and handled in similar ways (e.g., constructing a poster and giving an oral presentation on kites at school).

When dealing with the second man, her cognitive controls perceived stimuli presented by him (his physical appearance and warm greeting) which, however, were construed by another personal metaphor concerning loss and separation which also included Uncle Charlie (a metaphor that probably surfaced with the anniversary of her uncle's death). In coordinating the prescriptions from context and metaphor, her cognitive controls responded more to the requirements of the metaphor and centered on his eyes, skin color, and thinness. Her controls selected these details from many others and fused them with images of her uncle in the last months of his life. As a result of this coordination, her response was, "Let's go, Dad," and she plodded home. In this encounter, then, her cognition became constricted and inhibited accompanied by sad affect. How this particular experience modified her metaphor of loss and separation, is left to conjecture. In the year following her uncle's death, she experienced goodbyes (by relatives visiting for a day, by her older brother returning to college) with tears, withdrawal, and constriction. But apparently the metaphor gradually restructured since in later years such experiences were followed by more context-relevant behavior.

The theory presented here conceptualizes highly mobile cognitive structures as mediating between the requirements, opportunities, and limitations of reality and those of the personal world of metaphor. When adequately developed, these cognitive structures enable a normal/neurotic child to develop continually a personal world, while at the same time dealing with reality demands in an organized process that fosters adaptation, personality development, and learning. This model is the roadmap that guides the rationale of CCT to which we turn in the next chapter.

Chapter 3
The Rationale of Cognitive Control Therapy

The preceding chapters introduce CCT within prevailing views of cognitive therapy, the population of children for whom the method is proposed, and a model of cognition in personality and adaptation which integrates cognition, metaphors, and contexts. Translating this model into a rationale for therapy, CCT is framed by several interlocking propositions diagrammed in Figure 3.1.

BROAD PROPOSITIONS OF CCT

In normal development five hierarchically ordered cognitive controls differentiate with experiences, and are preadapted to meet the demands of average as well as unusual environments. They copy information and its requirements simultaneously from both external environments and metaphors. These two sets of requirements are coordinated to guide responses (in action, fantasy, and language modes or some combination) that deal with information as it is, as well as symbolically, that benefit from experimentation in pretending, and that are embedded in types and levels of affect which are optimal for learning and adaptation (e.g., curiosity, assertion, anxiety). The outcome of actions taken are appraised and assimilated, resulting in further differentiation of cognitive controls and metaphors, the development of additional alternative responses, and excitement and pleasure in learning. As a result of growth in one's personal world and in cognitive tools, the individual is prepared to deal with more complex demands.

In abnormal development, cognitive controls, initially immature because of mismatches during the first three years of life between stimulation and cognition, remain mismatched with the demands of usual and unusual environments, resulting in painful stress, anxiety, or aggressive tensions. To avoid or reduce these affects, cognitive controls coordinate reality and metaphor by rigidly avoiding information from reality and/or metaphors.

FIGURE 3.1. CCT and Normal and Pathological Cognitive Functioning

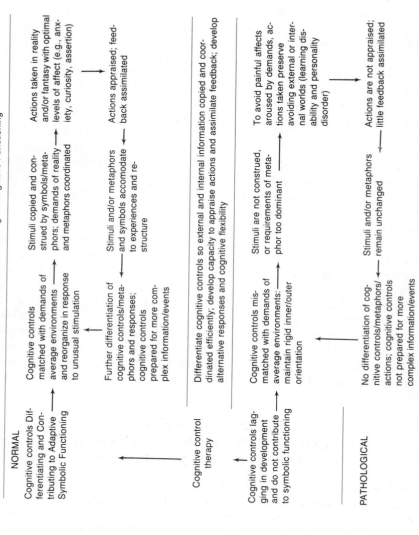

32

As a result, reality information is not copied efficiently (if the requirements of metaphor/symbols dominate), or information is not expanded into new knowledge, (if metaphors and symbols do not construe it). Therefore, actions taken as a result of pathological cognitive functioning preserve avoiding the requirements of either reality or metaphor. Further, there is an inability to appraise and assimilate the failure of responses so that neither cognitive controls nor metaphors/symbols differentiate, and possible alternative responses are not developed. Cognition remains ill-equipped to deal with more complex stimuli and perpetuates this maladaptive cycle.

Children for whom CCT is intended have difficulties that result from various disabilities at several points along this process. These disabilities are treated by having the child work on graded tasks designed to rehabilitate and differentiate cognitive controls so they become more efficient in copying and coordinating external and internal information, and more effective in contributing to symbolic functioning, pretending, and manipulating information physically and mentally, in ways that serve learning. While the child deals with these tasks, not only do cognitive controls become more efficient, but the child also learns to observe and become aware of his pathological cognitive operations and when and how alternative responses are possible. By acquiring new cognitive tools and insight, the child is equipped to change how he experiences and acts in the environment and, when indicated, to benefit from a more nondirected process of verbal/play therapy. With CCT, then, the goal is to interrupt the pathological cycle so that cognitive controls begin differentiating with experiences, contribute to the growth of a child's personal world, and provide tools for efficient learning and adaptation. From these broad propositions we consider next the coordination maintained by cognition between reality and fantasy over the course of normal development, and the different pathological forms this coordinating function takes.

NORMAL AND ABNORMAL COGNITIVE COORDINATION OF REALITY AND METAPHOR

Observations suggest three phases in the coordination maintained by cognitive controls within long-term personality development. Before the age of four years cognitive controls are oriented toward information from the world of fantasy (inner-oriented) so that information in the environment is typically experienced in highly personal terms (e.g., a 3-year-old moves and uses a shoebox in play as if it were a truck). During the first half of latency (ages 5 to 9), tempo regulation, scanning, selecting relevant information, constructing memory images, and categorizing, steadily

and increasingly work on and become more oriented towards information in reality (outer—oriented). In this position coordination provided by
cognitive controls enables the child to keep a distance from, and limit the
interference of, emotionally laden fantasies and wishes. By emphasizing
work on reality information, cognitive controls facilitate the growth of
other personality functions (e.g., identifying with and internalizing the
standards of parents and teachers and stabilizing mechanisms of defense).

During the second half of latency (age 9 to adolescence), cognitive controls shift to a position that is both outer- and inner-oriented. Now when
registering body percepts, regulating motility, scanning, articulating relevant from nonrelevant, comparing images with present stimuli, and categorizing information, the older child responds more flexibly to the requirements of external reality, as well as to those of metaphors and symbols.
While cognitive controls remain stable from one usual situation to another,
they also become flexible and mobile, shifting regressively (e.g., to more
narrow scanning) or progressively (e.g., to more broad scanning), or between fact and fantasy, as the environment and internal world change.
In flexibly responding to both worlds of information, cognition in the older
child and adolescent broadens the source of knowledge, contributes further to personality development, and adapts to changing environments.

An opposite course has been observed in the coordination unique to
clinical groups. By the age of nine years, cognitive controls are either excessively occupied with information from fantasies, wishes, and impulses
(inner-oriented), with external information inefficiently copied, or they
are excessively occupied with external stimuli (outer-oriented), limiting
the contribution of private thoughts and fantasies. Of equal importance,
cognitive controls in these rigid orientations fail to shift back and forth
from reality to metaphor in keeping with opportunities, limits, and demands. As a result, efforts to adapt usually are limited whether the task involves learning in school, in psychotherapy sessions, or from experience.

The Origins of
Pathological Cognitive Orientation

Several types of mismatch between a person's unique cognitive make-
up and his/her environments are proposed as accounting for a pathological
cognitive orientation. In one type an unusual environment, which persists over a long period of time, interferes with a child's negotiating key
developmental issues. For example, an 18-month-old requires a hip cast
for over a year, limiting motility and physical experimentation with the
environment, behaviors that are critical for further development. In another example, a child is hospitalized for surgery at the age of four resulting in a cognitive shift toward the inner world at a time when the

orientation of cognitive controls is about to shift rapidly towards external information. In both instances the mismatch is a function primarily of the developmental state of the child and "environmental accidents." In another type of mismatch, the content and form of a child's environment, from infancy, is uniquely ill-suited given the child's make-up. For example, the child's caretaker is regularly depressed or ambivalent and inconsistent in responding to cues from the child. In this instance the mismatch is a function primarily of the state of the environment.

If the atypical environment persists, the long-term adaptive process (discussed in Chapter 2) gradually takes hold. Cognitive controls accommodate to the situation, fail to differentiate and to develop the capacity to coordinate metaphors and reality. Further, these dysfunctional controls become autonomous and persist long after the unusual environment disappears. For example, if, during the first two years of life, a child is continuously stimulated by a vigorous caretaking style that is excessive and ill-timed in terms of the child's unique make-up, the child could adapt by directing attention toward narrow segments of stimulation in order to attenuate it. In this way, a level of focal attention, characterized by passive-narrow scanning would be structured, becoming a slowly changing, habitual cognitive strategy. This strategy would then be employed years later in average environments (e.g., first grade) where it would fail to coordinate the requirements of the classroom.

Last, brain injury incurred in utero or in the first years of life could, of course, contribute to the formation of a pathological cognitive orientation. However, from the view of CCT, the issue would still be how the child's cognitive functioning, now influenced by brain injury, becomes structured to coordinate external and internal information in terms of the child's capacity for complexity and change in information, the child's unique personal world, and the unusual environment surrounding him/her.

Types of Pathological Cognitive Orientation

The rationale of CCT takes a further step and distinguishes between dysfunctions in cognitive orientation that occur before the age of three years, and those occurring after, a distinction which converges with the onset of attention deficit disorders proposed by DSM III (see Chapter 1). For convenience, pathological cognitive orientations that are structured by the age of three years are referred to as Type I, and those structured after as Type II.

In the first type, information from reality and metaphor is copied inefficiently and remain segregated. As a result, by the third year of life the child shows significant failures in one or more of the following capacities:

(a) delaying motor activity, a prerequisite if symbols are to be included, along with external stimuli, in constructing reality; (b) being aware of standards and requirements of stimulation in the environment; (c) being aware of one's actions and ability to meet these standards; (d) symbolic functioning-pretending (i.e., transforming information that has been copied into something else with the use of symbols); and (e) connecting thoughts, beliefs, and verbal statements to fantasies and actions. Observation suggests that Type I pathology is associated with children viewed nosologically as personality trait disorders, developmental deviations, and attention deficit disorders.

In the second type of pathological orientation, information is copied more or less adequately, whether from external stimuli or metaphors, and there is some capacity to pretend, to symbolize experiences, to appreciate the requirements of stimulation and how actions taken satisfy these requirements. The cognitive dysfunction of these children resides primarily in the inability to coordinate the requirements of reality and metaphor and is recruited to control information in the service of primary neurotic conflicts and the solutions they prescribe. Because these children leap back and forth between reality and metaphor, and fail to assimilate experiences, metaphors remain fixed, continually construing events and prescribing responses and affects that work against learning and adaptation (neurotic metaphors). Observation suggests that Type II pathology is associated with children viewed nosologically as severe anxiety and obsessional disorders with learning disabilities, and with either hyperactivity and flight of ideas, or physical and mental constriction and inhibition.

Subtypes of Pathological Cognitive Orientation and Therapeutic Approaches for Each

There are three subtypes of Type I pathology. Each is treated with a particular therapeutic approach as shown in Figure 3.2.

Subtype I. Outer Orientation: A pervasive, rigid, outer cognitive orientation which limits the accessibility of metaphors to discover new information as well as the contribution metaphors could make in serving adaptation. Cognitive controls are excessively occupied with external, discrete, usually concrete stimuli, while metaphors and their calls for action are avoided and rarely included in responses. For these children the therapeutic approach emphasizes rehabilitating cognitive controls to perceive and assimilate the requirements of metaphors efficiently and to integrate these requirements with those of the external stimuli.

Subtype II. Inner Orientation: A pervasive, rigid, inner cognitive orientation which limits the contributions and requirements of external information and the extent to which various opportunities and limitations provided

FIGURE 3.2. Type I Pathological Cognitive Orientations and Therapy Models for Each

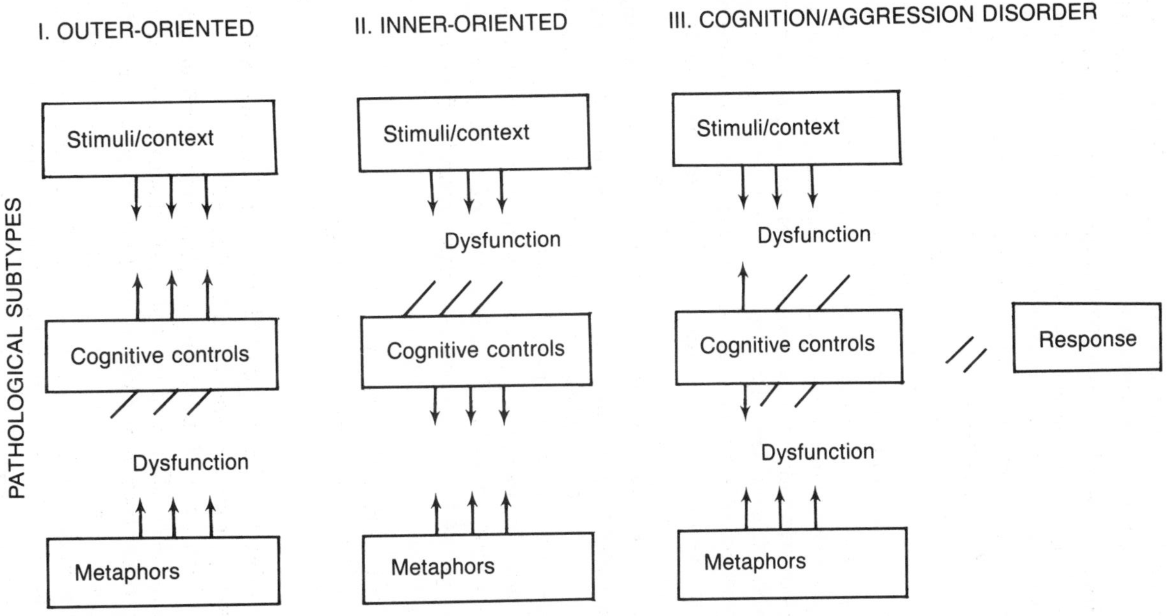
I. OUTER-ORIENTED
II. INNER-ORIENTED
III. COGNITION/AGGRESSION DISORDER
PATHOLOGICAL SUBTYPES
Stimuli/context
Cognitive controls
Dysfunction
Metaphors
Stimuli/context
Dysfunction
Cognitive controls
Metaphors
Stimuli/context
Dysfunction
Cognitive controls
Response
Dysfunction
Metaphors

THERAPY MODEL

I. Restructure cognitive controls to perceive, assimilate, and integrate requirements of metaphors with external world

II. Restructure cognitive controls to perceive, assimilate, and integrate requirements of external world with metaphors

III. Integrate aggressive action into cognitive activity and widen range of information used from environment and metaphors by the environment could be taken advantage of in experimental actions. For these children, the therapeutic model emphasizes rehabilitating cognitive controls to perceive and assimilate the requirements of external stimuli and to integrate these requirements with those of metaphors.

Subtype III. Cognitive Pathology and Aggressive Disorders: Excessive aggressivity, usually physical, which interferes with gathering and coordinating information from both metaphors and external stimuli. While these children may have access to external stimuli and metaphors, their cognitive controls are usually myopic, centering on narrow details in reality or in metaphors and exaggerating their prescriptions. The therapeutic model followed for these children emphasizes integrating aggressive actions within mental cognitive activity, thereby rendering aggression under the influence of cognitive control, reducing the disrupting influence of physical actions on thought, and promoting an increasingly widening range of information from external and internal environments.

Subtype IV. Excessive Shifts in Cognitive Orientation: There are two types of Type II pathology as diagrammed in Figure 3.3. With the first, while these children tend to achieve cognitive control maturity when a metaphor is perceived, cognition rapidly shifts to an outer orientation, centering on a reality detail *unrelated* to the metaphor, as a way of avoiding its prescriptions. Similarly, when a reality detail and its requirements are perceived, cognition immediately shifts to an inner orientation, centering on a detail from fantasy *unrelated* to the external stimulus.

To aid these children, therapy emphasizes capturing the inner metaphor from which the child escapes by centering on an external stimulus (or conversely, capturing the external stimulus from which the child escapes by centering on a fantasy) and in a stepwise fashion connecting each external stimulus and its associated metaphor, coordinating, and integrating their respective prescriptions.

With each of the four subtypes, once the primary goal of the respective therapy model has been met, the final phases of CCT (Model V) focus on techniques that address appraising the actions taken and assimilating the outcomes of these actions so as to modify metaphors and/or situations in the service of learning and adaptation. Each of these therapy models and the techniques employed are detailed in the chapters that follow.

THE PROCESS OF CCT:
PRESENTING GRADED TASKS

Since CCT is conceptualized and conducted as a variation of psychodynamic psychotherapy, the next discussion considers why CCT, while retaining some tenets of psychotherapy, departs from others by presenting the child with particular tasks and materials.

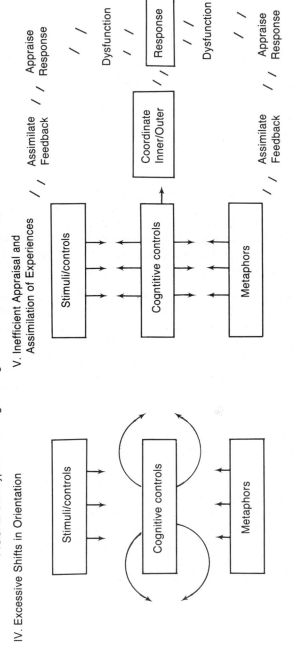

FIGURE 3.3. Type II Pathological Cognitive Orientations and Therapy Models for Each

The method of psychotherapy evolved by Freud shaped the approach of psychotherapy with children that allows the child the freedom to do in a playroom whatever he/she wishes (save for a few restrictions). With the benefit of this freedom, the child gradually repeats in play and verbal behaviors conflicts, unconscious attitudes, wishes, and feelings that are transferred to the therapist. The child resists reflecting on and understanding her behaviors in favor of repeating them. With the help of the therapist (primarily in the form of interpretation), the child gradually overcomes this resistance and learns about her conflicted wishes and fantasies, which have been outside of awareness but prescribing maladaptive behaviors. As a result of this insight or education, the child is free to modify (reform) the methods she has been using to conduct her life.

But, this nondirected treatment process has been reexamined over the past four decades by psychoanalytic ego psychologists. These therapists have observed that some adults and children cannot make use of a nondirected relationship with its deprivation of external stimuli (represented especially by lying on a couch). Some of these persons repeatedly describe daily details of life, rarely reporting dreams, daydreams, or fantasies. Others become quite stressed and frightened by the flood of thoughts and fantasies they experience and must sit up and keep a connection with the therapist and physical surroundings. In the first chapter we considered a girl who initiated checker games, session after session, in order to remain connected with external stimulation and to avoid fantasies. And, we considered a boy who became stressed and frightened by the flood of fantasies and emotions he experienced, racing about the playroom colliding with one experience after the other.

From the view of CCT, these children and adults cannot make use of a nondirected treatment situation because of their pathological cognitive orientation. The person who clings to reality details may need therapy in learning how to image and symbolize external stimuli without being overwhelmed by intense anxiety. And, the person who is flooded with fantasies may need to learn how to perceive external stimulation and its requirements without becoming panicked. As already noted, to accomplish this, CCT sets a task before the patient with which she is asked to work, rather than leaving to the patient the job of organizing some activity or set of thoughts. As an example, with one program (see chapters that follow), the child is asked to walk along a pathway at various tempos. With another program a child is asked to survey 30 geometric cutouts and retrieve particular shapes. In so doing, CCT departs from one proposition of psychodynamic therapy stated by Freud that "it is wrong to set a patient tasks." The rationale for this departure comes from two particular concepts within psychoanalytic ego psychology which are also useful

guides in conducting the techniques to be described. One is the concept
of cognitive autonomy, which, in turn, relates to symbolic functioning.
The other is the concept of stimulus nutriment and the structuring of
cognition.

The Concept of Cognitive Autonomy from Reality and Fantasy

In normal development, cognitive functioning is viewed as autonomous
both from fantasies and drives and from stimulation in the external environment.[1] Cognitive functions are guaranteed autonomy from the influence of fantasies by virtue of the fact that from birth these functions are
inherently preadapted to and "fitted with" reality stimulation. Many
studies illustrating that infants, in the first days of life, track moving targets
and scan increasingly complex patterns, could be viewed as examples of
cognitive functioning inherently fitted to stimuli in reality. On the other
hand, cognition's autonomy from the environment is guaranteed by the
human's constitutionally-given ability to transform and represent stimuli
in symbols and fantasies. Studies have shown that representational behavior surges at 12 months (e.g., the child tilts his head back, pretending
to drink from an empty cup). A person's representational growth, then,
is viewed as protecting the person from becoming stimulus-bound and
a slave to environmental requirements.

We discussed above that cognition's autonomy shifts through the course
of development: (a) from a phase when autonomy from the representational world is less and symbols are dominant in creating reality; (b) to
a phase when autonomy from reality is less and environmental stimuli
are dominant in defining reality; (c) to a phase when cognition maintains
flexible autonomy between reality and fantasy.

What do we mean behaviorally when cognition is conceptualized as
autonomous from fantasy and reality? Consider the following behaviors
of a 36-month-old preschooler who shows he has emerged from the first
three years of life free of Type I pathological cognitive orientation and with
solid capacity to exercise cognitive autonomy. He postures his body, extends his arms, and walks from a table to shelves across the room. There
he surveys a large number of toys and then focuses on a 3-inch plastic

---

[1]This discussion relies upon and elaborates one aspect of Rapaport's theory of ego
autonomy (Gill, 1967).

figure of a spaceman. He rubs the head of the figure saying, "No helmet." He continues surveying, picking up and returning objects. Finally he takes a plastic spaceman, which now has a helmet, carries it back to his table, and sets it next to another identical figure.

At another time, the same child stands on all fours, tossing his head and opening his mouth wide. He crawls slowly across the floor, each forward movement of his arms and legs suggesting power and determination. He scans an array of toys and objects on the floor, crawls to a short wooden stick, leaves it, goes to another, growls, picks up the stick with his teeth, and carries it back to his "den." There he drops the stick from his mouth next to a 12-inch wooden figure of a man, the stick and figure are the same length. He raises his head again, growls ferociously and says, referring to the stick just dropped, "Me killed him, too."

Both vignettes would be viewed as moments of play. In the first, the play involves cognitive functioning that deals with information as it exists. In the second, the play involves cognitive functioning that deals with information as it is imagined. What is critical for us is that *the same cognitive controls are operating in both episodes, in one they function relatively autonomous from fantasy and in the other relatively autonomous from reality.*

Body ego–tempo regulation is operating in the first episode when the boy extends his arms and walks across the room, and in the second when he crawls, tossing his head and posturing a fierce animal. Focal attention is operating in the first episode when the boy surveys the toys on the shelf, and in the second episode when he scans objects on the floor. Field articulation is operating in the first episode when the boy articulates relevant/irrelevant stimuli, selectively attending to a particular plastic figure, and in the second when he selectively attends to a particular stick. Leveling-sharpening is operating in the first episode when the boy compares the perception of the figure he picks up with an image (of a spaceman with a helmet), and in the second episode when he compares the perception of a stick with an image (of one of a particular length). Equivalence range is operating in the first episode when the boy sets the spaceman figure next to one that is identical, and in the second when he lays the stick next to the wooden figure referring to them as belonging to the same category ("Me killed him, too.").

These vignettes illustrate that by the age of three years, a normal child achieves the capacity to handle stimulation from reality and fantasy, using cognitive controls with autonomy. Since this capacity is achieved during the time when pathological cognitive orientations are formed, we need to take a closer look at when and how a child symbolizes. A formulation of this process contributes to a rationale of the tasks, materials, and methods used in CCT to treat children.

Symbolic Functioning:
When Does Pretending Emerge and
What Makes It Possible?

In the following discussion it is important to recall the distinction made in Chapter 2 between the construction of symbols and metaphors.[2] Constructing a symbol involves a relatively molecular process, which represents a single object, person, or event. Constructing a metaphor involves a more molar process, which represents a complex developmental issue by using a pattern of behaviors and symbols that is persistent and habitual. First, a word about the ingredients of symbolic functioning.

When a symbol is constructed, something "is presented again" in some way other than its original form. In this process a referent, which is some meaning as it exists in the mind of the person constructing the symbol, is conveyed by a vehicle which is the mode of behavior used to carry that meaning. Different behaviors can serve as vehicles (e.g., body movements, images, drawings, spoken language), and the vehicle carrying one meaning can consist of a combination of behaviors. For example, a child takes a wooden cube, "John," places it on a ruler, shouts, "Five, four, three, two, one—blast off," and slowly raises the ruler and cube. In terms of symbol construction, the cube, ruler, spoken words, and movements of the objects are all part of the vehicle conveying the referent "a spaceman in flight."

The sensory form of vehicles may or may not bear a relation to a quality of the referent. A child may place a pot on his head, or a wash cloth, as vehicles conveying the meaning of space helmet. The pot is viewed as a more conventional symbol, while the wash cloth as a more personal one, since the sensory attributes of a pot are more similar to those of a helmet. Linguistic vehicles have the least relation with their referents. Many words like "Philadelphia" or "kill", as they are, do not necessarily reflect qualities of the meaning a person may have in mind when saying, "You'll kill them in Philadelphia." Some words, especially vocalizations such as "boom," "pow," "zap," bear a closer similarity to their probable referents.

While symbolic functioning has been observed during the first year of life (e.g., a child opens its mouth as a vehicle to convey the meaning of a drawer opening), there is a sharp increase during the second year, as the child initially constructs conventional symbols (e.g., holds a toy bottle to a doll's face; covers a doll in a crib with a piece of cloth). After the second year, personal symbols mushroom (e.g., the child manipulates a

---

[2]This discussion relies in particular on observations reported by Kagan (1981) and others (Smith & Franklin, 1979).

spoon to convey a bat hitting a ball, a tool fixing a toy truck, and a rocket ship soaring through space), and the child sustains pretending for at least 15 minutes.

By the third year, then, cognition achieves a two-fold capacity, illustrated by the earlier anecdotes. Cognition remains autonomous from fantasy, copying information as it is and symbolizing it with conventional symbols. And cognition remains autonomous from reality, transforming information into highly personal terms that are quite discordant with the actual sensory properties of the information. And, the child can sustain pretending for over an hour, shifting between information as it is and as it is transformed with conventional and personal symbols, orchestrating the activity around a continuous theme. In developing this two-fold capacity, the child has the tools to serve the requirements of reality with the benefit of rehearsals in thought and to serve the requirements of fantasy with the benefits of trial actions in reality.

What cognitive capacities are prerequisites for the emergence of symbolic functioning? During the second year of life the child can regulate body tempos to perform intentional acts, scan information, articulate particular pieces in a field, compare a perception of a present object with an image of one encountered in the past, and categorize objects in terms of some physical similarity or usage. But while these cognitive functions develop, a network of other related functions also develop that implicate cognitive functioning.

One function concerns the capacity to be aware of standards defined by others and to be aware of when, whether, and how one's actions meet or violate these standards. Kagan has observed, for example, that during the second year of life children show awareness of alterations in materials (e.g., a cracked toy, a spot on one's shirt, a paint chip on a cupboard) and express behaviors that suggest standards have been violated.

Using these observations and other data, Kagan proposes that this awareness, in turn, requires the capacity *to infer* that the chipped paint, for example, was caused by someone's action and that certain actions violate standards. The capacity to infer emerges by 17–18 months. By the end of the second year the child is capable of inferring a psychological state in another person or the reasons for material or stimulation to be in some particular arrangement. Inferring, of course, requires recalling earlier experiences and relating these to present perceptions. Awareness of standards required by others and inferring whether and how one's actions meet these standards could be viewed as part of the process by which the child articulates external reality.

Other developments are more related to a child's inner world. One concerns the ability to treat objects as symbols. During the second year of life the child has the ability to substitute one object for another. Here the child must distance herself cognitively from the object and replace it with an alternative, the replacement selected initially because it shares some attribute of the original object.

The capacity to substitute one object for another relates to the capacity to assume different points of view and to shift from one to another. For example, by the age of three, a child can engage a glob of clay, as clay, assume another point of view and engage the clay as pizza pretending to eat it ("Yumm!"), assume another point of view and engage it as feces ("Yuk!"), and assume another point of view and engage it as a snake, with the child shrinking back in fear. It is important to note that with each point of view accompanying each transformation of the clay, the child assumes a different role and experiences different fantasies and emotions.

The Concept of Stimulus Nutriment and the Structuring of Cognition

During the first three years, as the child shifts between dealing with information as it is and as it is transformed and construed by fantasy, other cognitive controls gradually differentiate so that with each experience they become prepared to deal with more complex information. A formulation of this process also contributes to a rationale of the tasks, materials, and methods used in CCT.

To address this question, CCT uses the ego psychological concept of stimulus nutriment (Gill, 1967), which extends Piaget's concept of alimentation. When the environment presents a new stimulus, more complex than previous ones, an already existing cognitive structure accommodates to it until it is fully assimilated. It is during this process of accommodating to and assimilating the more complex information that the cognitive structure undergoes differentiation. Cognitive structures differentiate, then, depending upon the availability of particular stimulation, which Piaget refers to as "aliment" and ego psychology as "stimulus nutriment."

One study, which observed that infants of different ages prefer to look at checkerboards of different complexity, serves as an illustration. Three-week-old infants look longest at a 2×2 checkerboard, 8-week-old infants look longest at an 8×8 checkerboard, and 14-week-old infants prefer a 24×24 checkerboard. From the viewpoint of stimulus nutriment, cognition of the youngest infants was structured and adapted to the simplest organization of information (2×2 checkerboard) which therefore was sought after and preferred over the other displays. With an increase in age, cognition was more differentiated and therefore sought nourishment in progressively more complex information.

In normal development, cognition seeks out a level of complexity in information that is only slightly greater than the complexity of existing cognitive structures, and when accommodating to and assimilating this information, the structure undergoes further differentiation. Ego psychology elaborates this process by suggesting how cognitive structuring takes place in abnormal development as well as normal, and why deviant cognitive structures lag in differentiating.

To illustrate, consider the example discussed in the previous chapter in which focal attention is structured to engage in passive-narrow scanning as one way of handling a pathological degree of mismatch between the child's attention system and the tempo and complexity of information. Here, passive-narrow scanning serves the goal of avoiding encounters with information so that stress and anxiety are kept at some tolerable level. Therefore, unlike instances of normal development where, as proposed by Piaget, cognitive structures are nourished by more complex organizations of information, the structure of narrow-passive scanning is nourished by freedom from stress and anxiety by this mode of scanning when information is avoided. In another example, it a patient's cognition centers on external stimuli, excluding the contribution of fantasies, this pathological outer orientation is nourished by freedom from stress and anxiety achieved by the orientation when fantasy is avoided.

THE RATIONALE OF CCT:
THE COGNITIVE FUNCTIONS
ADDRESSED IN THERAPY

The several cognitive capacities achieved in normal development by the third year of life can be summarized: (a) static, dynamic (moving), and anticipated information in reality is copied by a range of cognitive processes which involve the body, regulating motion, surveying, selectively attending, comparing images of information with present perceptions, and categorizing information; (b) the relation between perceptions and images and between actions and outcomes are inferred; (c) the same information is approached from different points of view; (d) information is transformed by symbolic functioning, which involves constructing conventional and personal symbols using various vehicles to convey meaning (e.g., body postures, gestures, images, words); (e) with symbolic functioning the child develops standards of behaviors permitted and prohibited in reality, which, in turn, influence rehearsals that take place in fantasy as well as actions selected for experimentation in reality; and (f) when each experience is assimilated, cognitive structures differentiate, search for, and are preadapted to deal with more complex stimulation.

As discussed in the first chapter, CCT takes the position that children who have failed to develop these capacities are limited in the use they can make of nondirected, verbal/play therapy. Their very developmental failures limit the efficiency with which they can initiate copying and transforming information in the service of exploring and reforming the requirements of their inner worlds, experimenting in reality, and assimilating new experiences in preparation for more complex ones. Their pathological cognitive orientations, whether excessively inner- or outer-oriented, persist, nourished by the freedom they bring from intense anxiety and stress, which is aroused when situations press them to coordinate and integrate the requirements of reality and metaphor.

To treat these children, CCT takes the position that at the start the therapist initiates and directs tasks and the therapeutic process. With these tasks, each dysfunctional cognitive control, which is failing to differentiate, is rehabilitated in a developmental sequence beginning, if indicated, with body ego–tempo regulation and progressing through the hierarchy of controls to conceptual thinking (equivalence range). Therefore, a treatment program has been designed for each cognitive control.

While the task requirements vary from program to program, each of the programs address the same set of functions as outlined in Figure 3.4. The tasks require the control process being treated to: (a) copy information that is static, dynamic, and anticipated; (b) infer relationships between an image and a perception of a stimulus; (c) assume different points of view; (d) participate in symbolic functioning, constructing both conventional and personal symbols and using alternative modes as vehicles; and (e) participate in shifting among points of view during a process of pretending.

To promote the differentiation of a cognitive control while it is dealing with each of these functions, the child is presented with a series of tasks graded in a stepwise fashion according to several variables: from simple to complex patterns of information; from requiring physical activity to requiring mental activity, with physical actions subordinated; from requiring little delay to requiring more delay; and from requiring that few standards be met to requiring careful appraisals of when and how the child's responses meet the requirements of the task and of her personal world.

Figure 3.4 also shows that the sequence with which these functions are addressed honors the child's presenting pathological cognitive orientation. For children who are outer-oriented, each program begins with tasks consisting of neutral information and then gradually consisting of information that arouses and invites the participation of fantasies and the construction of symbols, first conventional ones and then highly personal ones. For children who are inner-oriented, each program begins with tasks that emphasize transforming information first with highly personal symbols and later more conventional ones; then a reverse sequence is followed as the tasks address each of the other functions, gradually reaching a point where the child copies information as it is without the participation of fantasy.

Last, at each step of a program, with each series of tasks, the child is

cctc–c

FIGURE 3.4. Cognitive Functions Addressed in Each
Cognitive Control Therapy Program

Tasks Graded within Each Function

A. Simple   _____ Complex

B. Physical Actions   _____ Mental Actions

C. Little Delay   _____ Much Delay

D. Responses not Evaluated   _____ Responses Evaluated

Cognitive
Orientation

Inner   *Outer*

Begin   End

1. Process static information as it is.
2. Process dynamic information as it is.
3. Anticipate information as it is.
4. Infer a relation between an image of information and a perception of a stimulus.
5. Assume different points of view when engaging information; reason by analogy and categories.
6. Develop symbolic functioning—pretending
   A. Assign stimuli meanings (referents) that are usual (conventional) and unusual (personal); increase independence from external stimuli; increase distance of representation from events to which they refer
   B. Express meanings using a progression of (nested) vehicles: from body actions to fantasies to language; transform one inanimate object to another and an inanimate object to an animate object
   C. Shift flexibly among meanings (referents) and behaviors expressing meanings (vehicles)
   D. Shift flexibly among roles (identities) while pretending

End   Begin

trained bit by bit to observe, evaluate, and become aware of his/her responses, when and whether they serve learning and adaptation, and to coordinate the outcome of responses in order to reform the requirements of metaphors and/or reality stimulation. When the child shows the capacity to engage all cognitive controls with flexible autonomy from reality and fantasy characteristic of the normal 3-year-old (described above), the therapist relinquishes giving direction and the child initiates and organizes activities for treatment. In the last phase, then, CCT resembles nondirected verbal/play therapy.

The next chapter discusses techniques and procedures that apply to all CCT programs. The chapters that follow (5 to 9) describe the tasks and techniques for each of the programs developed to treat one of the cognitive controls. Chapter 10 discusses the last phase of treatment, when the process takes on a more nondirected format, and the child initiates and organizes the activity.

Chapter 4
General Procedure in Cognitive Control Therapy

The general procedures discussed here apply to each of the programs detailed in the next chapters and with these techniques, and concepts considered, define the practice of CCT.

STEPS IN CCT

The goals of CCT are to promote the efficiency with which cognitive controls (a) copy and coordinate information in reality and fantasy, (b) participate in the process of symbolic functioning, and (c) participate in evaluating and assimilating actions taken and in modifying maladaptive responses and pathological metaphors. To achieve these goals two broad steps are followed. First, treatment programs are conducted in a directed format (outlined in Chapters 5–9) to restructure dysfunctional cognitive controls so that they become more efficient when dealing with information as it is and as construed in symbolic functioning and pretending. When cognitive controls become efficient tools, treatment then shifts to a nondirected format (outlined in Chapter 10) in which pathological metaphors are articulated and reformed.

The programs designed to treat the five cognitive controls are listed in Table 4.1. The tasks and techniques unique to each of these programs are detailed in the next chapters. To facilitate discussing general procedure, only a sketch is presented here. Following the theory and rationale presented previously, the tasks of the five programs form a hierarchy of complexity and of the level of cognitive-developmental maturity required by them. The tasks used to treat body ego–tempo regulation (the programs, *Who Is Me? Where Is Me?* and *Moving Fast and Slow*) are the least complex and require the child to use the earliest cognitive control (experiencing and defining the body in static and dynamic positions and in motion). For example, the child is asked to stand on one leg, or to walk over a pathway, or to move her hand toward and through an imagined cloud of smoke,

Table 4.1. Cognitive Therapy Programs Prescribed for Each Level
of the Hierarchy of Cognitive Controls

DEVELOPMENTAL LEVELS OF COGNITIVE CONTROL FUNCTIONING	COGNITIVE THERAPY PROGRAMS
5. *Equivalence Range*	5. *Where Does It Belong?* Categorizing information that is near/present and far/absent, into conceptual groups: from narrow physical and functional realms to broad conceptual realms.
4. *Leveling-Sharpening*	4. *Remember Me.* Constructing images of information in memory: from simple, global information to complex, differentiated information.
3. *Field Articulation*	3. *Find the Shapes.* Deploying attention selectively: from narrow fields of information containing little irrelevant information to broad fields with many distractions and much irrelevant information.
2. *Focal Attention*	2b. *Which Is Big? Which Is Small?* Tracking information actively: from narrow to broad scanning in macro-space and microspace.
	2a. *Follow Me.* Tracking information passively: from narrow to broad scanning in macrospace and microspace.
1. *Body Ego-Tempo Regulation*	1b. *Moving Fast and Slow.* Regulating motor tempos: from those involving body through space to those involving objects across a table to those involving a pencil across paper.
	1a. *Who Is Me? Where Is Me?* Building cognitive schemata: from those involving the total body to those involving small parts of the body.

Note. From *A Biodevelopmental Approach to Clinical Child Psychology: Cognitive Controls and Cognitive Control Therapy* (p. 487) by Sebastiano Santostefano, New York: Wiley Publishing Co. Copyright © 1978 by Wiley Publishing Co. Reprinted by permission.

and to define the body sensations experienced and express associated fantasies. The tasks used to treat the focal attention control (the programs *Follow Me* and *Which Is Big? Which Is Small?*) require the child initially to track various moving targets with her body, later only with visual attention, and still later to actively survey and scan displays of information while remaining seated.

The tasks used to treat field articulation require the child to sit still, actively scan, and sustain attention on stimuli that have been defined as relevant while ignoring existing stimuli that have been defined as irrelevant. For example, the child surveys a matrix of 25 cut-outs of varied colors, shapes, and sizes and searches for and retrieves only the medium blue triangles. Similarly the child searches for and retrieves only circular yellow paperclips from a display of 40 paperclips, varying in shape, size, and color. The tasks used to treat the leveling-sharpening cognitive control are even more complex and require a still higher level of cognitive-developmental maturity. For example, the child is asked to study and remember patterns of geometric cutouts, or paper clips, or squares of sandpaper, varying in color, texture, and shape and then to reexamine the display sometime later and determine whether or not a change in the pattern has occurred. The tasks used to treat equivalence range functioning (*Where Does It Belong?*) are the most complex and require the child to employ the developmentally most advanced cognitive control (categorizing and conceptualizing information). For example, the child identifies and lists the physical attributes and uses of a decorated porcelain vase, and then locates other objects in the room which contain one or more of the attributes and uses identified. Next the child forms groups of these objects, and conceptualizes how the objects of each group belong together.

In addition to the developmental progression represented by the five treatment programs, the tasks within each program, form a graded series of seven main steps. With each step the child is required to use the particular control mechanism being treated, but with each step the task stimuli and requirements vary as follows: Step 1—static information is copied and produced; Step 2—moving (dynamic) and/or ambiguous information is copied and produced; Step 3—information is anticipated and managed while the child assumes different points of view; Step 4—information is managed while it is embedded in stimuli which arouse fantasies and emotions; Step 5—the information presented is construed by the child as something other than what it is; Step 6—information and tasks are managed by the child while the child enacts a fantasy directed by the therapist; Step 7—information and tasks are managed within a fantasy directed by the child and enacted by the child and therapist.

Diagnostic Data to Prescribe Therapy

To prescribe a program of CCT, the first task is to diagnose which cognitive control is dysfunctional and which subtype of pathological cognitive orientation is handicapping the child. The presenting problem, history, free play interview, and intellectual and projective tests aid in this diagnosis. Evaluations conducted by the author and colleagues have also relied on tests developed to evaluate each cognitive control (Santostefano, 1978). Multiple types of data are needed because we have observed repeatedly that different cognitive control deficits underlie similar clinical symptoms, and, conversely, the same deficits underlie different syptoms. Therefore, the presenting symptom alone may not be sufficient to select one of the cognitive therapy programs.

Because of space limitations, and because the reader may not have access to tests of cognitive controls, highlights are presented here of data that could be obtained from history, intellectual and projective tests, and CCT tasks employed as diagnostic instruments in the first sessions of therapy.

Diagnostic Data from History. Discussions in Chapters 2 and 3 make clear why a history of the first three years of the child's life is invaluable. The therapist should focus questions for parents on possible mismatches between the child's unique make-up and unusual/usual environments, and on whether these mismatches interfered with the child's achieving, by the age of 4 years, the cognitive capacities outlined.

The following questions are offered as illustrations: Was the child hospitalized, moved to some very different environment, or exposed to a marked change in caretaking style for an extended period of time (e.g., an aunt with a low-keyed, depressive style cared for the child from 18 to 24 months because mother was undergoing surgery and recovery)? Did the child show behaviors suggesting failure to develop an awareness of standards and whether and how her actions met them (e.g., the child regularly showed no reaction to behaviors such as tipping over a large container of juice while reaching for a spoon)? Did the child show that attentional activity was beginning to take a deviant course (e.g., at 24 months a child sustained attention for 30 minutes while lining up identical pieces of Legos, but regularly closed her eyes when held before fish tanks at the aquarium; at 18 months a child frequently blinked her eyes and turned away from garments of bright colors worn by her or others)? Did the child show difficulty substituting one object for another and become excessively stressed if a particular plastic figure could not be found? Did the child tend not to pretend when using toys and materials; or did he use them in ways that suggested attributes of the toys were totally lost (e.g., beginning at age two, a child regularly "played" by stacking and lining up various materials, sometimes constructing patterns but rarely pretending; another child used materials, such as a spoon, almost exclusively in highly personal ways, for example, as a car, piece of BM, candy)?

When focusing on the first three years of life, parents of children with severe learning and adjustment problems frequently report two types of behavior that appear to be diagnostic markers of early cognitive pathology. With one type the parents report that the child showed unusual interest and skill with some circumscribed domain of information. One child, for example, could identify a wide range of foreign and domestic cars by the shapes of the grill and another by the hubcaps. Another child, by the age of 4, had developed the ability to name the day of the week on which each member of the family and relatives had been born. Parents view these behaviors as suggesting high intelligence and accordingly express confusion as to why their child now has difficulty learning. Such early competence, which the author refers to as the "hubcap phenomena," represents the child's attempts to reduce the external world to some circumscribed, manageable level of complexity and to avoid experimenting with information. Later these children typically develop excessive inner or outer orientations, frequently tuned out or occupied with external, trivial details.

The second type concerns isolated but repeated acts of physical aggression that occur between the second and third birthdays and exceed what common sense would view as appropriate. One child twisted off the heads of animal figures and rubber dolls, pushed his 20-month-old sister down a flight of stairs, and dropped many items into the toilet bowl. Another child gave the household cat "haircuts" on several occasions, cutting its hair, an ear, the tail, and skin. While these children display no other particularly unusual behaviors at this time, during these aggressive moments they show indifference, lack of appreciation for the things or person aggressed against and the outcome of their actions. Some parents view such behavior as "peculiar" but sustain the belief that "he is getting his feelings out," others become stressed and punish the child severely. Whatever their response, parents are usually struck by the child's indifference. These behaviors are understood as reflecting failure in a combination of developmental issues which implicate cognitive functioning: the awareness of standards and whether one's actions meet them; the capacity to pretend; and the beginning of pathological cognitive autonomy where the boundary between reality and fantasy abruptly collapses resulting in behaviors totally prescribed by fantasies.

Diagnostic Data from Psychological Tests. For our purposes, data from traditional tests are useful to aid in diagnosing whether or not a child is handicapped by a pathological orientation. In general, compare a child's efficiency and level of anxiety/stress when dealing with items that are structured and "external" (i.e., do not require imaging and fantasy, such as Wechsler tests; copying geometric designs) versus items that are unstructured and "internal" (require imaging and fantasy, such as Rorschach; telling stories to pictures). Extreme differences in performance signal a pathological cognitive orientation.

The child *handicapped* by a *pathological outer orientation* generally performs better with tasks that fit this orientation and shows a profile of differences illustrated by the following:

1. When dealing with the requirements of structured procedures,
   a. efficiency of performance relatively adequate, sometimes exceptional (e.g., drawings of geometric designs are nearly photocopies of the standards; high ability to repeat digits forward and backward);
   b. little or no anxiety/stress, affects of pleasure and industriousness while performing, conveys she is "really into" the tasks;

c. affiliated and related to the examiner as a person;
d. quick reaction times and responses developed with little hesitation.
2. When dealing with the requirements of projective tests,
a. efficiency of performance relatively inadequate, for example, with the Rorschach, difficulty in producing images; constructing images which, though suggesting some dynamic content, are global in organization in terms of developmental expectations (e.g., "creature," "butterfly," "bat," "bunch of colorful flowers," "clouds," "explosion"); with picture tests, stories are constricted and brief and essentially descriptions of the picture;
b. much anxiety/stress; affects of "boring," "This is hard," easily fatigued or sleepy while performing;
c. withdrawn from the relationship with the examiner (e.g., slumps in chair, little eye contact);
d. long reaction times and many hesitations while responding, or quick responses to escape the task; quick to say, "No," "I don't know" in response to inquiries.

The child handicapped by a *pathological inner orientation* generally performs better with tasks that fit this orientation and shows a profile of differences illustrated by the following:

1. When dealing with the requirements of structured procedures,
a. efficiency of performance relatively inadequate; for example, lower Wechsler I.Q.'s than would be expected from child's behavior and history; low performance with tasks presenting discrete, external information (e.g., repeating digits forward and backward, answering questions to the Information Subtest); when copying designs the child may embellish and animate the design or spontaneously share a fantasy (e.g., while copying a Bender Design A, "These are two space ships crashing in space.");
b. much anxiety/stress; affects of "boring," "This is hard," easily fatigued or sleepy while performing;
c. withdrawn from the relationship with the examiner (e.g., slumps in chair, little or no eye contact, slips into thought);
d. long reaction times; many hesitations while responding; very quick responses with little interest in remaining engaged with the task; quickly responds to requests for elaborations with, "No," "I don't know," "That's all."
2. When dealing with the requirements of projective tests,
a. efficiency of responses relatively adequate; for example, with the Rorschach, readily constructs differentiated images (e.g., "two people jumping up and down, beating on drums," "a man on a motorcycle, his hair blowing back; he's waving to somebody."); with picture tests readily constructs long narratives; however, responses are

sometimes excessive; with Rorschach, images take excessive liberties with the stimulus (e.g., to Card I, "This is a person in the middle with his arms up, the king is on this side saying to him, 'Climb
up,' the queen is on this side saying, 'don't climb up'; all the people are cheering and wondering what will he do; the wind is blowing smoke all around them."); similarly, the picture test stories constructed sometimes quickly leave the stimulus and introduce persons
and/or animals and events that have no referent in the picture, resulting in an elaborate, highly fanciful tale;

b. little or no anxiety/stress; affects of pleasure and excitement while
performing; conveys she is "really involved" with the task;

c. affiliated and related to the examiner as a person,

d. quick reaction times, responses developed with little hesitation.

The child handicapped by pathological *shifts in orientation* shows both
highly efficient and very inefficient moments of performance with both
structured and projective tests, showing a profile illustrated by the following:

1. When dealing with the requirements of both structured and projective
procedures,

a. characteristically shifts from the cognitive orientation required by the
task at hand to the opposite orientation (e.g., while copying a geometric design, the child abruptly stops, begins discussing a TV movie
about "a guy like Darth Vader who could turn people into puddles
of water," or while responding to a Rorschach inkblot, the child
abruptly stops and asks the examiner, "Did you make these pictures
on the wall?" or, referring to a pen set on the examiners desk, "Did
someone give you that for a present?"); other forms of such shifts
are also observed (e.g., a child periodically interrupts constructing
images to inkblots or telling stories to pictures in order to reposition
carefully a tissue box on the table; another child interrupts the same
processes to rub carefully his index finger over pencil marks on the
table for many seconds; a child produces two relatively elaborate differentiated images to a Rorschach inkblot and then abruptly shifts
and focuses on a tiny detail construed in global, concrete terms—
"This is like a tiny bump," "These are tiny specks of something.");
similarly, the child interrupts an elaborate story to a picture and becomes occupied with a concrete detail in the picture (e.g., "Does this
guy have buttons on his shirt? Yeah. No, I can't tell.");

b. much anxiety/stress with both types; rapid shifts in affect while performing, from moments of pleasure and excitement to moments of
boredom, fatigue/sleepiness, and complaints that the task "is hard";

c. frequent shifts in the quality of the relationship with the examiner;
from moments of being allied and engaging to moments of being in

opposition to the examiner and avoiding the relationship (e.g., refuses a task, stares out the window for several minutes);
d. shifts in reaction time and the ease with which responses are delivered (e.g., with the Block Design Test, a child quickly begins constructing an easy design, completes one half of it, then hesitates and shows confusion while attempting to complete it; with the Rorschach, very quick reaction times to some cards and long delays to others).

Diagnostic Data from the First Treatment Sessions. The first three or four sessions can be used diagnostically to clarify which therapy program and steps within it should be prescribed for a child. As discussed above since cognitive controls, and the programs designed to treat them, represent a hierarchy of cognitive activity, from less to more complex and differentiated, the therapist can easily experiment to select an appropriate program. Similarly, the graded steps and tasks that make up each program lend themselves nicely to this purpose.

Initially, a treatment program is selected and administered that fits the child's developmental competence. Then, depending upon the child's response, the treatment shifts to a program that requires more or less complex cognitive activity. For example, assume a therapist, using her "best guess" introduces treatment in field articulation (Chapter 7), presents a relatively simple display of eight cutouts of two shapes and two colors, and asks the child to search for and retrieve only red circles. The child glances at the therapist, yawns, walks away and begins manipulating material on the shelf. The therapist encourages the child to return to the table and repeats the instructions. Now the child asks for a drink of water. Because of the child's behavior, the therapist shifts to the developmentally lower, focal attention program.

Our next illustration considers diagnostic experimentation by shifting tasks from one set within a program to another step in that same program. The therapist selects the field articulation program as suitable, and again using her "best guess," presents a task from Step 1, consisting of a display of 24 geometric cutouts of multiple shapes, colors, and sizes, and asks the child to retrieve all the small, blue diamonds. The child performs the task efficiently and with no signs of stress. The therapist moves to Step 4, presents an array of cutouts now surrounded by pictures which arouse fantasies/emotions (e.g., a baby nursing on a bottle, a child eating an ice cream sundae) and asks the child to retrieve all of the medium, green triangles. The child picks up two cutouts, stops, fidgets, looks away, continues picking up a large, green triangle (an error), looks away, etc. The child's behavior now makes clear that the field articulation function is not operating as efficiently as when there were no pictures surrounding the display. Emotions/fantasies are not being balanced effectively, interfering with cognitive activity. With this observation, the therapist shifts back to Step 2. The child is presented a display of 20 buttons of three sizes and colors and asked to locate all of the smallest green buttons immediately next to medium white buttons.

Planning and Conducting a CCT Program for a Child

Using diagnostic data as a guide, the therapist selects a program and a level within that program, the complexity of which matches the child's developmental cognitive capacities, and continues in a stepwise fashion to programs requiring developmentally higher cognitive capacities.

To facilitate our discussion, consider children outlined in Table 4.2, referred for assistance because of learning disabilities and behavior problems and who show one or another cognitive dysfunction (e.g., short attention span, highly distractible, unable to stick with a task, forgetting assignments). Mary has difficulty using her imagination (outer-oriented), struggling with writing make-believe themes. Tom shows an inner orientation, frequently lost in thought and tuned out. John frequently aggresses verbally and physically and is extremely restless. Sally is excessively distractible, frequently shifting between the content of school tasks and fantasy.

Because observations and history indicate Mary's developmental failure occurred at all stages of cognitive control functioning, her program begins with treatment in the developmentally earliest cognitive control, body ego—tempo regulation, and accordingly with the *Who Is Me? Where Is Me?* program. As Mary develops some ability to attend to body perceptions and construct images representing them, the next program in the hierarchy is phased in (*Moving Fast and Slow*) and then the next (*Follow Me*), and so on, progressing systematically to therapy in conceptual thinking. In this way, her course of therapy proceeds in a stepwise fashion with each developmentally higher program phased in as Mary gives behavioral evidence that the cognitive control being treated has developed competence.

But we have already noted that each program consists of several steps: from those where the tasks require that the cognitive control being treated manage information as it is to those where the tasks require that the cognitive control manage information that is transformed in the process of symbolic functioning and pretending. Therefore the next consideration concerns the sequence in which Mary is administered the steps of each program. The guideline followed in CCT is that the pathological orientation of a child determines the sequence in which the steps of a program are conducted. The outer-oriented child begins with tasks that initially fit the child's tendency to avoid the prescription of fantasies, and gradually moves to those that require the information be processed while engaged

Table 4.2. Planning the Starting Point and Course of CCT

ASSESSMENT OF COGNITIVE CONTROL	MARY	TOM	JOHN	SALLY
Equivalence Range (ER)	Narrow, concrete	Narrow, concrete	Narrow, concrete	Narrow, concrete
Leveling-Sharpening (LS)	Unstable images	Unstable images	Unstable images	Adequate
Field Articulation (FiAr)	Indiscriminant attention deployment	Indiscriminant attention deployment	Adequate	Indiscriminant attention deployment
Focal Attention (FoAt)	Narrow passive scanning	Adequate	Adequate	Adequate
Body Ego–Tempo Regulation (B–T)	Global body schema, poor regulation of tempo	Adequate	Adequate	Adequate
Assessment of Orientation	Subtype I: Outer Orientation	Subtype II: Inner Orientation	Subtype III: Aggressive	Subtype IV: Shifts in Orientation
Treatment Prescribed	1. Restructure all cognitive controls 2. Follow guidelines for outer orientation	Restructure FiAr, LS, & ER Follow guidelines for inner orientation	Restructure LS & ER Follow guidelines for aggressive disorders	Restructure FiAr & ER Follow guidelines for shifts in orientation

in fantasy. The inner-oriented child follows an opposite sequence, beginning with tasks that initially fit the child's tendency to engage in fantasies and avoid the requirements of reality information, and gradually moves to those that require the cognitive control being treated manage information without the participation of fantasy.

In our example, Mary is handicapped by an outer orientation. Therefore, each program administered would begin with steps presenting "outer-oriented tasks" and gradually shift to steps presenting "inner-oriented tasks." In this way, the requirements of each program initially respect and fit Mary's pathological orientation and gradually promote flexibility and autonomy from external stimuli.

Continuing with the examples listed in Table 2, Tom's profile indicates adequate development in the first two cognitive controls and dysfunctions beginning with field articulation. Accordingly, his treatment begins with the program *Find the Shapes* and gradually phases in the programs *Remember Me* and *Where Does It Belong?* in that order. Because of his pathological inner orientation, each program begins with "inner-oriented" steps and gradually shifts to the "outer-oriented" steps. The description of each program presented in Chapters 5 through 9 include instructions to introduce the outer- and inner-oriented child into treatment.

With the next illustration, John shows dysfunctions in two developmentally advanced controls which call for therapy to begin with the program *Remember Me* and continue with the program *Where Does It Belong?* Because John also shows a major aggressive disorder, these programs are conducted using techniques, described in Chapter 10, which integrate John's aggressive actions, fantasies, and language within the tasks. Sally shows dysfunctions in field articulation and equivalence range, illustrating a case in which cognitive controls in need of treatment are not sequenced. Her treatment would first consist of tasks from the program *Find the Shapes* and then from the program *Where Does It Belong?* To restructure Sally's pathological shifts in cognitive orientation, each program is conducted using special techniques, also described in Chapter 10.

As these examples illustrate, all children may not require each of the therapy programs, but when two or more programs are required, they are conducted in a sequence following the cognitive control hierarchy. In this way, therapy in the first program administered fosters cognitive capacities that are prerequisites for the next. Further, once a program is selected, a child may require all or a few of the steps of that program and may require many or a few sessions with a particular step before moving to the next. How does the therapist determine whether a child successfully meets the requirements of a particular step?

Criteria for Success. The steps of each program are defined by tasks containing fairly explicit requirements representing various levels of complexity. Exceptions are the program *Who Is Me? Where Is Me?* and *Where Does It Belong?* where the cognitive competence being developed is clearly defined but the task requirements are less structured and left more to the clinical judgement of the therapist. With programs that contain fairly explicit task requirements at each step, the following quideline is recommended: before moving to a more complex task, *a child should successfully handle three trials or tasks in succession at the same level of complexity without showing disruption in the cognitive process required and/or high levels of stress/ anxiety or other affects* (e.g., fatigue, boredom, opposition). For example, if a child, treated with the program *Find the Shapes*, accurately retrieves in three successive trials particular cutouts designated by the therapist from a field of 15 (consisting of two shapes, two colors, and two sizes), and shows some pleasure in working, the therapist could introduce a more complex field of 20 cutouts (consisting of three shapes, three colors, and three sizes).

Materials Used in the Tasks. The tasks of each program make use of materials such as geometric cutouts; rods; black, white and primary colors; lines and contours; buttons; pieces of cloth; and other familiar objects. These materials are selected because, as mentioned earlier, the cognitive controls of children being treated were compromised during their first three years and engaging information results in stress. Therefore, to rehabilitate dysfunctional cognitive controls, the materials and tasks should "take the child's cognition back" to an earlier phase during which cognition functioned in a "conflict-free" sphere of experience dealing with shapes and patterns similar to those an infant engages in the first two years. The materials and tasks used, such as pursuing a moving cube or discriminating a field of cutouts, are not ends in themselves but means to an end—namely fostering the cognitive control of information from reality and fantasy as a psychologically nourishing, pleasurable activity.

The programs also require material, such as a toy spider and pictures of a wounded soldier or of a baby feeding, as a way of arousing fantasies/ emotions. These stimuli create stress for the outer-oriented child whose cognition automatically turns away from and defends against fantasy/ emotions. But these very stimuli are welcomed by the inner-oriented child for whom geometric cutouts are stressful since for her cognition automatically turns away from and defends against the requirements of external reality.

The stress a child experiences in response to stimuli and task requirements is a function, then, of the child's cognitive orientation. Therefore, the therapist should be aware of when a pattern of geometric cutouts to be remembered is a welcomed stimulus, readily assimilated by a child, while a pattern of rubber, mythical creatures is rejected and vice versa.

Conducting a Program and Developing a Child's Self-Observation. Instructions to introduce a program and explain the tasks of each step are provided in the chapters to follow. The therapist should, of course, modify the statements suggested to suit the child's language ability. Moreover, given the view maintained by CCT of the place language holds in cognitive therapy, the therapist is urged to keep verbalizations to a minimum initially and to learn which words have "steering power," or those words which influence or modify a child's behavior.

During the first session, and whenever indicated thereafter, the therapist actively cultivates the child's understanding of the reason for asking her to deal with particular tasks, rather than to play, and attempts to indicate what the child and therapist hope to accomplish. The child should eventually understand that the treatment program is intended to change how he/she thinks and what interferes with the control and use of information, whether from reality or fantasy. In the next chapters, the goals of each program are stated in the language of therapists. The therapist's job is to convey these goals in the child's language. One way to accomplish this is to use the name of the program from the beginning. When a child is told, for example, "We are going to play a game called *Follow Me*" and then immediately is asked to track a target moved by the therapist, the activity coupled with the name *Follow Me* begins to set the stage for the child's understanding that the goal of the treatment is to develop further the ability to sustain attention on moving information. Similarly, the name of the program, *Remember Me*, along with the first task begins to cultivate an understanding that the goal is to remember increasingly larger fields of information and to compare what one remembers to perceptions of present information.

The understanding a child cultivates of the treatment goals relates to the task of developing a child's capacity for self-observation, a major aspect of CCT. Self-observation emerges within a treatment process that is cultivated by a therapist with clinical flexibility, skill in interpersonal relating and negotiating, and careful management of transference and resistance, each a hallmark of psychodynamic therapy. Therefore, although the steps of each program are described in structured, mechanistic terms, the programs should not be conducted in a mechanistic manner within a relationship that takes on the quality of an instructor and pupil. Rather, the tasks should be administered as arenas within which child and therapist transact and negotiate, creating a process in which the child has the freedom to relive pathological modes of thinking and adapting, become conscious of these behaviors, and modify them.

Because the tasks make use of simple materials and require specific cognitive/behavioral responses, they provide a child with an excellent opportunity to make fairly molecular observations of his/her cognitive functioning and the factors that disrupt its efficiency. In terms of developing a child's self-observation, the course of treatment defines three phases. In the first, the therapist encourages the child *while engaging tasks* to observe repetitive behaviors/emotions that compromise the efficiency of the particular cognitive control being treated (e.g., walking away to pick up a toy while tracking a moving target; vigorously scratching while actively scanning two rods set far apart; suddenly throwing or banging task materials; yawning with fatigue and/or boredom; hurling vindictives at the tasks or therapist). As the child develops the capacity to observe, the therapist, in the second phase, helps the child establish connections between these behaviors and the particular ingredients of tasks that increased in complexity and therefore increased stress (e.g., the target to be tracked moved through a curvolinear path versus a linear one; two rods to be scanned and compared were set 6 feet versus 3 feet apart; the number of geometric cutouts to be remembered increased from six to nine). When the child shows capacity to observe the relation between behaviors/affects that interfere with cognitive efficiency and ingredients of the tasks, the therapist, in the final phase, helps the child relate tasks and behaviors in the office to similar situations and behaviors that occur at school and home. It is only in this last phase, when the child shows a solid ability to observe and generalize behaviors, that the therapist includes interpretations that integrate aspects of the child's personality dynamics, the styles of other persons (teachers, parents), and ingredients of situations that usually result in maladaptations.

The Use of Modeling. Throughout each program the therapist is urged to demonstrate and model the response required by a task. Previous chapters detail the proposition that in structuring psychological behavior, the action mode should dominate initially, and the child should initially assimilate the actions of models. The programs, *Who Is Me? Where Is Me?* and *Moving Fast and Slow* in particular require the therapist "to speak" with his/her body, modeling postures and gestures. While other programs subordinate body movements, the therapist should still be active, modeling the task requirements. The therapist who is inclined to conduct therapy primarily verbalizing requirements, or by engaging a child in verbal interactions, is encouraged to be aware of this tendency and to use modeling as often as indicated as a way of interacting. This issue is stressed because in normal development before age 3 the structuring of cognitive controls and of a flexible cognitive orientation does not take place as the child responds to and assimilates verbal statements. Rather, important structuring takes place by the second birthday—long before language is fully developed (see Chapters 3 and 11).

The Last Step of a Structured Treatment Program. Once the outer-oriented child reaches those steps of a program that provide therapy within symbolic functioning, and once the inner-oriented child reaches those steps that provide therapy with information that does not require pretending, each child participates in a final step where the therapist prescribes and directs a fantasy the child is asked to enact. The therapist embeds within this fantasy various tasks that require the child to use the particular cognitive control that has been treated. Gradually the therapist relinquishes giving direction and passes on to the child the freedom to invent play themes, fantasies, and activities, which similarly involve the cognitive control process treated. This step is included to cultivate the child's cognitive flexibility and autonomy, both from the requirements of reality and fantasy, making available the particular cognitive control as a tool to serve efficient learning and adaptation. This step is also included to provide a bridge to a phase of nondirected play/verbal therapy, if indicated, within which the child articulates and restructures pathological metaphors that have been a source of maladaptation. Techniques for this nondirected phase are discussed in Chapter 10.

DURATION/FREQUENCY OF SESSIONS AND LENGTH OF TREATMENT

In a majority of cases the duration of each session has been the traditional 50-minute hour. However, in a number of cases presenting severe degrees of cognitive and emotional pathology (e.g., borderline states, autistic and/or schizoid features), we have made use of sessions lasting only 15 or 20 minutes but conducted several times a week (or even two times a day in residential programs).

As for frequency, for severe cognitively disabled children, fewer than two sessions a week is ineffective. Three or four sessions per week is highly desirable, especially with inpatient populations, with each session abbreviated to 20 or 30 minutes. If the cognitive deficits are less severe and/or if CCT techniques are blended within a course of traditional psychotherapy, one session a week could be effective.

The duration of treatment varies, of course, with the severity of the child's cognitive pathology and adjustment problems and therefore no guidelines are available. In our experience the CCT method has been effective with some cases when applied for about twelve months (weekly sessions) while in many cases, because of the severity of the pathology, 2 or 3 years of treatment have been required to turn the tide.

GENERAL ARRANGEMENTS

Any typical playroom or clinical office is an appropriate setting for CCT. However, if a child requires therapy in body ego–tempo regulation and in focal attention, a space as large as 10 by 20 feet may be required, and an even larger space, such as a school gym, is desirable. The only pieces of furniture required are a table about 4 feet long and suitable chairs.

Except for the materials used in CCT, there should be a minimum of toys and play materials present during the first phase of treatment. One reason for suggesting that play materials not clutter the office is that in addition to the therapist, the geometric cutouts, rods, and other materials described in the next chapters take on significance in the transference. Because the geometric cutouts, for example, are the information the child must process, and because the child has experienced lifelong stress and conflict between cognitive structures and the demands of information, the cutouts become the target of transference and resistance. Material unrelated to the tasks could interfere with this transference development. The manner in which the child experiences and behaves with the material used and how the child fights against and flees from the task, allows the therapist to teach the child about ingredients that underlie school failure and related personal problems.

THE TECHNIQUE OF
DIRECTED FANTASY

As noted above, in the final step of each program, the therapist directs the child in constructing and enacting fantasies which include the cognitive control process being treated. When this step is introduced, the child has already achieved the capacity to use the control mechanism to manage information as it is and as it is when transformed with conventional and personal symbols. Therefore the child is equipped to extend this competence into sustained pretending.

By engaging in cognitive activity within sustained pretending, the child cultivates several developmental skills achieved by the normal 3-year-old (see Chapter 3) (e.g., flexibly substitute objects with others; infer what ingredients make the substitutions possible; appreciate the requirements of reality and fantasy; enact the requirements of fantasy in experimental action and accommodate to the requirements of reality in experimental fantasy; sustain pretending and experimental action for a period of about one hour). A phase of sustained pretending also provides a bridge to a phase of nondirected verbal/play therapy in which the child reforms key pathological metaphors.

Each program description includes examples of fantasies the therapist could direct, and Chapter 10 describes examples of sequential motifs that occur in a nondirected format and the techniques used to reform metaphors. Therefore in this section, we list only the key steps followed in the technique of directed fantasy. In considering these steps, it may aid the reader to review the concept of metaphor presented in Chapter 2.

Step 1. The therapist describes a situation, events, and characters (human and/or animals; mythical figures). The content of the fantasy relies upon observations gathered while conducting the structured steps of the program and knowledge of the child's adjustment problems and past history.

Step 2. The therapist assigns a character (identity) to the child and one to the therapist and prescribes a task that emphasizes the cognitive control process being treated.

Step 3. Child and therapist *enact* the prescribed roles and pretend events.

Step 4. As the fantasy is enacted, the child is encouraged to elaborate its ingredients with directed questions, e.g., "Who else comes along?" "What happens next?" "If the detective can't do that, what does he do next?"

Step 5. The therapist helps the child extend the fantasy to include other situations/characters/events, or to prescribe another fantasy that may be manifestly different. In the structured form of this technique, the therapist insures that the new activities included emphasize cognitive control functioning (e.g., scanning an array of wooden cutouts, which child and therapist pretend are various weapons hidden by the enemy in a cave; examining this array of cutouts to determine whether they are the same as a cache of weapons found earlier).

Step 6. As the fantasy is extended and/or transformed into others, the therapist is active gradually guiding the child in measured steps to include several ingredients in the sequence noted below.

1. The fantasy articulates that a "good force" is opposed by a "bad force" each represented by one or more fictitious characters.
2. The unique powers of the bad force are elaborated along with its intentions and the behaviors and activities it prescribes.
3. The good force is provided initially with defenses capable of providing protection against the unique powers of the bad force (e.g., special suits that have the power to deflect dangerous beams of "green light" that come from the evil force).
4. As the bad force is elaborated and the good force equipped with special defenses, the good force is assisted by allies—other characters with attributes that are particularly suited to deal with the evil force.
5. These allies give rise to the identity of an "ego ideal"—a character who is usually the leader of the allies (e.g., "the king's highest servant," "the queen's First Commissioner," "the assistant of the village chief").

The ego ideal embodies special powers and represents standards concerning rules and regulations, honesty, civilized behavior, the value of effort in succeeding. Frequently the child assigns the role of the ego ideal to the therapist, and later alternates the roles of good force and ego ideal with the therapist. Of course, sometimes the child also assumes the identity of the character representing the bad force.

6. The good force, assisted by the ego ideal enacts a solution in which the bad force is gradually overpowered, reformed, and civilized. The intentions and behaviors of the bad force are changed, and the bad force becomes an ally of the good force.

Step 7. Interpretation and insight. When this technique is used in a short-term phase of therapy, the therapist does *not* make interpretations. Usually a child is not aware of the meaning of particular symbolic characters and happenings nor of the possible relationships between the child's real maladaptive behaviors and those imputed to the evil force. After enacting a series of fantasies, some children spontaneously identify a relationship between the symbolic bad character and themselves or an acquaintance, suggesting that some issues are surfacing to awareness (e.g., "That Charlie Chink—a fictitious character representing a bad force—is just like Tommy; he's always swearing in school and breaking everybody's things."). The therapist acknowledges these relationships, and at most clarifies them, but does not interpret a relationship to the child or some motivation/dynamic/wish on the part of the child.

The "insight" the child gains during a short-term phase of directed fantasy is primarily "behavioral," "nonverbal," and "nonconceptual" and represents a corrective experience. Following discussions in previous chapters, it is assumed that as the child assimilates the identity of the ego ideal, and the imaginary experience of protecting against and eventually overpowering and reforming the bad force, some aspect of the child's pathological metaphors undergo change and begin to prescribe less maladaptive ways of construing events and behaviors/emotions to deal with them. Interpretations are included, as outlined in Chapter 10, when a sequence of fantasies are recycled during a more long-term, nondirected format.

To conclude this section, several additional issues should be noted. A single directed fantasy, or even two or three, usually cannot cover all of the steps listed above. However, a single fantasy could include the first five steps as illustrated in the examples given in the next chapters. To benefit from these five steps, the child ideally should engage in cognitive control activity within several fantasies enacted over several sessions. Many more sessions and directed fantasies are needed to engage Step 6 efficiently during which the child elaborates good and bad forces, defenses required by the good force, an ego ideal that comes to its assistance, and the final reformation of the bad force.

One child may require only one or two sessions with Steps 1 through 5 and readily move into Step 6. Another may be capable of engaging in only two or three directed fantasies following the first five steps. Last, the more the therapist joins the child in acting roles and elaborating pretend situations and events, the more effective the technique. The therapist accustomed to treating children from a chair will need to reconsider his/her style to make optimal use of this method.

EVALUATING SYMBOLIC FUNCTIONING

Each treatment program includes tasks that require the child to construct symbols representing body positions and tempos and materials the child manipulates within cognitive control functioning. During these tasks, the therapist is required to help the child evaluate the symbols constructed. Three guidelines are followed, which have proven effective with children as young as 6 years old, as well as with adolescents. When evaluating symbols in terms of these guidelines, the child should not believe that "there are right and wrong answers." Rather, the guidelines are designed to help the child understand how symbols can vary as representations carrying meaning and as communications to others. The goal over the course of treatment is to help the child develop an appreciation of the requirements of reality and fantasy and understand how the two can be related. The discussion that follows assumes the reader has reviewed material on symbolic functioning in Chapter 3. The examples given come from a study of the symbols children constructed when construing how they might use a thin green wooden stick (from a Lincoln Log® game set) and a paper clip. Examples involving objects used in the treatment programs are given in the next chapters.

Evaluating the Fit Between a Symbol and Attributes of Objects Symbolized

With this guideline a child is asked to articulate the physical or functional attributes of the object symbolized and determine how they fit the symbol. For example, when asked to imagine and pretend what one could do with a green stick, one child noted "You can open a can of paint with it," and another, "You can use it like a spoon and stir things like lemonade." With the first, the child is helped to evaluate that the stick would likely break if the can has never been opened and could probably open a loose lid. With the second, the evaluation would point out that the properties of the stick fit the pretend usage.

Similarly, when asked to pretend usages for a paper clip, one child said, "You can stick it in your nose," another, "You can hang a key on it." In evaluating these responses, each child develops the understanding that the properties of the paper clip fit each pretend usage. The child who produced the first usage was also helped to understand its highly personal meaning. (See below.) In contrast, a child who pretends "It's a saw you cut wood with," would be shown that the paper clip is small, does not have cutting teeth like a saw, and so on.

Evaluating Whether a Symbol Is a General or Specific Statement of the Attributes Construed

With this guideline the child cultivates an understanding of when symbols are overly extended, or global, versus specific. For example, in pretending usages of a green stick, one child responded, "You can hit someone on the head with it," and another, "You can make a straight line like a ruler." Evaluating the first, the child is helped to see that the pretend usage is a general statement, since many different objects can be used to hit someone on the head (e.g., a rock, a book, a marble, a shoe). The second symbolic use is more specific to the properties of the stick. With the paper clip as a stimulus, the symbolic use, "You can stick it in your nose," represents a more general statement, and the child is helped to understand that many other items can be placed in one's nose (e.g., a button, a marble, a crayon); while the use, "You can hang a key on it," is more specific. Similarly, if a child pretends, "You can do a magic trick with it and make it disappear," the child is helped to understand that as construed, the symbolic use is a general statement since many other similarly small items can be used in magic tricks. In contrast, "You can clip it on your fingernails," is a relatively specific symbolic use of the properties of a paper clip.

Evaluating Whether a Symbol Is Conventional or Personal

Here the child cultivates an understanding of when and how a symbol communicates to others as well as to oneself, and that conventional symbols are readily understood by most persons while personal symbols are more likely understood only by the person or a close friend.

Using examples given above, pretending to use a stick to open a can of paint or to stir lemonade, although differing in the degree of fit, represent conventional symbols since someone else is likely to understand the symbolic use. In contrast, pretending to use a stick, "to build a farm," or "to make the stomach of a puppet," or as "a bridge over a river," represent personal symbols, the meanings of which are not readily understood by someone else. Along the same line, pretending to use a paper clip with others to make a necklace is a conventional symbol; while pretending to use it "to make a castle and this is the top part of it," or putting it in one's nose, are more personal symbols, the meanings of which are not readily understood by others.

MANAGING TRANSFERENCE
AND RESISTANCE

As the clinician would guess, it is frequently not possible to conduct a prescribed course of therapy as planned. At various times along the way, the child regresses and resists working with tasks. CCT ascribes to the psychoanalytic view that managing and resolving transference and resistance is necessary in order to modify and reform behavior.

What is meant by transference and resistance? While interacting with the therapist, the child repeats, bit by bit, the methods she has used to conduct her emotional life and to engage in learning. These methods are developed from past experiences with caretakers and environments. When repeating past behaviors, the patient construes and experiences the therapist as if she were one of these past caretakers, a process Freud referred to as transference.

Resistance to change represents the other side of the same coin. Freud observed that resistance is often graphically displayed by a patient in transference experiences with the therapist. By experiencing the therapist as someone else, rather than as a therapist, the patient is justified in using old, maladaptive ways of coping and therefore refuses to suspend these habitual ways of behaving and to assimilate stimulation and persons as they exist, rather than as they are imagined. Thus, much of a person's behavior in the transference is viewed as serving resistance to change; and from this view transference becomes synonymous with the process of resistance.

While the patient's transference behaviors block change, they simultaneously make available unique opportunities to promote change. As the patient relives unsuccessful ways of behaving, experiencing the therapist as someone else, the therapist can behave in ways that are different from past caretakers and therefore restructure the maladaptive behavior. An early statement by Freud emphasizes the importance of this process in psychotherapy and also serves to clarify CCT as a psychodynamic process, distinguished from methods of perceptual training and behavior modification.

. . . we must (eventually) treat his illness not as an event of the past, but as a present day force. This state of illness is brought, piece by piece, within the field and range of operation in the treatment, and while the patient experiences it as something real and contemporary we have to do our therapeutic work on it . . . (Freud, 1914, *Collected Works*, Standard Edition., Vol. 12, p. 151)

In ascribing to the management of transference and resistance as the nexus for change, CCT proposes that with cognitively disabled children, the conflict to be resolved does not exist between wish and defense but between cognitive structures and information in the environment and/or fantasy. These children habitually use immature cognitive control behaviors (e.g., narrow scanning or an outer orientation), which may have adaptively managed environments and caretakers in the past, but are now maladaptive in assimilating present stimulation and persons. The mismatch between cognition and current stimulation results in stress and flight and fight behaviors, which the patient repeats in the treatment situation, experiencing the therapist and the therapeutic tasks as carbon copies of earlier caretakers and situations. These maladaptive modes of functioning are tenaciously repeated, rather than examined, and thus become resistant to change.

Since the cognitive dysfunctions being treated were structured during the first three years of life, it would follow that the transference behaviors these children reveal repeat modes of negotiating that derived from that period. What we need, then, to organize observations in the treatment room and guide technique is a developmental model of mother–infant interaction during the first three years of life. The model the author has adopted for this purpose derives from the work of Louis Sander (1962, 1964, 1976).

Sander's Model of Mother–Infant Interaction

On the basis of longitudinal observations, Sander has proposed that infant and mother "negotiate" nine "issues," defining developmental periods which contribute to the structuring of the infant's ego functions (e.g., perception, motility, expressions of earliest emotions, and style of seeking and avoiding stimulation and caretakers).

Initial Adaptation (0–3 Months). This issue concerns fitting together mothering activities (e.g., affects, type, and timing of stimulation) with cues the baby gives (e.g., states of alert inactivity, various cries, smiling, fussiness) with each influencing, assimilating, and accommodating to the other. Successful negotiation of this first issue is reflected in the infant's organized rhythm of feeding and sleeping, and the extent to which mother feels she "knows" the child.

Establishing Reciprocal Exchange (3–6 Months). This issue concerns the extent to which interactions between mother and infant include active-passive exchanges (e.g., during feeding and around the infant's rapidly developing smiling response) and the extent to which mother can allow the child to play or pursue some activity by himself.

Early Directed Behavior (6–9 Months). The baby takes more initiative directing his own behavior and the behavior of others, intends to engage a person or stimulation, anticipates a response or stimulation, and attempts to control stimulation that is approaching, avoiding, or disappearing. One major accommodation required of mother is that she should honor the infant's preferences by removing or bringing particular objects within reach.

Focalizing the Caretaker (9–15 Months). The infant negotiates the unconditional availability of mother by making increasingly more explicit requests for particular types and rates of stimuli and for protection from danger and stressful stimulation, a dominant need as the child becomes physically more mobile and explores larger space. Mother's responses may require physical contact or only cues revealing her attention and awareness. By focalizing and guaranteeing mother's availability and trust, the child establishes a base from which he can move away from mother and explore larger environments.

Self-Assertion (12–20 Months). With a secure feeling that he can separate from mother yet have her available, the child begins to assert himself *in opposition* to mother, showing more negativism, possessiveness, and exhibitionism in various negotiations (e.g., toilet training, returning a toy to a sibling). Mother phases in limits and permission, responses that vary in consistency, ambivalence, and guilt as well as in the inventiveness she uses to suggest alternatives (e.g., offering a less dangerous but related kitchen utensil the child insists on using). To negotiate self-assertion, the child must sense that his victory can be accepted by the mother. If mother's behaviors are severely limiting, the child could surrender self-assertion and active exploration.

Initial Testing of Destructive Aggression (18–24 Months). The child experiments with explicit aggressive behavior (e.g., destroys a toy, scatters material) performed with a sense of triumph ("John John do!") and followed by "making up" (e.g., sticking a piece of scotch tape on broken china). Mother should distinguish among the child's various destructive intentions (biting in play versus in anger), phase in alternative behaviors the child could employ (banging a toy hammer against a pot instead of a refrigerator) and initiate making up (engage the child in repairing a damaged object).

Modification of Aggressive Intent (24–36 Months). The child gradually accommodates to and internalizes the caretaker's standards, begins to show socially acceptable aggressive play, modifies his omnipotence in keeping with reality testing, and strengthens his identification based upon parental modeling, gains which are tested while aggressing in other environments (e.g., preschool).

Extending Secondary Process Functioning in Interaction (12–36 Months). Negotiations serving earlier issues also help the child elaborate speech, symbolic representation, and pretending. The mother understands, responds to, and stimulates the child's pretending, and the child internalizes pretend communications provided by mother. In solidifying their relationship through symbols and pretending, mother and child develop an understanding of each other's intentions and the alternatives available for mutual exchange.

Consolidation of Body Image (0–36 Months). Throughout the 3-year period the child constructs and solidifies a body image and sexual identification, expressing curiosity in his body and the bodies of others in exhibitionistic, seductive, and autostimulating behaviors. Parents respond with stimulation and prohibitions and communicate about the body and its parts. Through these transactions the child develops cognitive schemata of body and a sense of self.

Guidelines to Negotiate Transference and Resistance

Relating Sander's model to our earlier discussion of transference and resistance leads to the following assumptions: when in a therapeutic process, the child resists changing his pathological modes of functioning by transfering behaviors from issues noted above, which were not adequately negotiated with caretakers during the first three years of life (i.e., before language was fully developed). In other words, when coping with a conflict between the competence of her cognition/personality and the pace and complexity of stimulation, the child regresses to one or more of these issues repeating old, maladaptive ways of negotiating. Accordingly, the resistant behavior does not give way to verbal interpretation as much as to *interactive* behaviors by the therapist which engage the child in re-negotiating these issues. Common forms of resistance shown by children who require CCT include testing aggression and excessive self-assertive-ness or its opposite (e.g., passivity, fatigue, engaging in stereotyped activity). These behaviors serve to control the therapist and stimulation and to preserve old ways of behaving.

By adapting Sander's model to our needs, several technical guidelines are suggested.

Initial Adaptation. The therapist works to "know" the patient's unique postures, rhythm of activity, and preference for pace of stimulation and to understand the degree to which the therapist's own rhythm matches that of the child. Examples: One child habitually engaged tasks with a slow tempo; another regularly pierced space like an arrow, and after vigorously engaging a task, slumped in a chair and withdrew. The therapist accom-modated to these rhythms. One child commented that the lights were too bright and a wall decoration "crazy with too much color." The therapist changed this stimulation.

Reciprocal Exchange. The therapist searches for opportunities to engage the child in active-passive exchanges, especially with affects that match the child's range and intensity. Examples: One child exclaimed, "Wow!" and threw up his arms in pleasure when he correctly identified which of two beakers contained the most water. The therapist spontaneously imitated the child's pleasure. When a child showed increased resistance to mem-orizing patterns of geometric cutouts, the therapist invited the child to give him a pattern to memorize.

Early Directed Activity. The therapist is alert to being passive in response to the child's directions, especially as the child attempts to seek or avoid therapeutic tasks. Examples: One child insisted that the work take place on the floor instead of the table; another that the tasks be located on the left side of the table; and another directed that while she worked on a task the therapist sit at the far end of the room. The therapists followed these directions without interpretation.

Focalizing. The therapist insures his/her availability and awareness of the child's unique needs, responding initially with behaviors and later ver-bally. Examples: One child repeatedly broke the point of a pencil and then looked to the therapist who sharpened the pencil each time; another posi-tioned her arms to bring attention to an assortment of minor scratches. The therapist showed concern and applied Band-Aids®. Another child climbed to the top of a cabinet whenever the cognitive task became difficult. Each time the therapist lifted the child to the floor expressing concern for his safety.

Self-Assertion, Testing Destructive Intentions, and Modifying Aggressive Behavior. The therapist views the child's assertive and aggressive behaviors as part of a process in which the child establishes autonomy, acquires pleasure in achievement, and pursues information with excitement and curiosity. The therapist accepts without ambivalence the child's sense of victory after showing defiance, carefully discriminates among aggressive behaviors, and provides alternatives that render aggression more socially appropriate. Whenever possible, the alternative behaviors should integrate some aspect of the child's aggression with aspects of the cognitive task at hand. Examples: One child suddenly became aggressive, throwing geometric cutouts across the room, when his task was to point to cutouts named by the therapist. The therapist set up a box across the room and invited the child to try "to win points" by throwing the cutouts named into it. Gradually, several boxes were set up each offering different points. Then, the therapist designated that the highest score is earned by throwing the cutout into the box in a slow arch and the lowest by hurling the cutout in a direct path. Over several sessions the child gradually modified his aggressive behavior, eventually continuing with tasks by pointing to the cutouts rather than throwing them. In modifying aggression with the help of these "games," the child pretended aggression on some occasions, playfully flipping a cutout across the room. The therapist raised his eyebrows and smiled. The child beamed victoriously and continued with the task.

Extension of Secondary Process Functions in Interactions. The therapist cultivates an understanding of the child's unique symbols and cultivates the child's use of pretending. Further, the therapist introduces verbal statements and symbols to help the child become aware of the stress experienced when managing tasks, the cognitive/behavioral strategies the child uses to reduce stress, how behaviors observed in the office resemble those that occur in school and home, and which alternative behaviors are possible.

Case Illustrations: Managing Resistance in Psychotherapy Versus CCT

To illustrate the approach proposed to manage resistance, let us compare the management of resistance by a neurotic child in psychotherapy with that by a cognitively disabled child in CCT. At one point in treatment a young girl, suffering from neurotic symptoms, sat under the therapist's desk, placed several cardboard boxes around it, and declared she did not want to come anymore to "this stupid place." The therapist commented she was hiding from him and protecting herself with a wall, and maybe they could find a way of telling him what the hiding was all about.

In the next session, while sitting silently under the desk, she began passing "notes" (one or two words conveying no meaning) to the therapist. Bit by bit, the therapist noted it seemed she had secrets she wanted to share yet also hide, that maybe she imagined she would be punished if she revealed her secrets, and that as her doctor he wanted to help her with her worries. When this interpretation was fully constructed she came out from her enclosure and engaged in doll play, with parent dolls angrily scolding and spanking a child doll for being "naughty" and "dirty," and because sometimes the child doll "touches things she shouldn't."

This sequence is familiar to clinicians practicing child psychotherapy. The child resisted by crawling under the desk, refusing to engage the therapist. The resistance was resolved as the therapist made several statements guided by a model of intrapsychic conflict: that by hiding under the desk the child was hiding from past and contemporary behaviors forbidden by internal standards, that she had transferred onto the therapist punitive attitudes that belonged to others, and that keeping these behaviors and wishes hidden maintained guilt and anxiety at a tolerable level. The resistance was resolved when the child's guilt, and fear of punishment by the therapist, were brought into awareness and distinguished from the therapist as a helping figure. Resolving the resistance enabled the child to elaborate her internal conflicts further in doll play and to continue participating in the treatment process.

In a course of CCT with an 8-year-old boy the therapist had been conducting tasks which involved regulating various body tempos and scanning moving targets. At one point the therapist presented a new, more complex task, asking the child to scan two rods, set about six feet apart, and to point to the taller one. The child pushed the rods to the floor, proclaiming he "doesn't want to play that stupid game" and is going to color instead. Whereupon he took crayons and paper, sat under a table, and busied himself "drawing." The therapist again set the rods on the table and asked the child to look them over. Before the request was finished, the child shouted, "Go (expletive deleted) yourself!" clearly keeping the therapist and his demands at a distance. Yet, on two occasions, the child held up his paper, obviously directing the therapist to lines he had drawn. The therapist showed pleasure with a reassuring nod.

During the next session the child again located himself under the table and busied himself drawing. Again the child blasted the therapist whenever he made contact but also brought the therapist's attention to particular designs. The therapist expressed an interest and waited, drawing lines himself with colored crayons. The child then mumbled to himself that he could not find a crayon. The therapist obtained the crayon and placed it next to the child. The first time the child tossed it across the room. On the next occasion he used the crayon without acknowledgement. Another time he broke a crayon while drawing lines. Without comment the therapist taped the two pieces together and left the crayon which the child subsequently used.

In the next session the therapist asked the child to challenge him by drawing two lines or circles, and the therapist would try to figure out which is bigger. The child accommodated with delight, taking great pains to make nearly identical drawings. With each task the therapist puzzled, searching for the bigger drawing. Then the therapist asked the child, "to take a turn." The child accepted, working with a set of lines the therapist presented.

In the next session, child and therapist continued taking turns examining lines the other had drawn. The therapist noted it was difficult to tell which line was longer when they were made of different widths, colors, etc. and asked the child to set up two rods because then they could be more sure of the length of each, the distance between them, and so on. The child accommodated and then took a turn. This time the therapist set up rods closer together than several sessions ago when the child first resisted.

Reconstructing this example in terms of the rationale of CCT, the child resisted treatment by pushing the rods to the floor and drawing while sitting under a table. Rather than conceptualizing this behavior in terms of intrapsychic conflict, the therapist viewed it as resulting from conflict between the child's cognitive dysfunction (narrow-passive scanning) and the task complexity he was asked to manage. The child had been visually tracking objects. When given a more complex task (actively scanning two rods), he regressed and resisted. The task represented a strong push for change and created stress. The child managed the stress by angrily rupturing the process of reciprocation and avoiding the therapist as the source of stressful stimulation.

To manage and resolve the resistance, the therapist negotiated reciprocity, focalizing, and self-assertion. In drawing lines with crayons, the therapist imitated the child's behavior, a precursor of reciprocating. In responding to the child's first designs, in locating particular crayons, and in repairing others the therapist insured his availability and focused behaviorly on aspects of the child's needs. Throughout all of these interventions the therapist did not respond to the child's angry vindictives but stepped past them, displaying interest and showing the therapist's integrity was intact.

After insuring his availability, the therapist invited the child to challenge him in a game of judging lines, allowing the child to take the initiative, experience self-assertiveness, and participate in a "game," (pretending). Then suggesting they take turns drawing and judging lines, the therapist provided the child with an opportunity to reenter a reciprocal relationship with child and therapist alternating between active and passive positions. Last, having negotiated reciprocation and self-assertion, the therapist modified the activity the child initiated so that it took on features of the cognitive task the child had abandoned. By negotiating these several issues, resistance was resolved, and the child returned to the therapeutic task until the next, more complex demand led to new resistance and another phase of negotiations.

Two additional points should be made before leaving these anecdotes. When the child returned to the task the complexity was reduced in an effort to create a better fit between the child's cognition (the two rods were placed closer together), increasing the likelihood that the task would be assimilated rather than rejected. Second, the therapist refrained from making interpretations. In CCT interpretations are used to resolve resistance only after the child has developed considerable awareness of his behaviors and affects when dealing with tasks. At a later time the therapist might say, "When rods are almost the same and placed far apart, figuring out which is taller is very hard so you get nervous and mad." Then, when the child has become aware of the connection between the complexity of information and unique behavioral/affective responses, the therapist points out to the child that he manages nervous and mad feelings by "quitting" the relationship and the task, and by keeping the therapist away "with swear words," and "easy drawings." In the final stages the therapist teaches the child how behaviors in the office are the same as behaviors in school and at home, and guides the child in constructing and experimenting with alternatives.

A Main Technique in Resolving Transference/Resistance

As the preceding example illustrates, in addition to negotiating issues, the major technique used to resolve transference/resistance involves *integrating the resistant behavior within the response process of the cognitive task* at hand. As noted earlier, the most common resistant behaviors are exaggerated self-assertion and aggression, whether expressed directly or indirectly. Because sublimated forms of self-assertion and aggression are critical aspects of successful learning and competing, it is important that in resolving resistance the therapist not require the child to surrender his/her self-assertion, but promote, bit by bit, a modification of the child's aggression and recruit sublimated aggression within cognitive activity and learning.

In addition to the previously described anecdotes (e.g., the boy who hurled the geometric cutouts), the following examples illustrate the technique in resolving direct forms of assertive-aggressive resistance. One child refused to continue working with tasks, sat silently in a chair at the far end of the room, and angrily scraped the geometric cutouts used in the tasks with her fingernails and with wooden doll figures. While this behavior could be viewed as hostility displaced from the therapist to the wooden cutouts (she was symbolically scratching the therapist), the therapist did not interpret this possible motivation but set out to integrate the resistant behavior into the response process required by the abandoned task. Over a period of time the therapist asked the child to take a file and scrape the cutout that had changed in a display the child was asked to remember (see Chapter 8), then to take a piece of sandpaper and rub it over the shape that had changed, and still later to take a piece of cloth to rub the shape. Another child refused to continue working, took a dart gun, and shot darts at the walls, ceiling, puppet figures, and occasionally at the therapist. Over time the therapist asked the child to shoot darts at the rod judged to be taller, then to hold the dart in his hand and hit the rod selected according to a dimension designated by the therapist, and then to point to the rod with his finger. Another child refused to work by breaking a rod in two. The therapist set thin sticks alongside of each rod and asked the child to break the stick next to the rod selected in response to the task, and then later to twist one of the coat hangers placed alongside the rods, and still later to straighten out one of the coat hangers.

The following examples illustrate the technique in resolving indirect (passive/inverted) forms of assertive-aggressive resistance. One child, who often complained of being sleepy or tired, rested her head on the table, declared she was sleepy, and refused to continue working. With playful affect the therapist offered that the wooden rods the child had been engaging were also sleepy and wanted a bed to sleep in. The child readily accepted the therapist's invitation that they make beds of cloth. With the next tasks the child was asked to take the rod designated (e.g., taller, thicker) and put it to bed. Later the rods were placed on "beds" of cloth, and the child was asked to "wake up" the rod containing the attribute designated. As "sleepiness" was handled in this imaginary way, the child gradually began to express the anger her sleepiness had masked. When "waking up" a rod, she sometimes exclaimed in anger, "Hey! who woke me up?" Then she began to swat the rods off the pieces of cloth exclaiming, "Hey! Who knocked me out of bed?" As she expressed pretend ag-

gression more directly, versus through sleepiness, she soon angrily refused to engage the task. The therapist was now faced with resolving
another form of the same resistance, but throughout the child was not required to surrender any one form of self-assertion/aggression.

Patience, Ingenuity, and Rebuilding the Alliance

Since children treated with CCT are also handicapped by severe personality disorders, an episode of resistance may sometimes require 10 or
12 sessions to resolve. Throughout, the therapist perseveres, tries one
technique, waits, tries another, and waits until the resistance is resolved.
Once resolved, at least partially, the therapist works on rebuilding the
alliance. One technique that frequently helps is role-reversal or, in psychoanalytic terms, inviting the child to identify with and assume the role
of the aggressor. In CCT the child is invited to present the therapist with
cognitive tasks which the therapist works on, readily accepting the non-
authoritarian role.

Play as Resistance in the Child

Children who are less impaired by character disorders frequently leave
the task and engage in spontaneous play. The therapist needs to determine whether the play is serving resistance or working through some
emotional conflict that would facilitate progress in CCT. This issue is a
potential stumbling block especially for those who practice play therapy.
When first conducting CCT therapists often gleefully pursue some play
activity the child introduces, especially if it appears "dynamically rich."
But, considerable experience dealing with such developments suggest that
by "playing" the child is frequently attempting to control the therapist
and avoid the tasks.

To determine when play is serving resistance, the following guidelines
are suggested:

1. Over several sessions the play is stereotyped and repetitive, failing to
   elaborate and organize around an issue (e.g., the same formboard game
   is played many times; numerous "snowflakes" are cut out and hung
   on the wall).
2. The play does not include elements of the abandoned cognitive task
   or does not relate to the child's learning and adjustment problems.
3. The child is sleepy or irritated, for example, when dealing with treatment tasks but hums with pleasure while drawing the 10th tulip or
   carefully aligning furniture and dolls.

Play as Resistance in the Therapist

Training others in CCT methods, the author has observed some therapists become bored by the specificity, analytic rigor, and attention to molecular cognitive activity required by CCT. To find relief, these therapists follow the child's "more interesting dynamic activity" or initiate play as a diversion. When a therapist retreats into play, he/she is responding much like the cognitively disabled child who retreats into drawings and games to escape the demands and stress of slowly and steadily engaging a graded series of tasks in the service of promoting cognitive growth. Analyzing and reforming cognitive deficits are meticulous and sometimes tedious work, but no more tedious than playing the same "puppet show" for the 20th time.

Play as a Means of Resolving Resistance

As examples provided earlier and in the next chapters illustrate, play may also be useful to resolve resistance and return the child to the hierarchy of tasks being conducted. In CCT the therapist identifies the psychic conflict contributing to the resistance and designs a game for the child to play which integrates the conflict with an element of the cognitive task.

The previous example involving "putting rods to sleep" illustrates brief moments of play. An example of a more sustained use of play is provided by a child who, usually preoccupied with war fantasies, yet readily guilty when asserting, refused the tasks and began drawing elaborate pictures of battlefields filled with exploding bombs. Since the child had been dealing with tasks that required particular shapes be removed from stacks of geometric cutouts (see Chapter 7), the therapist designed a game in which stacks containing particular cutouts were time bombs that would explode unless found and "defused." The child readily engaged the game, pretended he was a special soldier, while scurrying about and examining towers of cutouts the therapist had placed on the floor.

Making Up After an Episode of Resistance

The therapist should be active making up after an episode of resistance, providing the child with opportunites to experience the fact that her achievements are accepted. Making up also contributes to the child's internalizing the therapist's standards. If resistance includes destructive behaviors, the therapist engages the child in repairing the damaged object. Sometimes a child will make bids to make up, for example, tidying materials in the office or becoming preoccupied with a small tear in a hand puppet.

Insight

The same considerations discussed above in the section on the technique of directed fantasy apply here. When resolving transference and resistance in CCT, the therapist, in the early phases of treatment, refrains from making interpretations. The insight the child acquires is nonverbal and derives from corrective experiences (i.e., from assimilating the behaviors and standards of the therapist who did not react or behave as did early caretakers or as imagined by the child).

SPECIAL CONSIDERATIONS FOR CHILDREN WITH SEVERE PSYCHOLOGICAL LIMITATIONS

CCT methods have been used to treat children who are severely retarded, autistic, or clinically psychotic. The methods used most often derive from the programs in focal attention and field articulation in an attempt to bring the child's cognition more in touch with reality and/or more able to use fantasy and symbolic functioning as means of rehearsing action.

Because these children frequently refuse or fail to respond to treatment tasks, the therapist conducts a preliminary phase of treatment designed to cultivate the child's ability and willingness to perform the response required. To illustrate, assume an autistic child is presented with a display of black and white cutouts and asked to place the black circles in a box. The child refuses and/or fails to respond.

1. The therapist places the cutouts in the box, repeating the demonstration several times, and makes a few comments, if indicated, drawing the child's attention to the demonstration.
2. If the child does not respond, the therapist takes the child's hand and guides it gently but purposefully to the designated cutout, helps the child grasp the cutout (placing the child's finger over it if necessary), and guides the child in carrying the cutout to the box.
3. If the child does not appear to be looking at the display, the therapist gently directs the child's head toward the display with one hand, while removing cutouts with the other or guiding the child's hand through a response.
4. The therapist gradually relies on more subtle forms of physical guidance (e.g., nudging the child's elbow or placing a child's hand near a cutout) and later on verbal instructions.
5. The therapist provides demonstration and physical guidance until the child purposely completes a response successfully. When the child

removes designated cutouts (by tapping them; displaying a standard) on his/her own initiative, the tasks are slowly increased in complexity following the guidelines described in the next chapters.

All of the considerations given to the issue of transference and resistance apply equally when treating these children. The case report presented in Chapter 11 contains graphic descriptions of behaviors displayed by an autistic boy and the techniques used to manage them.

Chapter 5
Therapy With The Body
Ego–Tempo Regulation
Cognitive Control

The cognitive control of body ego–tempo regulation concerns the manner in which a person uses images/symbols to represent the body and regulate its motility. As formulated by both psychoanalytic and Piagetian theory, the ego (cognition) is first a body ego. The body provides information and behavior modes by which the child formulates experiences, becomes a vehicle that carries meaning in the process of symbolic functioning, and contributes to a sense of self, all of which form the first layer of cognitive structuring.

Two programs, *Who is Me? Where is Me?* and *Moving Fast and Slow*, described in this chapter are designed to restructure and rehabilitate this cognitive mechanism so that it functions efficiently when body information is perceived and experienced as it is, as well as when this information is transformed by symbols and fantasies within the process of symbolic functioning and pretending. If a child's diagnostic evaluation indicates a need for therapy in body ego–tempo regulation, it is often effective to include parts of both programs in each session, moving to the steps of each program as defined by the child's progress and needs.

Sometimes extremely hyperactive children experience difficulty working with *Who Is Me? Where Is Me?* probably because the program requires the child to focus attention on kinesthetic sensations. In these cases, the first sessions are devoted to the program *Moving Fast and Slow*. When the child demonstrates some capacity to regulate different motor tempos, the program *Who Is Me? Where Is Me?* is introduced. Both programs are guided by common goals: to train the child to direct attention at and register body sensations and movements and to cultivate increasingly differentiated images and symbols that represent these perceptions and movements. At first glance, the therapist who has not conducted this form of treatment may not appreciate the importance of repeatedly and patiently directing the child's attention to some aspect of body sensation. Remember that the child who requires therapy with this mechanism has not yet differentiated clear body boundaries and a sense of body self. The child is also inefficient in registering information provided by the body, resulting in the diffuse body ego with which he/she engages experiences.

PROGRAM 1A: *WHO IS ME?* *WHERE IS ME?*

Purpose: To develop the child's capacity to perceive and describe body sensations; to develop the child's capacity to use body gestures as symbolic vehicles which organize and formulate aspects of external reality and his/her personal world; to develop the child's appreciation of how gestures are understood by others.

Materials: Chairs; tables; magazine pictures of individuals, adults, children, animals depicting or engaged in various activities and conveying various emotions; pipe cleaners; and other materials as noted.

Introduction and General Procedure

The program consists of seven main steps summarized in Table 5.1. With the first three the child is asked to engage the entire body, then large parts of the body, then small parts of the body, and then the body in relation to objects, all involving both static and dynamic positions. Beginning with Step 4, the child is introduced to therapeutic activities that cultivate the body as a source of meaning and as a vehicle for expressing meaning in the process of symbolic functioning. To facilitate discussing these steps, terms used are defined here (further elaborated by Barten, 1979), along with related considerations.

Expressive gestures consist of movements of the hands, face, and postures of the whole body that express feelings and intentions. Inactive gestures consist of movements that represent actions upon objects or actions performed with objects (e.g., pretending to catch a fish or comb one's hair). Instrumental gestures are movements intended to regulate or change the behavior of others or to direct someone to do something (e.g., a child raises his arms to indicate that he wants to be picked up). When first asking the child to perform some gesture, the therapist relys upon images conveyed by the child in earlier steps, or suggests the child ''be some animal'' since children readily image animals. If the child has exceptional difficulty performing expressive and inactive gestures, the therapist invites the child to prescribe various activities, emotions, and meanings and then performs gestures to convey them. The therapist should draw from

Table 5.1. Steps in Therapy with Body Ego: *Who Is Me? Where Is Me?*

Step 1. Child perceives and describes the body in static positions
    Part A Entire body (e.g., standing; sitting; lying)
    Part B Large body parts (e.g., arms extended; legs apart)
    Part C Small body parts (e.g., finger extended; eyes shut)
    Part D Child and therapist evaluate responses

Step 2. Child perceives and describes the body in dynamic positions
    Part A Entire body (e.g., crawling; leaning)
    Part B Large body parts (e.g., flexing arms; tilting head side to side)
    Part C Small body parts (e.g., blinking eyes; tapping toes)
    Part D Child and therapist evaluate responses

Step 3. Child perceives and describes the body in static and dynamic relations to other objects
    Part A Entire body (e.g., wear various clothing; walk toward, around, through tangible and intangible stimuli)
    Part B Large body parts (e.g., move arm toward, around, through tangible and intangible stimuli)
    Part C Small body parts (e.g., place finger against cheek, in oil, in water)
    Part D Child and therapist evaluate responses

Step 4. Child performs expressive and inactive gestures, conveying conventional and unconventional meanings with body and body parts
    Part A Child gestures meanings requested verbally by therapist; therapists gestures meanings requested verbally by child (e.g., be an angry tiger; be a scared mouse, be a monster; be a boom)
    Part B Child gestures meanings requested nonverbally by therapist using concrete/abstract stimuli (e.g., dolls; pipe cleaner figures; penciled lines); Therapist gestures meanings requested by child using same method
    Part C Child gestures meanings requested by therapist using pantomime; Therapist gestures meanings requested by child using the same method
    Part D Child and therapist evaluate responses

Step 5. Repeat Step 4. Child performs expressive and enactive gestures conveying meanings in relation to other objects (e.g., catch this fish—a wooden stick; be a wolf fighting this sheep—a rubber figure; be this—a zigzag line—going toward and around this—a circle)

Step 6. Child performs multiple expressive and enactive gestures to develop multiple referents and vehicles
    Part A Child conveys multiple meanings using the same gesture and conveys one meaning using multiple gestures
    Part B Child and therapist evaluate responses

Step 7. Child performs expressive and enactive gestures shifting rapidly on command from one meaning to another and from one vehicle to another
    Part A Vary stimuli used to convey meanings (e.g., dolls; pictures; pipe cleaner figures; pencil lines; verbal commands)
    Part B Child and therapist evaluate responses

Step 8. Child performs a series of random expressive and enactive gestures using multiple referents and vehicles
    Part A Child imitates therapist and labels referent if possible
    Part B Therapist imitates child and labels referent if possible
    Part C Child and therapist evaluate responses

knowledge of the child's unique situation and history when suggesting possible representations to be enacted.

Most children easily perform the body positions and movements required. Remember that the goal is not to teach the child, for example, how to step over a book but to give the child *the experience* of stepping over a book many times while articulating the body sensations that accompany the activity and eventually the images and symbols the child constructs and ties to them. Occasionally a child is unable to perform a particular posture or movement required by a task. Here time should be taken to help the child achieve the response before the child is asked to use the posture as a symbol conveying some meaning.

The instructions given below for each step are intended only as illustrations. The language and demonstrations used by the therapist should suit the child's developmental status and style. This treatment program requires the therapist to be physically active and somewhat of a dramatist, demonstrating body postures, guiding and joining the child in performing some gesture. Therapists whose style may not fit these requirements should examine whether they are equipped to present the tasks adequately.

Introducing the Child to the Program

The Outer-Oriented Child. Verbal introductions to the program should be kept to a few remarks since words may not be particularly effective or meaningful for a child who requires this program. Say, "Johnny we are going to play a game called *Who is Me? Where is Me?*" The therapist stands at attention and asks the child to assume the same position. The therapist directs the child's attention to sensations experienced by the total body. For example, "Johnny, what do you notice when you are like this?" The child may respond, "I notice tight." The therapist replies, "That's good. Show me where it's tight." This request illustrates the main focus of treatment at this time: to direct attention at particular perceptions of the body and locate the sources of these perceptions. At this moment, and in future sessions, the therapist asks the child to continue directing attention and connect the sensation "tight" to perceptions of the legs or stomach, and so on.

If the child does not respond the therapist demonstrates, pushing the weight of her body against her feet, noting that she feels heavy at the feet, or by passing her hand along the back of her legs. The therapist might comment, "You see, we are going to learn how and what we notice with our bodies." Without further comment the therapist assumes the next body posture. For the child who makes few or no comments, an understanding of the activity and purpose of the program is conveyed best if the therapist waits for the child to share a perception and at that time confirms this is what the treatment is about.

During the first sessions, if the child uses a verbal symbol to convey a body perception, the therapist reserves it for later work. For example, while moving his hands and fingers (Step 2, Part C), one child described that his hands felt like "worms." The goal of the first three steps, then, involves both bringing the child's attention to body perceptions and helping the child build a vocabulary that describes them.

The Inner-Oriented Child. Introducing the child who is excessively withdrawn and physically inhibited requires special consideration. As discussed in Chapter 4, the therapist begins with the last steps of the program, which invite and permit fantasy, and therefore are fitted with the child's pathological cognitive orientation. Then gradually the therapist moves toward Step 1, which requires perceptions of the body without the participation of fantasy. To introduce the program, the first session is nondirective, and the child is given the freedom to move about the room and engage material. The therapist carefully observes the child, notes particular unique postures or gestures the child displays, and then imitates them while the child guesses what the therapist is pretending to be. For example, one child moved about the playroom swinging his body back and forth with short, choppy steps somewhat like the stereotyped sailor's gait. When the child was looking, the therapist imitated this gait and said, "Johnny, look at the way I am walking. What am I? Pretend I am something or somebody." Whether or not the child responded, the child was asked to make up somebody or something else and the therapist will "try to be that." After the therapist gestured what the child prescribed, the child was asked, "How did I do? Did I do it okay with the way I moved?"

Then the therapist said, "Now, Johnny you do something like I do." For example, the therapist rubbed his ear, "Do that and try to guess what I am saying and thinking." After the child performed and responded, the therapist labeled the gesture (e.g., "Doing what I was saying, I am trying to figure something out"). This general procedure is followed during the first sessions. The therapist waits for other opportunities to imitate one of the child's gestures, which the child is asked to label, and the child is asked to imitate and label one of the therapist's gestures. In this nonverbal way, the therapist introduces and structures the content and purpose of the program for the child (i.e., attending to body gestures and postures as a means of communication).

Specific Instructions

The sequence of Steps 1 through 8 is followed for the outer-oriented child. The reverse sequence is followed for the inner-oriented child as discussed below.

Steps 1 through 3. These steps focus on producing and copying perceptions of the body progressively from perceptions of the body in static positions, to dynamic positions, and then in relation to other objects or stimuli. Within each of these steps, another progression is followed from the child experiencing and perceiving the entire body, then large parts of the body, and then small body parts.

The therapist initially demonstrates various positions the child is asked to assume, being inventive while remaining sensitive to those positions the child finds difficult because of age, physical make-up, and agility. While assuming each position, the child is guided, bit by bit, to perceive various sensations from the body and to label and describe them whenever possible.

If postures are selected that are grossly mismatched with the child's development stage, the treatment fails to provide the child with experiences necessary to form the base for developing the body as a symbolic vehicle. For example, the therapist could ask a 10-year-old to produce and describe the following position: The left leg is flexed, the right knee is on the floor, the right arm is extended upward, the left arm straight ahead, and the head is lowered. This body experience would probably not suit a 5-year-old, or a 10-year-old with major dysfunctions in body ego.

The therapist should be especially artful in conducting Step 3 because body postures and gestures in relation to other objects eventually become vehicles of meaning in symbolic functioning, representing feelings (e.g., crouching in fear) and actions performed without objects (e.g., pretending to catch a fish). The more articulate a child's body experiences in relation to other stimuli, the more equipped the child is to learn to use the body effectively as a symbolic vehicle.

The child begins with experiences close to the body, (e.g., puts on a heavy wool shawl, then a light cotton shawl, then a plastic shawl, perceiving and articulating body sensations experienced with each). Then the child experiences the body in relation to tangible objects distal from the body by walking toward, around, and onto a wooden box. Then the child experiences the body in relation to intangible stimuli such as walking toward, around, and through music coming from a cassette player. Then the child moves toward, around, and through imaginary stimuli (e.g., an imaginary, narrow column of smoke and an imaginary, wide cloud of smoke).

The same progression is followed with small parts of the body. For example perceiving and articulating each experience, the child places a finger on her cheek, forearm, foot. Next she places her finger in honey, water, oil, fingerpaints, and then passes it around and through music coming from a cassette player, and finally she positions it in relation to imagined columns of smoke varying in size.

With each part of each step, the therapist incorporates the four principles (see Chapter 3) that define graded experiences (i.e., complexity; delay; physical-mental actions; and evaluating responses in terms of standards). The therapist emphasizes one or another principle in any particular task, but attempts to orchestrate all four when shifting the therapeutic experience to a higher grade than the previous one.

To illustrate, consider how each of these principles might be followed in Step 1, Part A. In terms of simple versus complex, experiencing the body standing is simpler than experiencing the body in the crouched position. In terms of delay, the child could be asked to assume the static position of sitting, in slower and slower motion. With the principle of physical-mental activity, the child initially assumes the body posture prescribed and is not encouraged to describe the perception (physical activity). Gradually the child is required to describe and label the posture (mental activity). As the child describes and labels postures, the therapist begins to emphasize evaluating the perceptions and descriptions. For example, while assuming a crouched position the child says at one time "hiding behind a bush," and at another, "getting ready to race." To evaluate the crouched position in terms of the descriptions offered, the therapist imitates the positions and engages the child in comparing the position called "hiding" with that called "starting a race," and asks the child to compare his positions with those assumed by the therapist. In this way the child is trained to evaluate the degree to which various aspects of body language fit what they are intended to communicate. At more advanced levels, the child not only begins to learn that some body positions and parts are relevant and some irrelevant for a particular gesture, he/she also becomes aware of the possibilities for limitations of the body for constructing gestures. At this point, Step 4 is phased in.

Step 4. These techniques focus primarily on the body participating in the process of symbolic functioning. With each part, the goal is to help the child use the body and its parts as vehicles carrying circumscribed meanings. In general, the therapist describes or conveys a meaning, which the child is asked to portray with body gestures, and the child is invited to describe a meaning, which the therapist conveys with body gestures.

In addition to using the four standard guidelines to construct graded tasks, the tasks administered within each part of Step 4, and from one part to the next are varied according to whether the meaning to be gestured is presented with stimuli that are verbal or nonverbal and concrete or abstract. With Part A the meaning to be gestured, whether an activity, a state, or a feeling is presented verbally (e.g., with younger children: Be a tiger; Show me how a tiger acts; Be a mouse; Be a mad elephant; Be a happy squirrel). Older children can make use of humans as well (e.g.,

Be a guy sleeping in a park; Be a guy on a motorcycle). With Part B the meaning to be gestured is presented nonverbally by manipulating material (e.g., the therapist moves a toy lion to convey prowling, or a toy giraffe to convey eating and says, "Be this; show me what it's doing"). The shift from verbal to nonverbal stimuli to be gestured attempts to bring the child's experiences closer to the nonverbal stimuli which infants first symbolize with body movements (e.g., an infant opens its mouth to symbolize a match box opening).

Within Parts A and B, the tasks shift progressively from requiring the child to gesture conventional meanings to requiring the child to gesture more personal, unusual meanings. For example, with Part A the child is asked, "Show me a horse walking"; later, "Show me a space creature walking"; and still later the child is asked to be, for example, a "Zip," and a "Boom." Here nonsense words are used to encourage the child to develop the capacity to use the body to gesture highly personal meanings.

The same progression is accomplished in Part B by shifting the stimulus used to convey the meaning to be gestured from doll figures of familiar animals and persons, to pictures of animals and persons, to pipe cleaners shaped by the therapist in the form of more familiar animals and persons in various postures, then "nonsense shapes," and then pencil lines drawn on a sheet of paper, first forming simple drawings of animals and persons, then "nonsense" lines, such as ⌐ ∿, to which the child is to assign meaning conveyed by gestures.

By systematically varying the stimuli that present the meaning the child is to gesture, from verbal to nonverbal, and from concrete to abstract, the child learns to convey meaning with the body when the meaning is concrete and conventional, requiring particular ingredients, as well as when the meaning is more unusual and abstract, requiring no particular ingredients and permitting the child to make use of highly personal gestures.

The tasks of Part C provide the child with experience which further cultivates an action base for the body as a vehicle expressing meaning. The therapist pantomimes some activity and/or affect and the child imitates it and notes what is going on. Examples are: directing traffic; chasing a butterfly; watering a plant; waving goodbye with sadness. The child is also invited to pantomime some event, and the therapist imitates it and notes what is going on.

During the latter stages of this step, the therapist becomes more active, helping the child evaluate whether and how the child's gestures, and those of the therapist, communicate and what changes might improve the gestures as vehicles to convey the meaning in question. When more abstract stimuli are used, the process of evaluating is frequently facilitated by having the child carefully examine the stimulus with touch perception (e.g., trace his fingers over the contours of a rubber animal, of pipe cleaners the therapist sculpted, or along penciled lines drawn on a sheet of paper). Including these touch perceptions helps some children construct more clear images which are then gestured more efficiently.

Last, with outer-oriented children it is best to start training in symbolic functioning by presenting verbally the meaning to be gestured (Part A) and then physically and nonverbally. With inner-oriented children, the therapist would begin with pantomimes (Step C) and gradually require more explicit gestures in response to verbally described meanings.

Step 5. The techniques of Step 4 are repeated but the meanings to be gestured now involve the body in relation to other objects. The following are examples of usual and unusual meanings a child is asked to gesture: show me how you catch this fish (the fish is a stick placed on the table); be a wolf fighting this sheep (a sheep doll is placed on the table); be a sponge in water (a beaker of water is placed on the table); show me how you can be a cold germ in somebody's lungs (the space under a table and chairs is defined as lungs). The following are examples of tasks that use literal and more abstract stimuli to convey the meaning to be gestured: two dolls embracing; pictures of animals fighting; pipe cleaners shaped to form a tennis player hitting a ball with a racquet; pipe cleaners shaped in various angles and contours but not conveying any obvious figure or activity; a straight line drawn toward a circle and then curving around it.

Step 6. This step is designed to cultivate the child's ability to construct a single gesture that could serve as the vehicle for several meanings and to construct multiple gestures that could convey a single meaning. The child is guided in appraising these gestures in order to learn whether and how multiple vehicles are understood by others.

Initially ask the child to use the same gesture to convey two meanings (e.g., "Use your body in one way that shows somebody who is strong, and somebody who is mad; Use your body in one way to show somebody who is throwing a fishline, and somebody who is swinging a tennis racquet"). Gradually the number of meanings is increased to three and then four (e.g., "Use your body in one way that shows somebody kicking a ball, kicking a tin can, and kicking a door"). And dissimilar meanings are gradually combined (e.g., "Use your body in one way to show somebody kicking a tin can and somebody kicking a feather"). Here the motion would have to result in a degree of vigor that would honor the requirements of both the meaning of kicking a feather and the meaning of kicking a can. As another example, "Use your body in one way to show me somebody cheering at a game and somebody who is crying because the team is losing." Here the facial expressions and body movements would have to blend the requirements of both cheering and being sad. The same procedure is followed to guide the child in cultivating different gestures to convey the same meaning (e.g., "Use your body in two ways to show me somebody who is mad; use two different ways to show somebody mad").

To help the child learn how to cultivate multiple vehicles, the therapist should demonstrate as often as indicated. For example, the therapist clenches his fist, then bares his teeth, then glares, each time asking the child for the meaning of the gesture. Demonstrations such as these facilitate discussions with the child of how different gestures can be vehicles for the same meaning.

As with the previous steps, the meanings to be enacted are usual and unusual ones, and make use of literal and less literal stimuli. For example, the therapist places two pictures on the table, one depicting a person walking through a park, and another an animal stalking. The child is asked to produce a single body gesture conveying both meanings.

Step 7. Ask the child to perform a series of gestures on command, rapidly shifting from one meaning to another (e.g., "I'm going to mention different things and I want you to be each one. Show me with your body. Ready? Be a sleepy tiger. Now be a mad monkey. Now be a kid at a birthday party. Now be a kid watching a falling star."). The therapist attempts to describe meanings that require gestures which use small body parts as well as the total body. With an alternate technique, the therapist performs a series of gestures and asks the child to describe what they mean, and "What's going on." Again, with some children it is helpful if the therapist initially demonstrates, performing a series of gestures in response to various meanings expressed by the child.

Stimuli used to convey the meanings are varied from verbal labels, to doll figures, to pictures of animals and persons, to a series of pipe cleaners forming various shapes, to a series of penciled lines. For example, if a series of pictures are used, the child begins by gesturing what is represented by the first picture; then the picture is removed without notice and the second picture is presented; the child gestures the meaning portrayed, and so on.

Step 8. With this step the therapist and child take turns performing a continuous series of random body movements attempting to convey various meanings. Child and therapist imitate the gestures of each other and guess the meaning the other is conveying.

Sequence of Steps for Inner-Oriented Child. The therapist follows a reverse course for the inner-oriented child beginning with Step 8 with modification and concluding with Step 1. The first task the therapist has is to enter the child's fantasy world through the cognitive process unique to body ego–tempo regulation. As noted in the introduction to this chapter, to accomplish this the therapist observes the child's unique gestures during the first sessions, selects one that consists of vivid features, and demonstrates it to the child who is asked to guess, "What am I being?" The child is also asked to imitate some gesture of the therapist and to guess, "What am I trying to say?"

To illustrate, when the therapist clenched his fist against his stomach imitating the child, the child noted, "It means you're shot in the stomach." And when the therapist imitated another child's gesture (rubbing the palm of his hand over the back of his head and neck) the child noted it means, "You're pushing a spider off your head." These examples illustrate that the inner-oriented child frequently assigns highly personal meanings to gestures. Moreover, these meanings are quite fluid, as might be expected, changing from time to time. And the gestures used do not accommodate to reality requirements and to whether or not they are understood. At the start of treatment the therapist accepts the meaning the child offers for various gestures and the particular gestures a child uses to convey a meaning. As a working relationship is established, the therapist gradually phases in Step 7. Here the child is required for the first time to perform particular gestures as vehicles for particular meanings, to develop the capacity to shift from one meaning to another and from one vehicle to another, and to begin evaluating whether and how gestures communicate. The therapist continues through the steps in reverse order until the child engages Step 1, perceiving and describing static positions of the body without the participation of images and fantasies.

PROGRAM 1B: *MOVING FAST AND SLOW*

Purpose: To provide the child with experiences in differentiating and regulating body tempos in large and small spaces; to develop the child's capacity to use body tempos as symbolic vehicles; to develop the child's appreciation of how these tempos are understood by others as representations.

Materials: Metronome; cassette player and recordings of various tempos; paper; masking tape; pencils; crayons; animal and human doll figures; various toy vehicles; mazes; wooden cubes; stop watch.

Introduction and General Procedure

This program extends the preceding one, emphasizing body tempos as symbolic vehicles. Gesturing is now integrated within total body movements which the child performs. The program consists of seven steps, outlined in Table 5.2. With the first two the child performs various tempos in unrestricted and restricted space with the aid of a pacer, such as the clicking of a metronome. Step 3 develops body tempos as symbolic vehicles, each tempo now connected to a particular image. The steps that follow gradually elaborate the development of tempo regulation within the process of symbolic functioning. Tempos, and their associated images, are experienced in relation to objects. Then multiple tempos are developed as vehicles for a single meaning and a single tempo as the vehicle for many meanings. The capacity to shift flexibly among tempos and their referents is addressed in the last steps.

Table 5.2. Steps in Therapy with Tempo Regulation: *Moving Fast and Slow*

Step 1. Child moves the body and substitutes for the body at regular, slow, and fast tempos through *unrestricted space*
Part A Entire body through macrospace
Part B Hand and arm move an object through medium space
Part C Hand and arm move a pencil through microspace
Part D Shifting from one tempo to another while repeating Parts A–C
Part E Child and therapist evaluate tempos in terms of standards
Parts A–D. Use external cadence as guide and then remove

Step 2. Child moves the body and substitutes for the body at regular, slow, and fast tempos through *restricted* space
Repeat Parts A–E of Step 1 with defined pathways that are gradually more complex

Step 3. Child constructs images as referents for specific tempos (vehicles) performed in restricted and unrestricted space. Multiple fast and slow tempos are differentiated
Repeat Parts A–E of Step 1 requiring child to cultivate multiple fast and slow tempos within each dimension of space and to connect a specific image to each tempo
Child shifts from one tempo to another on command in response to images therapist calls out

Step 4. Child performs tempos in relation to stationary and moving objects experienced as they are or construed as something else
Repeat Parts A–E of Step 1 (e.g., walk over to get this—a cookie; now this—a toy snake; pretend this—a wooden cube—is a hamburger, walk over to get it)

Step 5. Child performs multiple tempos to represent a single meaning (referent) and experiences multiple meanings conveyed by one tempo (vehicle)
Repeat Parts A–E (e.g., walk your fast way and pretend you are going to math class, then to the cafeteria, then to meet a friend)

Step 6. Child performs a series of different tempos in large and small space shifting rapidly from one to another vehicle and from one to another referent while experiencing a relatively elaborate fantasy

Step 7. Child performs a series of random tempos and therapist guesses who/what is involved and the meanings conveyed; Therapist performs a series of random tempos and child guesses who/what is involved and the meanings conveyed

---

To provide graded tasks with each step, the child is asked to move his total body through space, then move some object across a table, and then a pencil across a sheet of paper, at first through unrestricted and then through restricted space. In addition the child is required initially to produce only one slow or one fast tempo while walking through a large space, and a single image as the referent for each, and later to produce several slow and fast tempos and a more differentiated image for each.

With each step, child and therapist join in evaluating tempos first in terms of external standards (e.g., the click of a metronome; measured time), then in terms of whether and how a tempo fits some conventional meaning that is easily understood by others or some personal meaning that is less universally understood.

The seven steps are followed as listed in Table 5.2 when the program is administered to an outer-oriented child. In this sequence, the child begins experiencing body tempos without the participation of images and fantasies against which the child's cognition is defended. After the child establishes clearly differentiated tempos and observes, evaluates, and appreciates these behavioral achievements, the child is usually more receptive to connecting images to these stable body movements.

With an inner-oriented child, the reverse sequence is followed. Beginning with Step 7, the therapist attempts to find entry into the child's personal world through the cognitive process of tempo regulation. As the child observes the therapist imitate the child's tempos, and as the child imitates tempos performed by the therapist, an alliance is gradually established from which the therapist proceeds to the other steps. First the therapist helps the child develop the capacity to shift rapidly from one tempo to another as vehicles of meaning and to evaluate these tempos in terms of the meaning the child intends to convey. In this way the child includes the therapist more and more into her fantasy world, and the therapist at the same time edges the child closer to acknowledging the requirements of reality. When Step 1 is reached, the inner-oriented child develops the capacity to engage in tempo regulation without the interference of personal fantasies and in response to stimuli in the environment. With this achievement, the child can construct tempos that flexibly represent both personal metaphors and more conventional symbols, a tool which serves managing hyperactivity and, when indicated, the process of nondirected verbal/play therapy.

When working with an outer- or inner-oriented child, the image the child initially offers as the referent for a tempo should be accepted even if the image appears inappropriate to the therapist. Since these children lack an appreciation of the fit between a referent and the tempo which carries its meaning, it is not surprising that the first images offered are ill-fitted even when the child constructs a conventional symbol. For example, hyperactive children will frequently construct the image of a horse as the referent for moving slowly, and then offer a cat for moving fast, without distinguishing between them.

The therapist demonstrates tempos as often as is indicated, providing the child with models to imitate, and offers images as possible referents. The therapist also teaches the child whether or not the suggested image fits the tempo in question. In terms of the space requirements, the distance available should be at least 15 feet, but preferably larger. Some children require that aspects of this program be administered outdoors, in a gymnasium, or in a very large room.

The need for therapy in tempo regulation has been observed in both inner- and outer-oriented children. A child habitually lost in fantasy can be quite hyperactive and so can a child who avoids fantasy and who is stimulus-bound. Both types of children lack appreciation and awareness of the various speeds with which they move their bodies, both lack the capacity to tie tempos, as vehicles, to referents, and both are not oriented to whether or not others understand their movements. When an elaborate set of tempos are differentiated, each tied to an elaborate set of referents, the child's movements are now under cognitive control, hyperactivity diminishes, and the body movements become part of the process which makes available symbolic functioning for learning and adaptation.

Introducing the Program to the Child

The Outer-Oriented Child. Say, "Jimmy, we're going to play a game called *Moving Fast and Slow*. Watch me." The therapist walks across the room at a regular tempo. "I'm walking in my regular way. Now you try it. Walk in your regular way." When the child has performed, the therapist says, "That's fine. Now I am going to walk slower than my regular way. Watch me again." The therapist demonstrates. "Now you try it." After the child performs, say, "That's fine. Now I am going to walk fast, faster than my regular way. Watch me." The therapist demonstrates. "Now you try it."

Typically the child who requires this program shows little or no difference between "usual," "slow," and "fast" tempos. The therapist does not tell the child about this quality of the performance. Rather, as described below, the therapist introduces a pacemaker, such as a metronome, to cultivate a behavioral difference among tempos.

The Inner-Oriented Child. The therapist observes the child's tempos during the first session or two. At the appropriate time, displaying a tempo typical for the child, the therapist says, "Mary, watch me; watch how I move. What am I when I move this way?" Almost always the child reports an image/fantasy (e.g., "You're a ghost," or "You're a green man"). Then say, "Right, now you move like the ghost (green man)." After the child has performed, say, "Now you take a turn. Walk and be something else, and I'll try to guess what you are." In this way child and therapist join in displaying body tempos and expressing what they represent. In the beginning the tempos and images are only noted by the therapist. Gradually the therapist engages the child in evaluating them (e.g., "What makes that a ghost walk?" and "What is special about the ghost walk that is different from the green man walk?"). As the child and therapist share perceptions and an understanding of different tempos and their associated images, the therapist moves to Step 6.

Specific Instructions

Step 1. The goal is to cultivate behaviorally different tempos performed through unrestricted space: first the child moves through large space, then moves an object over the space of a table top, and then moves a pencil over a sheet of paper.

In Part A ask the child to move from one wall to another, "In your regular way." The child may take an indirect route or move very rapidly, almost running. At this point no mention is made of this behavior. Next ask the child to move from one wall to another "slow" and then "fast." After the child performs, say, "We can keep track of what's regular, slow, and fast if we write down how much time it takes." Engage the child in constructing a record sheet on which times will be recorded. Ask the child again to walk across the room in regular, slow, and fast trials; use a stopwatch to measure the time taken; and invite the child to write the number down. If the child cannot write numbers, the therapist could write down the number and note whether the time taken is greater or less than other trials. The therapist can also count aloud at one second intervals to give the child a sense of the amount of time that has elapsed for each trial.

After the child performs several regular, slow, and fast trials, the trials are compared. Frequently the times are very similar or overlap. After helping the child gain some understanding that the tempos are similar, point out there are ways "to help us learn how to move at different speeds." The therapist introduces an external signal, such as the clicking of a metronome, and asks the child to take a step with each signal. In addition to a metronome, recorded music, taps on a toy drum, hand claps and other such devices are useful.

Say, "Let's try to get these walks to be different by using this." The therapist shows the child how the metronome clicks at different settings. "If you take a step each time there is a click it will help you move at only one speed." Using the metronome or some other device, ask the child again to walk across the room at various tempos. With each trial, focus the child's attention on the body sensations experienced when performing various tempos and on the differences in the pace of each. It is sometimes helpful during this phase if the therapist walks alongside the child to demonstrate.

When performing the task, some children show unique body postures and movements which seem to be the first attempt to translate the meanings of slow, regular, and fast into behavioral terms. For example, some children walk, stop, remain still, walk again, stop, showing difficulty maintaining a continuous forward motion. Other children maintain a forward motion but hunch their bodies and stoop over. Other show peculiar gaits such as a camel walk or short, jerky steps. These postures and mannerisms are gradually brought to the child's attention during Steps 3 and 4 when the child engages in imaging. If a device has been used to provide cadence, these cues are gradually omitted. Ask the child "to think the clicks in your mind and walk to them." Children severely dysfunctional in tempo regulation may require from ten to twenty sessions before they have differentiated three stable tempos while walking across the room *without the aid of an external cadence.*

In Parts B and C the same procedures are followed. Ask the child "to walk a doll from one end of the table to the other at regular, slow, and fast tempos." Again the therapist demonstrates, and the child works on differentiating three stable tempos in medium space without the assistance of an external cadence. When this is achieved the approach is repeated again until the child differentiates behaviorally three stable tempos while moving a pencil across a sheet of paper.

In Part D after three tempos have been differentiated in each modality and space, the child is asked to shift from one tempo to another on command in each modality and space. Say, for example, "Now we'll play the game in a different way. While you are walking across the room shift gears. When I say 'regular,' move in your regular way. When I say, 'fast,' move in your fast way. When I say 'slow,' move in your slow way. Shift from one to another when I name that speed." As the child walks the therapist calls for different tempos in a random sequence.

Throughout each of these parts, the therapist joins the child in evaluating the tempos produced.

Step 2. Follow the same approach used in Step 1 and help the child achieve regular, slow, and fast tempos while moving through defined and limited space. With Part A chairs, books, wooden blocks, masking tape, and other material, can be used to define the space through which the child moves. Initially a wide pathway (e.g., 5 feet) is defined by large material (e.g., blocks) and gradually narrowed and defined more subtly (e.g., a thin strip of tape). The pathway should also be changed gradually from linear to C-shaped, to S-shaped, and then to more complex shapes. The length and complexity of the path is determined by the stage and needs of the child. To administer each trial, the therapist varies the tempo the child is requested to perform, the complexity of the pathway the child is asked to navigate, and the magnitude of the space through which the child moves.

Wooden blocks and tape can also be used to define pathways on a table top over which the child moves a doll or toy car at different tempos. For trials involving microspace, sheets of paper with mazes of varying complexity are ideal.

Step 3. With this step the child is introduced to body tempos as vehicles for carrying meaning. In general the child constructs a stable image for each tempo performed in each modality and space. In the last part of this step, images are used as commands to give the child experiences shifting from one tempo to another.

Say, "Jimmy, let's pretend to be something while moving. Watch me. I'm being a turtle walking slow." The therapist walks across the room. "Now you walk slow and be something. What are you?" This approach is followed to help the child construct a *specific* image as the referent for each regular, slow, and fast tempo.

Once this is achieved, ask the child to cultivate several images each connected to a particular slow tempo, as well as several images each connected to a particular fast tempo. For example, if the child connects the image of a turtle to the slow tempo, the therapist says, "Now walk like something else that is slower than a turtle." The child may display a "snail walk." When the child stabilizes the "snail tempo," as slower than the "turtle tempo," ask the child to be something that is faster than a turtle but slower than a horse (i.e., the child's image for the regular tempo). In a similar manner the child is asked to differentiate three fast tempos each connected with a specific image. To facilitate this process, the therapist may need to offer images and perform associated tempos, or introduce a metronome, music, and other forms of cadence. Again record time for each tempo and give the child feedback. The work continues in this manner using unrestricted and then defined space until the younger child reliably displays at least two slow and two fast tempos, each connected with a specific image and the older child three or four of each type.

When working with space defined by a table top, the process of connecting images with different slow and fast tempos can be facilitated by giving the child several types of vehicles or doll figures to move. In this way the child develops a slow tempo while pushing a vehicle such as a jeep and an even slower tempo while pushing a vehicle such as a tractor.

To conduct this step within the space provided by a sheet of paper, a line-drawing technique is used. Say, "Johnny, watch this line I'm draw-ing with the pencil. Figure out what the pencil is by the way it's moving." At a normal speed, the therapist draws a line similar to one of those il-lustrated in Part A of Figure 5.1. After the child responds and provides an image for that movement and that line, the therapist draws another line at another tempo. The therapist asks the child to draw a line, and the therapist tries to guess what the moving pencil represents. To cultivate different images to the same tempo and one image to different tempos the same line can be drawn at different tempos and different images assigned to it. (See Figure 5.1, Part A for examples.)

After the child has developed at least two slow and fast tempos in large, medium, and small space, and each tempo has been associated with a specific image, the child then executes a series of tempos, shifting from one to another on command. The therapist uses the images the child has constructed to indicate the tempos to be performed. Say, "While you're walking on the path, be the animal I name, and change the way you move each time I name a different animal. Ready, be a turtle . . . a snail . . . a zebra . . . worm . . . rocket, etc."

Step 4. Here the child is provided experiences regulating tempos and their associated images in relation to static and moving objects.

In Part A the therapist could say, "Now I want you to do one of your walks getting that book from the shelf." After the child performs the therapist asks, "Which walk was it?" The therapist then locates other items, which vary in valence (i.e., a cookie, a wooden block, a toy snake). Say, "Do one of your walks to get this cookie." In this way the child is introduced to the notion that movements are regulated differently in rela-tion to various objects. As the child progresses, the objects to which tem-pos are related could shift to imaginary things. For example, a wooden cutout could be labeled a hamburger, a 50-cent piece, and a sponge used to clean a table, a technique which embeds tempo regulation deeper within symbolic functioning and pretending.

The therapist also moves various objects across the room to give the child experience regulating tempos in relation to things moving at various tempos. For example, move a toy fire engine quickly, a toy truck slowly, and a wagon even more slowly across the child's path while the child pretends she is walking across the street. Also, a toy horse could be walk-ing or galloping down the road. When moving objects are introduced, the child is given some destination or task. For example, "Let's pretend you want to cross the street to go to that store (a bookcase), and this horse is galloping down the street. Do one of your walks." With each scenario the child is asked to share the image conveyed by the particular walk performed.

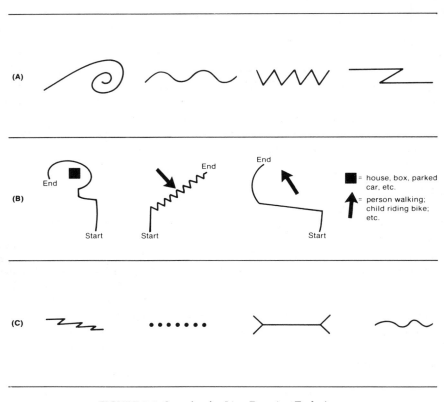

FIGURE 5.1. Samples for Line Drawing Technique

The various tempos performed by the child and the associated images offered are evaluated and compared with tempos the child showed previously as vehicles for those same images. For example, the child may say that his regular "horse" tempo was used to pick up the homework "from a teacher's desk," when the time the child took during the task was considerably slower than the horse walk at previous times.

With Part B various cars, doll figures, toy buildings, and furniture are located on a table to construct various scenarios and the child moves a vehicle, a person, or an animal figure in relation to either stationary or moving objects as the therapist prescribes. Again the tempos are timed and evaluated.

In Part C, the therapist makes use of the same pencil drawing technique using designs illustrated in Part B of Figure 5.1. For example, the therapist draws the square of the first figure, calls it a house, and then says, "Watch how the pencil moves toward the house. Figure out who or what moves that way." The therapist moves the pencil at a particular tempo following the course shown. The child determines who or what is moving. In a similar way the therapist can designate an arrow as a moving object (e.g., a car, a man walking, a child on a bicycle), and the child determines what the pencil is as it moves along the pathway in relation to this imaginary moving object (the second and third drawings in Part B of Figure 5.1). To stimulate imaging further with this technique, the therapist could use crayons to construct lines of different colors and thicknesses. Last the child is encouraged to draw similar designs and the therapist imagines what is moving.

Step 5. With gains made in constructing images conveyed by tempos, and in relating tempos to stationary and moving objects, the child is prepared to develop further the ability to perform multiple tempos as vehicles of a single image and to use one tempo to convey several images. If the child has not had therapy in body ego (the preceding program) integrating aspects of Step 4 of the program *Who Is Me? Where Is Me?* may be of benefit to the child at this phase of treatment.

In Part A with each task ask the child to imagine a particular situation and to enact various tempos within the imagined situation. To illustrate cultivating multiple tempos as vehicles for a single referent the child pretends that he is walking to the principal's office. First he walks at a fast tempo with hands clenched to his side, then at a slow tempo with his head bowed, and then at a regular tempo with a glare in his eye. To illustrate cultivating several referents for the same tempo, the child walks fast and pretends he is walking from one classroom to another in school, then pretends he is going to get a snack from the refrigerator, and then pretends he is meeting a friend.

Part B is conducted along the same lines as Part A. Objects are placed on a table to create a fantasized scene, and the child moves an object at one tempo, imagining several different referents. For example, the child moves an object, imaged as a girl on a bike, across an intersection, first on her way to school, then to a store, and then to a friend's house. Fantasized scenes are also set up in which the child moves some object at different tempos, each time imagining the same referent and experiencing different intentions (e.g., a boy is cutting the grass on a Saturday morning: "I have to get this done" [regular tempo]; "I hate to do this" [slow tempo]; "I want to meet my friend" [fast tempo]).

For Part C the line-drawing technique described above is used to train the child to construct multiple tempos for the same referent and a single tempo for several referents. For example, with the first drawing in Part B of Figure 5.1 the therapist suggests that the square is a box on the sidewalk and draws a line approaching it, first at a slow tempo, then another line at a very slow tempo, noting that the pencil represents a boy. With each trial, the therapist asks the child what the boy is thinking and feeling and what could be in the box. Then the child is invited to draw lines at various tempos in relation to some imagined object, stationary or moving, and to describe what is going on. To illustrate training the child to construct multiple referents for a single tempo, the therapist draws a single line moving slowly, which in the first trial represents a boy approaching a homework assignment, and in the next trial, an ant crawling across the sidewalk toward a crumb.

Step 6. The child performs different tempos in succession, shifting from one to another on command in response to elaborated referents. The major difference between this step and Step 3 is that now the child performs tempos, as representations, within a relatively elaborate fantasy initially directed by the therapist. For example, say, "Let's pretend this corner of the room is the principal's office; this is his chair, and here's the principal (a doll); this corner is the cafeteria, and here are sandwiches and desserts (wooden cutouts); this corner is the classroom, and these are math worksheets. Now stand here at the front door of the school and walk to each place, being the person I ask you to be. Ready? Be a girl who is going to the principal's office to get an award (the child performs). Now be a girl who has a stomach ache and is going to the cafeteria (child performs). Now, be a girl who loves math and is going to pick up a math worksheet (child performs)." The tempos a child performs within each imaginary episode are compared and evaluated.

Step 7. With this final step the activity resembles charades. The child forms a succession of different tempos, and the therapist guesses who is involved and what is going on. The therapist performs a succession of tempos and the child guesses. While inactive and depictive gestures are an integral part of the response, the child is encouraged to make major use of moving the total body or parts of the body across large and small spaces.

Concluding Remarks and a Note about Resistance

Once the inner- and outer-oriented child develops the capacity to use the body ego–tempo regulation process flexibly, responding to the requirements of information as it is and as it is imagined, the child has a mechanism to master hyperactivity, to learn and adapt, and also, when indicated, to serve the process of nondirected play/verbal therapy.

The transition from Step 3 to Step 4 for the outer-oriented child frequently provokes major resistance since the child must image the very activity cognition has avoided or has gained little practice in performing. Similarly, the transition from Step 4 to Step 3 for the inner-oriented child frequently provokes resistance since the child must begin excluding the participation of fantasies, the very activity cognition has used habitually to avoid the demands of reality. To handle these episodes of resistance, the therapist follows the model of negotiation discussed in Chapter 4.

In addition to these transitions as sources of resistance, brief periods of intense regression can punctuate therapy in body ego–tempo regulation because the tasks encourage the child to focus attention on his/her body and on the therapist's body, and because the therapist is physically active demonstrating body positions and sometimes making body contact with the child. The resistance observed frequently takes the form of sudden, intense diffuse hyperactivity or explicit agressive or sexual behaviors directed at the therapist. Examples: One child suddenly kicked the therapist in the leg; another, in a state of diffuse silliness, pressed her body against the therapist and tried to kiss him; another vigorously scratched the skin on her arm, resulting in some bleeding; another began to lick the palms of her hands.

These body gestures and movements are not yet connected to sufficiently elaborated and understood referents. Therefore, verbal interpretations are not used initially to manage them. Rather, in negotiating one of the issues, as discussed in Chapter 4, the therapist attempts to integrate the particular aggressive and/or sexual behavior within the content of the treatment program. For example, the child who began to scratch her arms was asked to scratch various objects in different ways, and the therapist tried to guess who was scratching and what was being scratched. Similarly, the therapist scratched the table top, a sheet of paper, the window pane, his head, etc., asking the child to guess what it means and what is going on. The child who pressed her body against the therapist was asked to press against the wall, a pillow, a chair, and the therapist, and with each experience to notice and compare the perceptions and feelings. Then, following the step being administered, these perceptions were labeled, alternative body gestures were constructed to convey the meaning, and so on.

These anecdotes illustrate that one goal in managing these episodes of regression is to provide the child with cognitive control over the meaning being conveyed by the body posture and movements involved and to develop alternative ways of conveying the same meanings.

Chapter 6
Therapy with the Focal Attention Cognitive Control

The focal attention cognitive control concerns scanning information to perceive its properties and attributes. Two programs are designed to restructure and rehabilitate this mechanism so that it functions efficiently when scanning external information as it is, as well as when information is transformed with symbols and fantasies within the process of symbolic functioning. One program provides the child with experiences in tracking moving information (passive scanning), a developmentally early part of the focal attention process, the other provides the child with experiences in actively scanning stationary information.

To benefit from these programs the child should have achieved, either in the course of development or with the assistance of the program described in Chapter 5, the ability to use the body and its movements as vehicles for communicating symbols and a stage-adequate sense of body self.

Although children for whom these programs are intended do not present hyperactivity as a major symptom, it should not be presumed that the child has developed adequately the body and its movements as vehicles for symbolic functioning. Therefore, some diagnostic assessment should be made of body ego–tempo regulation, and, if indicated, treatment with this control should be administered before the programs described here are introduced.

Relative to therapy in body ego–tempo regulation, the experiences provided by the programs in focal attention represent a major shift away from the body as a source of information. In developmental terms, this represents a shift from the use of proximal to the use of distal sources of information.

PROGRAM 2A: *FOLLOW ME*

Purpose: To provide experiences directing and sustaining attention on information that is moving; to develop the capacity for efficient, passive scanning during the process of symbolic functioning.

107

Materials: Various objects presented as moving targets. Examples of more neutral objects: wooden, geometric cutouts; beams from a flashlight; marbles; individual letters or signs printed on cardboard cutouts; recordings of tone beeps. Examples of objects with conventional meanings: toy cars, fire engines, police cruisers; animal and human toy figures; a pair of scissors; a knife; words printed on cardboard cutouts such as: *spider, mother, dad, blood*; flashlight projecting images of spiders; airplanes; recordings of various sounds (e.g., cars traveling, sirens, weapons firing); plastic figures of insects and mythical outer-space characters.

Introduction and General Procedure

The child is asked to orient her eyes and body in order to follow a stimulus moved through space by the therapist. For convenience the stimulus the child is asked to track is referred to as a target. The targets used require primarily visual perception but also auditory perception. Visual targets are presented first, since the visual mode is dominant, followed by auditory targets.

Seven steps are followed as outlined in Table 6.1. With the first two, the child tracks moving targets that are neutral and, therefore, likely to be perceived as they are, without images or fantasies aroused (e.g., a wooden square). The mode the child uses to track the stimulus is systematically varied. The child tracks the moving target walking alongside of it, then while standing or sitting and by moving only her head, and then while sitting and holding her head still, by moving only her eyes. With Step 1, familiar targets travel a relatively short distance and with Step 2, ambiguous targets, a longer distance.

With Step 3 the targets arouse images and fantasies. In this way the child tracks information while simultaneously experiencing and balancing affects and fantasies. The first targets used are less provocative (e.g., doll figure of a workman) and later more provocative (e.g., doll figure of a policeman or of a wolf). As discussed below, provocative targets are selected by the therapist according to the child's history, and the child selects targets that are especially potent in arousing fantasies and anxieties. When tracking these targets, the child may spontaneously convey a fantasy being experienced, but at this point these fantasies are only acknowledged. During this step, the focus is to provide the child with experiences in tracking while balancing fantasies and affects, a prerequisite for efficiently scanning in the service of symbolic functioning.

The next steps imbed the focal attention process within symbolic functioning. The child actively construes the stimulus being tracked as something other than what it is (Step 4), and, following the method of directed fantasy discussed in Chapter 4, cultivates a fantasy situation within which targets are tracked. In the last step the child initiates and directs increas-

Table 6.1. Steps in Therapy with Focal Attention–Passive Scanning: *Follow Me*

Step 1. Child tracks neutral, concrete, and familiar targets, perceived as they are, and moved through short distances by therapist
Part A Child walks alongside moving target while tracking target
Part B Child stands and/or sits and tracks moving target
Part C Child sits, holds head still, and tracks moving target with eyes
Part D Therapist and child evaluate child's tracking behavior

Step 2. Child tracks neutral/ambiguous, tangible and intangible targets, perceived as they are, and moved through long distances by therapist
Parts A–D Same as Step 1

Step 3. Child tracks targets that therapist continuously changes; Child required to anticipate information and shift points of view
Parts A–D Same as Step 1

Step 4. Child tracks targets that stimulate images, fantasies, emotions and that are moved through short and long distances by therapist
Parts A–D Same as Step 1

Step 5. Child tracks targets that are construed as something other than what they are and that are moved through short and long distances by therapist
Parts A–D Same as Step 1
Part E Child and therapist evaluate whether symbols constructed are conventional or personal and whether they fit attributes of the target

Step 6. Child tracks targets that are construed as something other than what they are, that are moved through short and long distances by therapist, while child fantasizes a situation and an identity
Parts A–D Same as Step 5

Step 7. Child tracks targets that are construed as something other than what they are while enacting a fantasy directed by therapist. The distance tracked and the mode of tracking are not restricted
Part A Same as Step 5, Part D

ingly elaborated fantasy situations within which tracking activity is emphasized.

When administering the program to an outer-oriented child, the steps are followed in the sequence described. In this way the child initially tracks information as it is, without the participation of fantasies against which cognition is defended and later develops the capacity to track information that arouses images and emotions and that is transformed by fantasy.

With the inner-oriented child the reverse sequence is followed. Beginning with Step 7, the therapist attempts to enter the child's fantasy world through tracking activity. As an alliance is established the therapist helps the child to track information that is construed in terms of conventional as well as personal symbols and to appreciate the difference. And, in the final steps the child develops the capacity to sustain attention on moving targets, perceived as they are without the interference of fantasies.

Once the outer-oriented child achieves Step 7, and the inner-oriented child Step 1, both children frequently engage in activities in which flexible tracking coordinates the requirements of stimuli and fantasies, shifting from one to the other. Passive scanning is now available as a tool to register information in everyday living as well as to serve the process of nondirected verbal/play therapy if indicated.

Throughout, the therapist is alert for opportunities to teach the child to observe and evaluate her tracking behaviors. For example, a child directs a fleeting glance at the moving target, looks away for several seconds, redirects attention at the target, and so on. Another may look away and appear "occupied," or stare out the window, or look at a picture on the wall; another may appear to be orienting himself and his gaze at the moving target but simultaneously vigorously scratch his legs. When such behaviors are noted, the therapist asks the child, "While you were looking at the (object), did you notice anything about the way you were looking?" As might be expected, the responses of children with dysfunctions in focal attention frequently reflect no awareness of such behaviors (e.g., "My eyes were hurting"; "I was looking hard"; "I was looking funny"; "The thing was flying through the air.").

Initially the therapist accepts such responses and repeats the inquiry at other appropriate moments. Also, when it is appropriate, the therapist offers observations, for example, "While you were looking at (target) you scratched yourself. Do you remember doing that?" Initially the therapist draws attention to large behaviors (e.g., walking away, moving about restlessly) and gradually to smaller ones (e.g., scratching an arm). As the therapist requests observation and offers observations, the child gradually becomes more observant and aware of his tracking behaviors.

When the child reaches those steps that require imaging the target, the therapist introduces the child to evaluating the degree to which the image fits the attributes of the target and whether the image is more conventional or personal. For example, while construing a paper clip, during Step 4, a child imaged it as a "key ring," and later as "something to stick in your nose; my brother did." Following the guidelines presented in Chapter 4, the child developed an understanding that the images of a key ring and something in your nose both fit the properties of a paper clip, but the first is a conventional and the second a personal symbol.

The age and developmental status of a child should be kept in mind when engaging the child in self-observation and evaluation. A 5-year-old would not be expected to sustain attention on a moving target over as great a distance as would be expected of a 12-year-old. With a 5-year-old attention is drawn primarily to the most blatant interruptions of the tracking process (e.g., the child walks away and picks up an item off the floor). With the 12-year-old, attention is drawn to more subtle behaviors (e.g., looking away for moments).

A word about the mechanics of presenting moving targets. Of course, the therapist can hold the target, stretch his/her arm out, and walk across the room for some distance. The therapist can also stand and move the target from right to left and vice versa, crossing the midline. In addition, we have found it useful to hang targets at the end of a long stick which the therapist holds while walking. This method is desirable for children who, when tracking, are disrupted by the proximity of the therapist's body (e.g., running away, becoming very sleepy).

Introducing the Child to the Program

The Outer-Oriented Child. Say, ''Mary, we are going to play a game called *Follow Me.* What am I holding in my hand? (Child responds.) That's right, it's a wooden square. I am going to move it through the air. You walk along and follow it; try to keep your eyes on it as long as it is moving.''

The therapist moves the target 4 or 5 feet. Then ask the child to move the target, and follow it, making appropriate comments such as, ''Do you see, Mary, I am following the square, and I keep my eyes on it all the time while you move it?'' This is repeated as needed to insure that the child understands the task.

The Inner-Oriented Child. Observe the child's behavior during the first session (or several sessions if the child is severely withdrawn) and note items the child handles more than others. Frequently these children bring some item of their own to the session which may also be used as a target. The therapist takes the item and says, ''Mary, follow this as it goes through the air. Keep your eyes on it as you follow it.'' After the child engages the task for a few seconds the therapist says, ''That's fine. Now you hold it and move it through the air, and I'll follow it. See, I keep my eyes on it all the time while I'm following it.'' This is repeated as often as the child's general behavior permits. Severely inner-oriented children may engage the therapist in this task only once in a session, refusing other invitations, and occupying themselves with some ''private'' activity. In such cases, while the therapist may relate to the child's private activity and to the child, the therapist remains patient and ever alert for opportunities to enter the child's world through the process of tracking. As these interactions increase, the therapist becomes familiar with ingredients in the child's private world and uses these to invent ways in which the process of tracking can be performed within that world.

Specific Instructions

Step 1. The goal is to develop the child's ability to sustain attention on targets moving through a short distance and perceived as they are. The task is made more complex by systematically varying the mode of tracking, the content of the target, and the pathway through which it moves. Each of these dimensions is varied within each part and from one to another. With Part A the child tracks a large, familiar target (e.g., wooden cube) which travels a linear course, by walking alongside of it. Gradually the size of the target is decreased (e.g., a marble), and the pathway it travels becomes "wavy" and then takes many complex turns. With Part B the sequence from large to small targets and from linear to curvilinear pathways is repeated, but now the child sits or stands and follows the target by moving only the head and eyes. When appropriate competence is achieved the child sits holding his head still and tracks the target by moving only his eyes (Part C).

In another variation of these techniques, a child may be treated more effectively if the same simple target (wooden cube) is used, and Parts A through C are followed. Then a slightly more complex target (marble) is used repeating the same parts.

If a child shows extreme difficulty tracking a target with only the eyes, keeping the body and head stationary, have the child straddle a chair backwards and rest her chin on a pillow placed on the back of the chair. This technique is usually effective in helping a child keep her head oriented forward while following the target only with her eyes.

While some children may not require large targets or tracking by walking alongside the target, it is usually best if a child receives at least a few trials, if only to orient the child to the task and to observe the child's unique tracking behavior. Conversely, because some young children, or those severely dysfunctional in tracking, become stressed when tracking very small targets, these would not be used.

The following examples of targets are intended to encourage therapists to invent targets that meet the special needs of a child: (a) lids of cooking pots, 12, 8, 6, and 4 inches in diameter, concluding with a circular cutout 1 inch in diameter; (b) a wooden cube is attached to a long stick. One side of the cube is painted black, another white, another half black and half white, and another in a 2×2 inch black and white checkerboard. The therapist rotates the cube while moving it through a pathway, presenting one or another side, and the child calls out "white," "black," "half and half," depending on the face of the cube exposed. In the early stages, this method helps to determine whether the child is watching and "sees" the target.

Step 2. Use the methods of the previous step but now present targets that are smaller, increasingly ambiguous, less familiar, and/or intangible. Examples of less familiar, tangible targets are ambiguous line drawings on 3×5 inch cards, pieces of metal from small motors, hair dryers, etc. Almost any piece of "junk" will do. Examples of intangible targets include a beam of light from a flashlight and recordings of tone beeps, ocean waves, or whistles. To present the latter, a cassette player or the microphone is moved through space. To maximize the sound as the target, rather than the microphone, the latter could be covered with gray cloth. The therapist, with electronic aptitude, could set up a series of speakers and a switch system that passes the recorded sound from one speaker to another, generating a stimulus of sound traveling through space. There is another, less complicated way of moving sound across space. The cassette player can be attached to a ring (or some other suitable fixture) located on a rope that is strung across the room. By pulling a string attached to the ring the cassette player is moved across space.

Step 3. The child tracks information while at the same time shifting points of view and anticipating information. The target is a six-sided cardboard or wooden block, attached to a stick, and containing various stimuli on the sides of the cube (e.g., numbers, letters, words, silhouettes of animals, and human figures). Stickers are ideal since they can easily be fixed to the block and then removed and replaced with others. As the block is moved through space, the therapist rotates the stick and therefore the cube, presenting one side and then another at uneven intervals. While tracking the block, the child calls out the name of the stimulus presented.

Since the goal is to provide the child with experience shifting among points of view while tracking, the therapist must be creative in constructing stimuli that fit the child's cognitive abilities and that require the child to shift without notice; for example, from the point of view of numbers, to types of animals, to profiles of famous presidents. In another approach one block could contain various living things and the child could call out whether the side displayed presents a mammal, an insect, a bird, and so on.

In the latter phases of this technique, the therapist presents stimuli that are symbols of some aspect of the child's difficulty and therefore bridges the next step, which emphasizes tracking targets that arouse fantasies and emotions. For example, if a child characteristically gets lost in fantasies of warfare, the therapist uses pictures of weapons as targets.

Step 4. This step emphasizes more formally the experience of tracking information while balancing emotions and fantasies. To select appropriate targets present the child with a wide array of objects. Examples are: doll figures of animals (e.g., wolf, alligator, snake); humans (e.g., policeman, worker, father, mother, infant); rubber figures (spiders, insects, monsters); a jackknife; a pair of scissors; an addition problem printed on a 3×5 inch card. Sound recordings that can be used as targets include: a baby crying; the siren of a fire engine; voices of children in a playground; and others readily obtained from sound effects records. Ask the child to share thoughts and feelings about each—those she likes or dislikes; those that make her feel happy, nervous, scared; those that make her "think of angry things or bad things." The child could also be encouraged to bring items into the office.

In addition, on the basis of an understanding of the child's difficulties, history, and behavior in therapy to this point, the therapist selects items as targets that are likely to arouse fantasies and emotions. For example, one child was suspended from school because he had carved "designs" into chairs and desks. At one point in this step, a jackknife (provided by the therapist) was used as a target. Another child focused much of his rage on an infant sibling so that a small infant doll and a picture of an infant nursing were used. Because a child had difficulty eating, frequently refusing food, pictures of food and toy replicas of food were used as targets.

The child tracks the targets selected following the same approach described in Step 1. Say, "Now I am going to move this (baby; jackknife; hamburger) through space. Try to follow it like the other things you followed. Let's see how you follow it." In general, the therapist follows a sequence presenting less provocative targets first, then more provocative ones, and reserving for the last phase those targets that hold a special connection with some current difficulty for the child (e.g., a jackknife for the child described above who carved school furniture).

During these trials, the therapist has the opportunity to help the child evaluate her tracking behavior comparatively by relating observations made with these emotionally arousing targets with observations made of previous, more neutral targets. During these evaluations the therapist begins to teach the child to observe how tracking information varies as the emotions/fantasies aroused by the information vary.

When tracking these targets, a child may make spontaneous comments, describing some recent event, or may express some fantasy. For example, while tracking a wolf puppet, one child exclaimed, "Watch out, he's going to bite!" While tracking an addition problem, another child exclaimed, "I hate math! Mr. (math teacher) is a (expletive deleted)." When this happens the therapist helps the child stick with the tracking activity. The therapist does not explore the fantasy or issue expressed. Rather, he reserves it for a later phase in therapy. For example, in response to the child who exclaimed that the wolf might bite, the therapist said, "Keep your eyes on him, Jimmy; let's make sure we know where he moves to so he won't come after us." In addition, this child became more restless and crouched, as if in a posture of vigilance. The therapist invited the child to creep along, tracking the wolf puppet "so you can watch his every move and be on guard."

Step 5. The process of tracking is embedded into the process of transforming information and symbolic functioning. To accomplish this the therapist uses as targets various cardboard cutouts or clay figures (much like 3-D inkblots) that vary in ambiguity, while at the same time lending themselves to being transformed. For example, a cutout or clay figure could lend itself to being construed as a "worm" or a "snake" or a "twisted stick." While another object might lend itself to being construed as a "bagel," a "dog's turd," or "a coil of rope."

The therapist says, "Mary, now I'm going to hold up something for you to follow, but as I move it tell me what it could be—what it reminds you of." Once the child has produced an image, ask the child to produce another, when appropriate. Repeated trials are administered, varying the targets used, and the distance and course of the pathway traveled by the target as outlined in Steps 1 through 3.

In addition to evaluating the tracking behavior displayed, the child and therapist also evaluate the degree of fit between the image/symbol produced and the physical attributes (form) of the target and whether the image is a conventional or a personal one.

Step 6. Embedding the tracking process within symbolic functioning is extended with this step. In addition to construing a target as something other than what it is, the child imagines a scene and assumes a pretend role within that scene and in terms of the construed target. Here the child may spend 15 minutes or a whole session with one target, scene, and role. Present the child with an ambiguous target and say, "This time I want you to imagine first what this could be or what it reminds you of." To illustrate, let us assume the child answers, "A snake." The therapist then says, "Fine. Now, think of a place where we could be and where the snake could be." The child responds, "The zoo; it's in a cage in the zoo." The therapist continues, "That's fine. Now pretend you are someone in that zoo with the cage and the snake." The child responds, "The zoo guy getting ready to feed it." The therapist asks, "What happens?" The child responds, "The zoo guy goes into the cage." The therapist continues in this way helping the child elaborate the scene and theme as much as possible. When the setting, role, and theme are established, the therapist says, "O.K., let's pretend the snake is moving around in the cage. You be the zoo guy and keep your eyes on him. Follow him carefully as you get ready to give him food. Let's make this (wooden cube) the food."

The therapist should look for opportunities within the imagined scene created by the child to incorporate dimensions used in other steps, such as moving the target through increasingly long distances that are linear and curvilinear, and varying the mode of tracking. As an example of the latter, after the child enacts walking around the cage while keeping his eyes on the snake, the therapist could direct the child to follow the target only with his eyes, "Let's say you came out of the cage and stood between two bars so your head and body are still and you watch the snake with your eyes to make sure he gets the food.''

Step 7. With this step the treatment process takes on aspects of the form of ''free play'' in which the child images a succession of scenes and a number of objects, persons, and animals. These scenes may be unrelated or they may become integrated into a theme. However, unlike free play, the therapist emphasizes within each scene and theme the process of tracking moving information. For example, one child centered a series of scenes on imagined warfare: In one scene the child tracked a large radar screen for enemy rockets (the therapist moved wooden cutouts through a large frame designated by the child); in another the child was in a field tracking the movements of enemy tanks. The therapist should be active helping the child create scenes that lend themselves to experiences with tracking moving information.

PROGRAM 2B: *WHICH IS BIG?* *WHICH IS SMALL?*

Purpose: To provide experiences actively and systematically scanning information; to develop the capacity for efficient active scanning during the process of symbolic functioning.

Materials: Wooden rods varying in length from 4 to 12 inches; clay; glasses containing water and varying in diameter and height; dishes containing water in varying depths and diameter; various materials that can represent differences in number, weight, density, texture (e.g., marbles, paper clips, balls made of varying materials).

Introduction and General Procedure

Throughout this program the child is asked to scan actively and to compare a series of two sets of information that vary in terms of one or more dimensions (e.g., height, number, weight, volume, with the left-right location of the pair randomized). When related to passive scanning (tracking) described above, the tasks described here require focal attention functioning at higher developmental levels. The aim then is not to train the child to estimate accurately the relative heights of two rods, for example, but to use the task of comparing rods as a way of promoting vigorous, systematic, and broad scanning.

The seven steps that make up the program, outlined in Table 6.2, parallel those of the preceding program. With the first two, the child actively scans and compares sets of neutral information that are not likely to arouse

Table 6.2. Steps in Therapy with Focal Attention–Active Scanning:
Which Is Big? Which is Small?

Step 1. Child scans and compares two sets of neutral, familiar information that vary in terms of one or more dimensions
   Part A Therapist locates two sets near together then increasingly further apart
   Part B Therapist presents two different sets and then increasingly more similar ones
   Part C Therapist does not restrict body movements while child scans and then gradually requires head and body to be stationary
   Part D Therapist does not restrict time child scans and then gradually restricts time
   Part E Therapist and child evaluate the child's scanning behavior

Step 2. Child scans and compares two sets of neutral, more ambiguous information that vary in terms of one or more dimensions
   Parts A–E Same as Step 1

Step 3. Child scans and compares two sets of information while shifting points of view and anticipating information
   Parts A–E Same as Step 1

Step 4. Child scans and compares two sets of information that arouse fantasies/emotions
   Parts A–E Same as Step 1

Step 5. Child scans and compares sets of information construed as something other than what they are
   Parts A–E Same as Step 1
   Part F Child and therapist evaluate whether symbols constructed are conventional or personal and degree to which they fit attributes of stimuli

Step 6. Child scans and compares sets of information construed as something other than what they are as part of a fantasy and pretend identity directed by therapist
   Parts A–F Same as Step 5

Step 7. Child scans and compares sets of information construed by the child and within a more elaborate fantasy. There are no restrictions on the number of sets of information compared, the distances between them, the degree of similarity among them, and the time taken to compare them

---

fantasies and emotions. Further, the tasks require increasingly more vigorous and active scanning as the distance between the two sets of information is increased and as the difference between them, reflected in some attribute, is decreased.

With Step 3 the child actively scans and compares sets of information in a format that emphasizes shifting points of view and anticipating information. These experiences prepare the child for the tasks in Step 4, which require scanning sets of information while balancing fantasies and emotions. With gains made in cognitive-affective coordination, a prerequisite for symbolic functioning, the child is prepared for Steps 5 and 6, which require the child to image situations and events and to assume fantasized roles within which the child engages in the process of active scanning and comparing information. The last step, resembling aspects of free play, guides the child in elaborating pretend themes consisting of a series of situations, but throughout every effort is made to emphasize the process of active scanning now exercised within elaborate pretending.

When administered to an outer-oriented child, the seven steps are followed in the sequence described. The child cultivates active, broad scanning while engaging information as it is and without the participation of fantasies against which cognition is defended. Then the child cultivates active scanning while flexibly shifting points of view and anticipating information. Flexibility is then applied in scanning emotionally arousing information. At this point the child is prepared to engage in active scanning within a deepening process of pretending and symbolic functioning.

With the inner-oriented child the reverse sequence is followed. The therapist begins with Step 7, modifying the technique as needed, and sets out to help the child invite the therapist into the child's private world. To accomplish this, and to set the stage for a treatment program that will restructure focal attention, the therapist asks the child to scan and compare sets of information that are part of the child's fantasy world. As the child observes the therapist scanning and comparing information, and as the child scans information designated by the therapist, an alliance is formed. With this alliance the therapist proceeds with the next steps. The child engages in active scanning within fantasies constructed by the child, but the fantasies become increasingly more organized, and the ingredients of the fantasies are brought closer to real events and stimuli.

Then the child gains experience shifting points of view as she scans and compares information that is transformed by conventional and personal symbols. As gains are made, the next steps emphasize tasks in which the child scans sets of neutral-ambiguous and then neutral-familiar information.

Once the outer-oriented child reaches Step 7, and the inner-oriented child achieves Step 1, they are equipped to engage in therapeutic activities and tasks which require them to actively scan information and flexibly coordinate the properties and uses of actual stimuli with those of fantasies associated with them. Active scanning as a tool can now serve more efficient learning and adaptation as well as the nondirected process of verbal/play therapy if indicated.

Throughout, the therapist is alert for opportunities to teach the child to observe and evaluate her scanning behaviors. The guidelines described in the previous program are followed. In the first sessions the therapist notes unique aspects of the child's scanning behaviors, gradually bringing these to the child's attention. For example a child gives each piece of information being compared only a fleeting glance and then looks away; a child looks at one piece of information for 15 seconds, looks away, looks at the other for 1 second, looks at the first again for 20 seconds, obviously centering on only one piece of information; a child directs attention at one set of information then, while looking at the other, blinks his eyes vigorously several times; a child shows unsystematic scanning and then "tunes out," seemingly occupied with private thoughts, or stares out the window, or becomes irritated, or scratches his arm nervously.

When such behaviors are noticed, the therapist asks the child whether or not she "noticed anything while you were looking at the two things." The therapist accepts the child's response and initially points out the most obvious part of the child's behavior. For example, "Johnny, you didn't notice anything. I noticed that you blinked your eyes very hard when you looked at that stick." Since children dysfunctional in focal attention usually are not aware of such behaviors, the therapist inquires, as often as is appropriate, and offers observations, until the child shows some capacity to observe attentional behaviors that occur immediately after or during a task.

In the early phases of treatment, attention is directed only to the child's behavior. In later phases, the therapist connects the dysfunctional scanning to a particular stimulus used in the task or to its complexity. For example, "When you said the stick was shorter than the policeman, did you notice what you did when you looked at the policeman?" The child responds he did not notice anything in particular. "Did you notice you blinked very hard, but you didn't blink when you looked at the stick?" As another example, "When you looked at those two sticks (differing in height by only ½ inch) did you notice anything about what you did that was different than before (the sticks differed in height by 2 inches)?" The child responds, "I did not look at the sticks as hard." "That's right. And, I notice that you began to jiggle your leg in that nervous way we talked about before. These sticks are harder to figure out and you got extra-nervous."

When the child is engaged in imaging the information being scanned, the therapist guides the child in evaluating the degree to which the image fits the attributes of the target and whether the image is more conventional or personal.

Again, the age and developmental stage of the child governs the requirements the therapist expects the child to meet in this evaluation process. For example, the scanning of a 5-year-old is expected to be more vigorous and systematic when the sets of information are 3 feet apart, but not as vigorous and systematic when 15 feet apart, while a 10-year-old would be expected to scan objects 15 feet apart, without showing disruptions in the process. The same issue would apply when the child is asked to evaluate the fit between an image and the attributes of the object in question. If a 5-year-old images a paper clip as a cup it may be sufficient to help the child articulate that the paper clip has round sides like a cup "but you can't put water in it." With a 10-year-old it would be appropriate to help the child articulate that the paper clip is not round like a cup.

Introducing the Child to the Program

The Outer-Oriented Child. Set two rods (one 8 inches and one 12 inches tall), for example, two feet apart, and say, "Mary, we are going to play a game called *Which Is Big? Which Is Small?* You see these two sticks? Look at one and then look at the other and then look at the other one again. Keep looking at each of them as many times as you need to until you are sure which is the bigger one." The therapist repeats these preliminary trials primarily to insure that the child understands the task format to be used. The more simple the task the better. Once the child understands the task, continue with Step 1.

The Inner-Oriented Child. Observe the child's behavior during the first session noticing which materials the child tends to manipulate or which material the child has brought to the office. Let us assume that the child tended to fiddle with paper clips while looking in a dreamy way at various items on the shelves. The therapist sets six paper clips on one sheet of paper, and three paper clips on another about 2 feet away and says, "Mary, look at these and look at these. Which has the most? Look at them as much as you need to, to tell me which one has the most."

Repeat tasks as often as possible until the child seems to be engaging the therapist and shows signs of inviting the therapist into her fantasy world. As noted earlier, some severely inner-oriented children may engage the therapist in a task only once in a session or refuse to perform, occupying themselves with "private activity." In such cases the therapist should be patient and look for other opportunities to engage the child. As the therapist becomes familiar with ingredients of the child's private world, the therapist should be in a position to introduce tasks that lend themselves to the process of active scanning while at the same time connect with the child's private world. As one example, while moving about the playroom a child showed that he was especially centered on lining things up straight. Therefore, the therapist constructed pairs of lines, asking the child which line was most straight. The more the therapist connects with aspects of the child's private world, the more a working alliance is established.

Specific Instructions

Step 1. The goal is to develop further the child's ability to scan neutral, familiar information actively and systematically while the tasks increase in complexity. The tasks are made more complex in a stepwise fashion by orchestrating four variables: (a) presenting two sets of information close together and gradually farther apart; (b) presenting two sets of information that are very different in terms of an attribute by which they are to be compared and then gradually presenting sets of information that are increasingly similar in terms of the attribute; (c) not restricting the child's body while the child scans and then gradually requiring the child to sit and hold his head and body stationary while scanning; (d) giving the child unlimited time to scan and compare the two sets of information and then gradually restricting the time.

Any neutral and familiar material that is easily varied in terms of height, number, size, weight, and texture can be used to form sets of information to be scanned and compared (e.g., wooden dowels or rods varying in height and thickness, paper clips varying in size, marbles, balls varying in diameter, color, and texture).

To illustrate how the four variables are orchestrated, wooden rods are used as an example. The therapist sets two rods upright, 2 feet apart (close together Part A); one 12 inches tall, one 6 inches tall (Part B very different in terms of height). The child, who is standing or sitting about 6 feet away from the rods, is asked to look the rods over and to point to the taller (or smaller one), taking as much time as needed, while the mode of scanning and time to scan are not restricted (Parts C and D).

In a later trial, the therapist sets two rods 4 feet apart (further away); one 12 inches, the other 8 inches tall (the rods are now more similar in height). The child is allowed to scan the rods for only 15 seconds (time is restricted), and asked to keep his body still and move only his head and eyes (body restricted). To limit time, the therapist places cardboard screens in front of the rods at the end of the time interval.

In a still later trial, two rods are set 15 feet apart (further apart), one 10 inches and one 11½ inches (more similar). The child is given 5 seconds to examine the rods (greater time restriction), and the child is asked to sit still, keep his head stationary, and move only his eyes while looking at the rods (greater body restriction). This illustration should be viewed as points in a sequence. One child may require only one trial with two items close together and another several trials.

In an alternative approach, only one or two of the variables are manipulated at one time if the child's needs indicate. For example, two rods are placed 2 feet apart (one rod 12 inches, the other 6 inches tall). The succeeding pairs are also placed 2 feet apart but the difference in their heights is gradually decreased (e.g., 12 and 8 inches; 12 and 10 inches; 12 and 11 inches; 12 and 11¾ inches), with the left-right location of the rods randomized. During these trials the child takes as much time as is needed and is not asked to restrict body movements. When the child shows efficient scanning comparing two rods very similar in height and 2 feet apart, the therapist repeats this approach now placing rods further and further apart, from trial to trial, while at the same time decreasing the difference in height. Next the therapist gradually reduces the amount of time the child is given to scan the information (e.g., 15, 12, 9, 6, and 3 seconds) while at the same time increasing the distance between the rods and decreasing the difference between their heights. Restricting the mode of scanning would be phased in last in the same way.

When other material is used, such as beakers of water and paper clips differing in size and shape, the task can be made more complex by manipulating two attributes simultaneously. For example, if large and small, circular and eliptical paper clips are used, the therapist could ask the child to point to the sheet of paper which contains the larger number of small, circular paper clips. Similarly, if balls of different diameters and textures are used, the child could be asked to point to the ball that is smoother and bigger or rougher and bigger. The more complex the comparison being made, the more vigorous and systematic the scanning required.

Using two different materials is also an effective way to increase the complexity of the task. For example, the child is asked to compare two clusters, each containing marbles and paper clips and to indicate which one has fewer marbles than paper clips. Two glasses that vary both in height and diameter when filled with water require more extensive, systematic scanning to determine which has the larger volume, than two glasses that vary only in diameter.

Throughout this step, whenever a child appears especially unsure, or makes many errors comparing the items, the therapist encourages the child to examine the items by touching them, counting them, and so on.

Step 2. Following the same approach described for Step 1, the child scans and compares information that is more ambiguous and whose designated attributes are more independent of external/physical properties. Examples of stimuli that are used in this step consist of cards on which are printed: (a) Mueller-Lyer illusions; (b) Delbeouf illusions; (c) wavy and zig zag lines; (d) rows of dots spaced unevenly. With each pair of cards presented, the child points to the longer stimulus, for example (e.g., wavy line versus rows of dots).

Step 3. The tasks are designed to require scanning while simultaneously shifting points of view. The stimuli used vary in terms of three or more dimensions and are placed behind cardboard screens. The therapist lifts the screens and calls out the dimension in terms of which of the two items are compared. The cardboard screens are returned for some seconds, the screens are lifted again, and the therapist calls out another dimension along which the same items are compared. This technique is repeated as often as is possible given the materials used. The time interval between trials is varied randomly.

As one example, the therapist places two balls that vary in diameter, density, texture, and color 4 feet apart. The therapist raises the screen, and says, "the heavy one." The child responds by pointing. The screen is lowered; after a delay of 10 seconds the screen is raised, and the therapist says, "the taller one." The child responds and the screen is lowered; after a delay of 4 seconds the screen is raised, and the therapist says, "the rough one," and so on. In this way the child actively scans in a state of anticipation and while shifting among the points of view of size, density, texture, and color.

Squares of cloth can be used in a similar way. The therapist asks the child to point to the "bigger one," "softer one," "heavier one," "smoother one," "darker one," etc. Other examples of stimuli are wooden, metal, and styrofoam cubes or cylinders; glasses of different heights and diameters filled with oil, syrup, water; squares and circles of construction paper; and cardboard varying in size, thickness, texture, weight, and color.

Step 4. The child scans sets of information while balancing fantasies and emotions aroused by that information. Present the child with pairs or clusters of the following material intended as examples: plastic insects, spiders, monster figures; doll figures of doctors, policemen, father, mother, infant; two glasses containing water colored with food dye (here, child and therapist participate in labeling the liquids; e.g., if the child labels the deep red liquid "blood," the therapist labels the pink-red liquid "a strawberry drink," or the reverse; see earlier discussion.); two glasses colored with brown food dye, one labeled "a chocolate drink" (light brown), the other "a BM" (dark brown); sets of knives and scissors.

As discussed in the previous program, *Follow Me*, the child participates in selecting and constructing material and shares thoughts and feelings about each item. For example, if the child labeled water tinted with red color "blood," the therapist colors another vessel of water lighter red, which the child indicates is a "strawberry drink." If plastic insects and animals are used the child identifies those that arouse intense anxiety or fear, those construed as "nice," "strong," "angry," etc. If doll figures are used the child identifies attributes for each (e.g., "mad," "nice," "strong," "bossy").

Pairs of these items are presented in various scanning tasks in terms of the attributes the child construed. For example, when the red liquid the child called blood is placed in beakers, the therapist asks the child to point to the glass "with the most blood." As another example, if the child construed an animal figure and a human doll figure both as mad, these items could be paired and the child is asked to point to the one that's "most mad.'' The variables of distance, mode of scanning, degree of difference, and time to scan are manipulated in these tasks, as in previous steps, to increase gradually the complexity. With this step the therapist also has the opportunity to explore pairing various emotions and attributes fantasized by the child and to note whether and how they effect the efficiency of scanning.

The therapist also selects material on the basis of the child's current difficulties, unique personality conflicts, and history. For example the child described in the previous program who carved ''designs'' into school furniture had also threatened a peer with a knife. This child was eventually presented with pairs of different knives (e.g., jackknife, hunting knife, butter knife, toy knife) and asked to point to the one that is ''sharper,'' ''can hurt someone more,'' ''heavier,'' ''longer,'' ''lighter.'' As might be expected, his scanning was much less efficient with these items than with others; he became very excited and took fleeting glances at a particular knife while centering on another; when asked which one could hurt someone more, he struggled, looked at the pair many times and concluded both could hurt someone equally. These scanning behaviors were brought to the child's attention and no interpretations were made, following the guidelines discussed in the previous program. And, the child was engaged in appraising the attributes of the knives presented (very sharp, dull, rubber blade) and whether and how they could hurt someone.

When engaged with this step children sometimes spontaneously produce fantasies, express comments about some event, and become quite emotional. When this happens the therapist helps the child remain focused on the task requirements and does not engage the child in addressing the fantasy or event described. Rather, the behaviors that disrupt the cognitive process are recruited into the task. For example, the child described above impulsively took a knife and passed the blade over the tabletop leaving the task. At this point, the therapist modified the task, setting a ball of clay next to each knife to be compared. When the child decided which knife was sharper, the therapist then permitted the child to test his conclusion by using each knife to cut the ball of clay.

Step 5. Scanning is embedded into the process of transforming information and symbolic functioning. The child points to one of three or more stimuli that are imaged as something other than what they are. Much of the same material used in previous steps can be used here (e.g., balls and cubes of different sizes, colors, textures; paper clips of different sizes and shapes; squares of cloth varying in texture, color, size, and thickness).

Three or more stimuli are presented and the guidelines that vary the distance between stimuli, the time allowed to scan them, and whether or not the mode of scanning is restricted are followed. To illustrate, the therapist presents four balls, varying in terms of several attributes, and says, "Let's pretend these are people. Point to the father. Point to the mother. Point to the uncle. Point to the kid." As another example, a set of balls is presented with the request, "Which one has a smooth face? Which one is strong? Which one is fat?"

These examples are intended to illustrate several issues. First, the scanning activity is now embedded in the process of imaging and pretending that an object is something else. Second, the therapist asks for designations that belong to one category or to several categories. The request for a father, mother, big brother, and so on, in one trial, concerns scanning and judgements that belong to the category of family. The dimensions to be designated could also shift from one to another category and point of view. In the illustration above, when the child points to the smooth face, the guiding category is facial features; and when he points to the "fat one," the guiding category is weight, and so on.

Later, with this step, the therapist asks the child to designate a category beforehand (e.g., present a row of cubes and say, "Let's pretend all of these are something, what could they be?" The child responds, "horses" or "spacemen" or "cars"). The therapist accepts the category and then invents attributes along which the items are compared (e.g., "Which one is the fastest, the slowest, the heaviest."). Here there is an opportunity to engage the child in evaluating the fit between the items selected and the attributes imaged.

Step 6. Scanning is embedded further into the process of symbolic functioning by including scanning activity as a major part of a fantasized situation. Ask the child to imagine material as something other than what it is, a situation in which child and therapist could be, and to assume a pretend role. For example, the child calls a cluster of paper clips "spaceships" and designates the setting as outer space. The therapist asks the child to pretend he is someone. The child responds he is king of the fifth world. The therapist then joins the child in organizing and enacting a pretend theme with scanning as a major activity. The therapist asks the child to give a different identity to each type of paper clip (e.g., friendly, enemy, warship, cargo ship) and indicates there are two places through which spaceships can enter; and the king has to keep an eye on things and notice who is trying to enter the fifth world. The therapist locates two sheets of paper as points of entry into the imaginary world, places various paper clips on each, and asks the king to determine which entry point has, for example, more cargo ships than spaceships. The distance is varied between the items compared by asking the king to pretend that the enemy has found other points of entry which are located further apart. The king could also be restricted in how much time he is allowed to examine the information and whether or not he can move his head.

Step 7. At this point the process takes on aspects of "free play" but active scanning remains a major ingredient. Frequently the scenes and episodes that take place in this phase are integrations of previous themes and scenes. We can use as an example the child who pretends to be king of the fifth world. Paper clips remain spaceships; marbles are transformed into spacemen—some are warriors, others repairmen, others pilots; pieces of cloth become space stations orbiting in the fifth world. The king has to keep track of everything and show everyone he has the greatest mind. The therapist spreads across the floor clusters of paper clips and squares of cloth containing clusters of different marbles, asks the king to point to that part of the sky where there are more of one type of spaceship or more space stations, and asks him to point to the space station on which there are more fighters or more workers and so on.

Concluding Remarks and a Note About Resistance

Once the outer- and inner-oriented child develop the capacity to track and scan information flexibly, managing information as it is and as it is imagined, the child has the mechanism of focal attention as a tool in learning and adapting and also, when indicated, to serve the process of nondirected play/verbal therapy.

Over a number of sessions the therapist begins to construct an understanding of the child's unique focal attention functioning. For example, one child may habitually blink vigorously while attempting to sustain attention in passive tracking or when scanning two sets of stimuli; another may direct a rapid series of dartlike glances; another may habitually rock her body; another may keep her body and head oriented away from the target while directing her eyes toward it; and other children may regularly become "sleepy," "bored," or "irritated" when scanning information. The therapist brings these habitual behaviors to the child's attention, bit by bit, later connects these attentional behaviors to an increase in task complexity, and still later to particular images, emotions, or fantasies experienced in response to stimuli. When these behaviors become obstacles to the treatment process, they are integrated within the task requirements as illustrated above.

It is not until the latter phase that the therapist begins to ask the child to explore possible connections between attentional behaviors experienced and observed in the office with behaviors experienced at school and at home. For example, "John, we notice again that you got very nervous and blinked hard when you were following that car. Can you think of a time when that happens in math class?" This comment illustrates that the therapist is as concrete and specific as possible in helping the child center on some recent moment and specific place. The question, "Does this happen elsewhere?" for the cognitively disabled child is too global and does not help the child construct connections between behaviors in the office and behaviors in other settings.

The outer-oriented child usually shows focused resistance in Step 4 of each program when tasks require tracking and scanning information that arouses fantasies and emotions. The inner-oriented child frequently shows major resistance when tasks require tracking and scanning ambiguous information while subordinating fantasies (Step 2 in each program). Episodes of resistance are managed following the technique discussed in Chapter 4.

Chapter 7
Therapy with the Field Articulation Cognitive Control

The field articulation cognitive control defines the manner in which a child scans, articulates, and responds to a field of information in terms of what is relevant and irrelevant for the task at hand (see Chapters 2 and 3). The program described in this chapter is designed to restructure and rehabilitate this control mechanism so that it functions efficiently when external information is handled as it is, as well as when information is transformed with symbols and fantasies within the process of symbolic functioning.

To benefit from this program a child should have achieved, in the course of development or with the assistance of the programs already described, stage-appropriate functioning in body ego–tempo regulation and in passive and active scanning. Therapy in field articulation emphasizes developmentally more advanced cognitive activity than required by previous programs: the child articulates and responds to fields of pieces of information that continually shift in relevance as the therapist designates the dimensions that guide how the information is to be considered and processed. In therapy with the developmentally earlier focal attention control, the child is asked to track moving targets and later to scan, for example, two rods and compare their heights. In performing these responses the child begins to withhold attention from various stimuli (e.g., pictures on the office wall). Nonetheless these tasks emphasize passive tracking and active scanning to develop efficient focal attention functioning, while body movements are regulated. In contrast the tasks of field articulation therapy require the child to use active, broad scanning and body movements are regulated within a process that deploys attention *selectively*, directing and withholding attention from information as it shifts in relevance.

The first distinguishing feature of this level of treatment, then, is that the child's responses are more differentiated *cognitive* manipulations of information. Sensory motor accommodations to information are subordinated and minimal while cognitive accommodations dominate. More complex than the task of comparing the heights of two rods set far apart, field articulation tasks contain complex organizations of contours, colors, spatial relations, and sizes to be surveyed, and more complex dimensions guide which information is to be responded to as relevant. With a second distinguishing feature the child engages information that is more confined to microspace. Fields of information are presented on the surface of a table and subsequently on sheets of paper.

PROGRAM 3: *FIND THE SHAPES*

Purpose and Goal: To develop the child's capacity to direct attention selectively at complex fields and configurations of information in terms of dimensions of relevance/irrelevance; to promote the efficiency of field articulation functioning with external information perceived as it is and with information transformed with symbols and fantasies in the process of symbolic functioning.

Materials: (a) plywood, cardboard, plastic cutouts of four geometric shapes (square, circle, triangle, diamond), three sizes (2×2, 3×3, and 4×4 inches) and six colors (red, yellow, blue, green, white, black); (b) $8\frac{1}{2} \times 11$ inch sheets of paper on which are printed geometric shapes, pictures, letters, arrayed in rows and randomly; (c) buttons and paper clips of various sizes and shapes, lego pieces of various sizes and shapes; and (d) various ambiguous shapes cut from construction paper each approximately 2×2 inches; with each shape the sides are linear, or curvilinear, or a combination.

Instructions and General Procedure

The therapist places an array of information on a table and instructs the child as to which dimension or dimensions of the information are relevant and what the child is to do with that information. In dealing with each array, the child uses two main responses; the information designated is removed from or located within the array. With younger children, it is useful to refer to relevant information as "the answers;" and whenever the task requires that relevant information be removed and located in a box, the latter is referred to as the "answer box."

The program consists of seven steps, as outlined in Table 7.1, each with a graded series of tasks that gradually increase in complexity. This is accomplished by following three guidelines either one at a time or in combination, once a starting point along these guidelines is selected that best suits the child's needs.

Table 7.1. Steps in Therapy with Field Articulation: *Find the Shapes*

Step 1. Child articulates fields of geometric cutouts in terms of dimensions designated by therapist and removes them

Part A Complexity of field surveyed increased by therapist
1. From few cutouts to many cutouts
2. From cutouts of one color to many colors
3. From cutouts located close together to far apart
4. From one type of geometric shape to four shapes
5. From cutouts of one size to three sizes
6. From displays without patterns to patterned displays
7. From an ordered array to a random array
8. From arrays of single cutouts to arrays of stacks of cutouts

Part B Complexity of dimensions defining information as relevant/irrelevant increased by therapist
1. From one to many dimensions defining relevant/irrelevant information

Part C Delay engaging relevant information increased by therapist
1. From little delay to much delay
2. From simple to complex tasks interpolated between instructions and performance

Part D Child and therapist evaluate field articulation behavior

Step 2. Child articulates fields of more complex stimuli in terms of dimensions designated by therapist which emphasize relationships among stimuli
Parts A–D Same as Step 1

Step 3. Child articulates fields of information, containing simple and complex stimuli, while shifting points of view and anticipating dimensions designated by therapist
Parts A–D Same as Step 1

Step 4. Child articulates fields of information that arouse fantasies/emotions
Parts A–D Same as Step 1

Step 5. Child articulates fields of information construed as something other than what they are as directed by therapist and then by child
Parts A–D Same as Step 1
Part E Child and therapist evaluate whether symbols constructed are conventional or personal and the degree to which they fit attributes of stimuli

Step 6. Child articulates fields of information within a fantasy directed by therapist
Parts A–E Same as Step 5

Step 7. Child articulates fields of information within nondirected fantasy and free play. No restrictions are imposed on the complexity of fields of information or the dimensions defining information as relevant/irrelevant

---

One guideline defines the degree of complexity represented by a field of information. For example, if geometric cutouts are used, the first array presented contains a few cutouts (e.g., six) all of one shape (e.g., squares), one size (e.g., large), one color (e.g., white), located close together (2 inches separate each cutout from others), and in rows and columns. A later array would contain more cutouts (e.g., 20), of two shapes (e.g., squares and circles), two sizes (e.g., large and small), and three colors (e.g., white, yellow, and red), located further apart (e.g., 6 inches separates one cutout from others), and in a more random array.

Another guideline concerns the complexity of dimensions used to define information relevant or irrelevant, and accordingly determines the complexity of the cognitive response the child is asked to perform in managing the task. Initially the therapist designates a few dimensions which define relevant information and, in a stepwise fashion, gradually designates more dimensions.

To illustrate, assume a child is presented with 30 cutouts of three shapes (squares, circles, triangles), two sizes (large and small), four colors (white, red, yellow, green) and arrayed in six columns of five rows, each cutout located 6 inches from another. This same array could be used to require that the child engage in a simple field articulation response and gradually in a series of increasingly more complex responses (e.g., the child is asked to remove: all the red cutouts; all the squares; all large, yellow triangles; all small, green circles and large, white squares; all small, green triangles next to either a large, white circle or large, yellow square. Or the child is asked to locate a small, blue diamond on each large, yellow circle and small, white triangle).

A close examination of the cognitive activity required by these examples helps illustrate how the child uses increasingly more differentiated field articulation responses as the number of dimensions defining relevant information is increased. With the first designation (red cutouts are relevant), the child scans the matrix, registers a blue cutout, withdraws attention, registers a yellow cutout, withdraws attention and so on—a process which subordinates as irrelevant the various shapes and sizes present and which actively withdraws from any color that does not qualify. Comparing this process with that required by the third task listed above (large, yellow triangles are relevant), the child scans the matrix, registers a large, yellow square, withdraws attention because the color is relevant but the shape is irrelevant; then registers a large, green triangle and again withdraws attention because the shape is relevant but the color is irrelevant; then registers a small, yellow triangle and withdraws attention because the color and shape are relevant but the size is irrelevant, and so on. The same micro-analysis could be applied to the field articulation activity required by the other tasks which use more complex designations to define relevant information.

A third guideline concerns cognitive delay which is superimposed on the other two guidelines. The therapist could permit the child to respond immediately once the relevant information is defined, or require the child to delay before responding, initially for 5 seconds, then 15, then 25, and so on. In addition the therapist could interpolate activities during these delays, asking the child, for example, to count to 10, read a paragraph, or draw a human figure.

These three guidelines are used in all steps of the program with some modification, except for the last. As discussed in Chapter 4, when a child has handled successfully three displays in a row at one level of complexity, the next display presented is made more complex by following one or more of these guidelines (i.e., increasing the complexity of the display, the number of attributes that define relevant information, and the delay imposed on the response).

The various steps in the program differ in terms of the degree to which information is articulated as it is or construed as something else. With Steps 1 and 2 the child deals with fields of information that are managed as they are. Steps 3 and 4 prepare the child for symbolic functioning by presenting tasks which emphasize shifting points of view, anticipating information, and balancing emotions and fantasies while engaged in the field articulation process. The child formally uses field articulation within the process of pretending and symbolic functioning in Steps 5 and 6. Step 7, as with other programs, is intended to be a bridge to a nondirected verbal/play treatment process within which the child resolves key pathological metaphors with the benefit of efficient field articulation functioning.

With an outer-oriented child, the seven steps are followed in the sequence described. In this way the child begins to restructure the field articulation mechanism by engaging information as it is without the participation of fantasy/emotions, which cognition habitually avoids. As the child's functioning becomes more efficient, the child is then asked to articulate fields of information that arouse emotions and fantasies, and eventually which require that information to be construed and transformed within the process of symbolic functioning.

With the inner-oriented child the reverse sequence is followed. The therapist begins with Step 7 and looks for opportunities to introduce field articulation tasks within the child's spontaneous fantasy activity. As an alliance develops, the therapist gradually moves to Step 6 and then 5, which require the child to construe information with symbols that are more conventional as well as highly personal. When the child's symbolic functioning becomes more flexible and responsive to attributes of external information, the therapist moves through the remaining steps helping the child develop efficient field articulation functioning while engaging information as it is, without the participation of fantasies and symbols.

Once the outer-oriented child achieves Step 7 and the inner-oriented child achieves Step 1, both children are more equipped with field articulation functioning as a tool to serve efficient learning and adapting. At this point, if indicated, therapy transitions to a nondirected verbal/play format to help the child work through and reform key pathological metaphors, a task which should be facilitated by the availability of efficient field articulation cognitive control functioning.

Introducing the Program to the Child

The Outer-Oriented Child. Begin with Step 1 and place a display of geometric cutouts on the table. Say, "Mary, we're going to play a game called *Find the Shapes.* Look these over and take all the squares and place them in this box." After the child performs, say, "Fine, let's try another one." The therapist removes the first display and presents another. "Now look this over and put only the small, yellow squares in this box." Once the child performs, the therapist introduces some explanation of the task since children who require this program frequently can assimilate some understanding of its purpose. Say, "The games we'll play go like this. I'll put cutouts and other things, on the table and I'll ask you to take certain ones away and to ignore others. When you do this over and over again, it will train your mind to concentrate better on the things that are important to get the right answers, and to push away (ignore) with your mind the things that are not important. Like when you read, you have to pay attention to the story and ignore other things. Let's try another one."

The Inner-Oriented Child. In one or more open-ended sessions, observe the materials the child tends to manipulate. As soon as an opportunity permits, construct a display with this material to form a field articulation task. Assume a child moves quietly about the room, ignoring the therapist for the most part, casually manipulating wooden human figures, toy animals, and puppets. On different occasions, the child presses and rubs one figure against another, places the wolf puppet on his hand, "bites" the pig puppet, and stands the wooden figure of a workman next to the pig puppet. The therapist takes 10 or 12 of these wooden figures, hand puppets, and animals, spreads them on a table in rows and columns, and says, "Harry, look these over; take all the ones that bite and are mean and put them in this box." After the child responds, the therapist returns the items to the display and says, "Now put all the ones that are nice in this box." The child responds and the therapist returns the items to the display. "Now all the ones that are the biggest."

   The therapist's initial requests attempt to use some aspect of the fantasies the child hinted were operating while manipulating the material. Then the therapist invites the child to designate an attribute. "What shall we take out next, Harry? You decide on something." Harry responds, "All the dirty ones." The therapist says, "OK take out the dirty ones. Which ones are those?" By repeating this procedure, the therapist begins to gain entry into aspects of the child's fantasies, which at this point are not fully revealed and which serve to defend against the treatment relationship. The therapist continues connecting with the child through field articulation tasks until an adequate alliance is established and the child is more receptive to interacting with the therapist. Then the therapist shifts to Step 6 and becomes more active, directing fantasized situations within which field articulation tasks become elaborated.

Specific Instructions

Step 1. The goal is to engage the child with tasks requiring the field articulation process and which become increasingly complex in a stepwise fashion. Wooden, plastic, or cardboard geometric cutouts are used initially as material because they are neutral stimuli and readily permit tasks to be graded in complexity. Tasks are made more complex by following the guidelines of Parts A, B, and C characterized in the introduction. With each task place a display of cutouts on the table and ask the child to remove particular ones and place them in the answer box. Later in treatment another response is added—the child is asked to place specific cutouts in particular locations within the array.

If a child is severely dysfunctional in field articulation, the guidelines of Part A (complexity of the field surveyed) are varied in the sequence noted in Table 7.1 while the guidelines of Parts B (complexity of dimensions defining relevant information) and C (delay) are held constant. The number of cutouts presented is systematically increased, and then the number of colors is increased as well. Next the distance between cutouts is increased within the number of cutouts and colors achieved in the previous trials; then the number of shapes and the number of sizes are increased in turn; then the arrays are constructed to contain patterns; then the arrays shift from an ordered arrangement of rows and columns to a more random arrangement; and last the arrays shift from containing single cutouts to stacks of cutouts.

The following example illustrates how these attributes are manipulated accumulatively. The therapist presents an array of: six cutouts (a relatively small number); of two colors (e.g., white and red); located close together (e.g., two inches separate each cutout); of one shape (e.g., all cutouts are squares); of one size (all cutouts are medium); the array does not form a pattern; the array is ordered in two rows and three columns, and the array consists of single cutouts. The child is asked to remove all the white cutouts and locate them in the answer box. If the child is successful with three trials of this level of complexity, the therapist increases the complexity by presenting a display of 12 cutouts (the number is greater). All other variables remain the same although the two colors and the sizes used would vary from display to display. Then the number of cutouts is increased to 20, for example, then 30, with all other variables remaining constant. When the child handles the display of 30 cutouts successfully, the therapist next increases the number of colors to three. First a display of 20 cutouts of three colors is presented, then a display of 30 cutouts of three colors. When the child is successful with this level, the number of colors is increased, for example, to five. First a display of 20 cutouts of five colors is presented, then a display of 30 cutouts of five colors. Throughout these trials, as color is manipulated along with the number of cutouts, the other attributes are held constant (e.g., close together, one shape, one size, etc.).

Notice that the number of cutouts is reduced to 20 (from the maximum number, 30, the child handled previously) each time the number of colors is increased. And then the number of cutouts is gradually increased again. This illustrates a technique that should be underscored at this point. Each time the complexity of the task is increased along some variable, the number of cutouts is *decreased* below the maximum achieved in previous trials and then increased again in a stepwise fashion. In this way the child is introduced to a new combination of variables, and therefore to a higher level of complexity, with a field of information that is initially less expansive than those of previous trials. When competence is achieved with the new variable, the field of information becomes more expansive.

Returning to our illustration, after the child successfully handles a display of 30 cutouts of five colors, removing all the items of a particular color as requested, the therapist introduces the variable of the proximity of cutouts. First a display of 20 cutouts of five colors is presented with the cutouts now 6 inches apart (versus 2 inches in the previous series). In the display to follow the cutouts are located 12 inches apart, and then 18 inches. With each task the child removes all the cutouts of a color designated by the therapist. Note if a large display is required with cutouts located very far apart, the display is located on the floor.

This sequence is repeated when the number of types of shapes is increased. The child has been working with displays consisting of squares. Triangles are added, for example, first in displays of 20 and then 30 cutouts of five colors, located initially near and then far apart. A third shape (circles) and then a fourth shape (diamonds) are added in the same way. When the child handles displays of 30 cutouts of five colors and four shapes, located near together and far apart, the therapist next introduces the dimension of size, adding a second size (e.g., small) and then a third (e.g., large), following the same procedure.

At this point, the child shows competence in field articulation functioning with displays of 30 cutouts of several colors, shapes, sizes, located close together and far apart. Now the task complexity can be increased further by constructing patterns of irrelevant information within the display. With one technique, colors and sizes that are *not* "answers" are arranged in some pattern that dominates the field to be surveyed. Examples: construct a frame of large, red shapes around the border of the display; locate a diagonal of yellow cutouts from one corner of the display to the opposite corner; locate two parallel columns of blue cutouts, extending from the top to the bottom of the display; locate four large, green cutouts in each corner of the display or cluster them in the center. The red frame, the yellow diagonal, the blue columns, for example, become dominant "figures" with the remaining cutouts the "ground." Accordingly more vigorous field articulation is required to subordinate these patterns while directing attention selectively at the information designated as relevant.

After presenting tasks that include patterns which modify the figure-ground relationships of the field of information, the therapist integrates the variable that concerns whether the display is ordered or random. Now instead of forming orderly rows and columns, the cutouts are arranged in increasingly random displays. For example, at first, three of the five columns in an array remain intact and the cutouts of the other two columns are spread out so that they cannot form rows and columns. Then all the cutouts are spread about in a random array.

The last technique used to introduce complexity into the field of information surveyed involves constructing displays of stacks of two or more cutouts instead of single cutouts. For example, instead of locating 15 single cutouts of several colors, sizes, and shapes in three rows and five columns, the therapist locates 15 stacks, each consisting of two cutouts, a large one at the bottom and a small or medium one at the top. To handle the task of removing yellow squares from the top of each stack, for example, more vigorous field articulation functioning is required. The child must repeatedly subordinate the bottom cutout and articulate the top cutout as relevant. A more complex variation of the same technique involves stacks of three cutouts (a large one at the bottom, a medium one in the center, and a small one on top.) The stacking technique is used with more complex tasks, discussed below, with which the child removes answer cutouts from either the bottom, the middle, or the top of stacks, or locates cutouts within particular stacks.

As noted earlier, with the severely impaired child, while the complexity of the arrays presented are increased, dimensions which define information as relevant remain constant (guideline, Part B). Accordingly with each task, the child has been removing information which has been defined as relevant in terms of one dimension, (e.g., all the red cutouts; all the squares; all the medium cutouts). When the child has achieved some competence with each of the variables listed in Part A, the therapist follows Part B and systematically increases from one to two the number of attributes which define relevant information (e.g., find all the green triangles), then to three (e.g., find all the small, yellow circles), then to more complex combinations (e.g., find the large, blue diamonds that are next to green circles; find red circles that are on top of red diamonds and under white squares).

With the last set of guidelines cognitive delay is introduced. While dealing with tasks which follow the guidelines of Parts A and B, the child has been allowed to remove the answer cutouts immediately after they were designated. Now the therapist requires the child to delay for increasingly longer periods of time before removing the cutouts (e.g., 15, 30, 60, 120 seconds). To introduce this guideline, say, "Mary, with the next game I'm going to ask you to wait before you find the answer shapes. After I tell you what shapes to find, wait until I say OK." After several trials with delay, invite the child to keep a notebook in which are recorded the duration of the delay, the level of complexity of the task, and whether or not the child made errors. Maintaining a notebook is one effective way of giving the child feedback on whether delaying influences the field articulation process.

With older children, the duration of a delay period can be an entire session. At the start of the session, an array is presented, and the answer cutouts designated. Then, the child goes on with other tasks. At the end of the session, the child returns to the array and completes the task, without the instructions being repeated. This technique relates to the second guideline for delay, which involves introducing interpolated experiences.

After the child has developed the capacity to delay two or more minutes, correctly removing the answer shapes, the child is asked to engage in some activity during the delay period. The interpolated activity could gradually relate to the child's problems in school and home and therefore form a bridge to later steps, which involve field articulation functioning while emotions are aroused. To illustrate, a progression of interpolated tasks could include playing tic-tac-toe, solving subtraction problems, drawing a picture of a person, reading a short paragraph about a plane crash.

When conducting Step 1 with children who are less impaired, or who are appreciably impaired but older, Parts A, B, and C can be orchestrated simultaneously. For example, from one task, or a series of tasks, to the next, the number of cutouts can be increased along with the number of colors, shapes, and sizes; the array can be patterned and then eventually contain stacks. And, with each more complex display, the number of dimensions defining the cutouts to be retrieved can be increased as well as the delay imposed before the cutouts are removed. When guidelines are combined, therapists frequently make the error of moving too quickly, presenting the child with a series of tasks that become too complex too fast. Therefore the child is cheated of the opportunity to repeat the field articulation process, over and over again, and to assimilate small degrees of increasing complexity with each repetition. To avoid this error, the therapist is encouraged to use the "rule" that the child should handle three tasks correctly in succession at one level of complexity, before being presented with tasks slightly more complex. In addition the therapist should be on the alert for signs of resistance, which suggest that the difference in complexity between one task and the next is too great.

Throughout this step whenever appropriate the therapist begins to draw the child's attention to noteworthy behaviors and expressions of tension and emotions that relate to efficiency and disruption in field articular functioning.

Step 2. Follow the same procedures, now making use of displays of more ambiguous information than is represented by geometric cutouts. The materials we have used most often, and which are readily located or constructed, include: buttons of various diameters, shapes, colors, sizes, and thicknesses; paper clips of various shapes and sizes; various shapes cut from construction cardboard in addition to circles, squares, triangles, and diamonds (e.g., hexagons, octagons, elipses); shapes with only linear or curvilinear perimeters, and with both linear and curvilinear perimeters; and various shapes in the center of which shapes are cut out.

These materials are used separately or in combination to form arrays and tasks following the guidelines of Step 1. A display of buttons and paper clips of many sizes, shapes, and colors arrayed as single items, or stacked, result in fields of information that are much more complex and ambiguous than those used previously. In addition to presenting more ambiguous fields of information, the therapist emphasizes task requirements that give the child experience articulating fields of information in terms of the relationships among the attributes located in the field. The following are examples of typical tasks: find small, round paper clips that are on large, round buttons and next to small, black buttons; find cutouts with six sides that are above a cutout with a square hole in it and to the right of cutouts with three wavy sides and one straight side.

Step 3. This step emphasizes experiencing field articulation while shifting points of view and anticipating information. This is accomplished by asking the child to retrieve a series of items, each member in the series defined by different attributes and, accordingly, belonging to a different category. When retrieving the first item named in the series, then the next, then the next, the child experiences using one point of view, anticipating and shifting to another point of view and so on. The arrays constructed contain materials used in Steps 1 and 2 in varying combinations that fit the child's cognitive status and therapeutic needs.

To introduce this step, say, "Now we are going to play *Find the Shapes* in a different way. I'm going to ask you to find three (or four or five) particular things. Put each one in the answer box as I name it. Find a small, green diamond (child responds); now a large, red circle (child responds); now a medium, blue triangle."

By combining the materials from Steps 1 and 2, tasks can be constructed that require shifting among points of view that increase in complexity. For example, ''Find a brown button that is on top a green square; (child responds); now a round paper clip that is on a yellow square; (child responds); now a paper cutout with only wavy sides that is on a blue diamond.'' Following the guidelines of Step 1 the first arrays would contain multiple colored cutouts, but of only one shape and size, on which buttons and paper clips are located; then gradually the number of shapes and sizes of the cutouts would be increased. As the items are located in a more random array, the dimensions of proximity can be included as a point of view, (e.g., find a paper clip on a green square that is near a blue circle; (child responds); now find a paper clip on a red diamond that is far from a yellow square). And, when stacks are used, the point of view of location can be included (e.g., find a small green square on the top of a stack with no button on it; now find a blue diamond in the middle of a stack that has a red button on the top of the tower).

Step 4. The child experiences field articulation functioning while fantasies and emotions are aroused and balanced, setting the stage for cultivating efficient field articulation functioning within the process of symbolizing. To accomplish this, various fantasy-arousing material is introduced while the child deals with tasks involving geometric cutouts as outlined in Step 1.

With one technique various pictures are located around the array the child is asked to manage. With a related technique, small pictures are taped on the top of selected cutouts. The content of the pictures is determined by the child's age, unique emotional make-up and difficulties (e.g., pictures of animals, persons, and mythical figures such as monsters and outer-space characters; pictures that portray nurturance, aggression, breaking rules, affiliation among peers). With another technique, as the child deals with a series of tasks, cassette recordings, which bear some relation to the child's unique personality issues, are played (e.g., recordings of racing cars, weapons firing, jet planes roaring, train engines, children crying or laughing, an adult shouting). With each task, after the child completes the requirements, the child is helped to share what the pictures or sound recordings brought to mind and what the child fantasized and felt.

When introducing this step, say, for example, ''Now when we find shapes, there are pictures around them (or on them). These pictures will make you think of things, and feel things, or remind you of things you have seen or done before. Your job is to find the shapes I name. So while you are findings the shapes you have to try not to let what you are thinking and feeling about the pictures get in the way of finding the shapes. After you put all the shapes in the answer box, you can tell me what the pictures made you think of and feel.''

Administer a series of tasks following the guidelines of Step 1 and systematically introduce various pictures or sounds. Select emotionally arousing stimuli carefully, and deal with the child's reactions therapeutically. Stimuli that are too disruptive run the risk of rupturing the therapeutic alliance. Initially use stimuli the child finds pleasurable and to which the child experiences no particular stress. Then gradually introduce stimuli that arouse a low level and then higher levels of stress and which increasingly provoke fantasies and emotions in the child. To determine which stimuli to introduce, the therapist relies upon his/her understanding of the child's emotional life and difficulties and observations made in therapy to this point. In addition, engage the child initially in examining a series of pictures and listening to sound recordings. Notice the child's spontaneous conversation and emotional expressions and conduct an inquiry (e.g., "Which one of these pictures is the most scary?") This preliminary exploration of the child's fantasies sets the stage for work in the next steps which make more use of directed fantasy.

Last during this step, begin to record the time a child takes to retrieve answer shapes and engage the child in comparing the times observed with different tasks and their respective "emotional distractions." If the task complexity remains the same, and the child takes twice as long to retrieve cutouts from a display surrounded by pictures depicting nurturance than from a display surrounded by pictures depicting power, there is an opportunity to begin pointing out to the child how particular fantasies interfere with his "concentrating."

Step 5. This step presents fields of information to be articulated, but the information is now construed as something other than it is. Using the same geometric cutouts, paper clips, buttons, and so on construct arrays, following the guidelines of Step 1, and introduce a symbol or image in terms of which the child construes the material. For example, present an array of 20 cutouts (three sizes, four colors and shapes, in an ordered array of rows and columns) and say, "With this game we are going to play *Find the Shapes* in a different way. Instead of asking you to find small squares, or yellow circles, I want you to pretend the cutouts are something else, and then I'll ask you to find all the things of a certain kind from the things you pretend. Let me show you. Pretend all of these cutouts are people. Put all the cutouts that are babies in this box." After the child retrieves several cutouts, the therapist engages the child in articulating the attributes the child used to fit the symbol of baby to the cutouts. For example, one child might retrieve all the small cutouts as babies and note that "the smallest ones are babies," another might retrieve all the red cutouts and note "they're babies because they always cry and get red." The therapist then asks the child, for example, to remove the "mother" cutouts, which are also examined in terms of the attributes the child uses.

As this work continues the therapist introduces various symbols from ones that are concrete (baby, father, mother) to ones that are more abstract (strong, weak). The therapist also varies the distance between the symbol used and its referent (e.g., brown buttons as farmers, blue buttons as policemen, and white buttons as nurses represent a close connection between the symbol and referent; while brown buttons as bad, blue buttons as happy, and white buttons as empty represent a more distant connection).

As the child becomes involved in this process of symbolizing the materials, tasks are presented within which the child designates the symbols to be used. For example, present an array of geometric cutouts and ask the child to pretend each type of cutout is something. In response the child calls the red diamonds, "fierce animals," the black squares, "fat elephants," and the white circles, "whales," and so on. The therapist uses these symbols in the task requirement (e.g., "Find a small elephant next to a medium whale."). When buttons, paper clips, and other more ambiguous material is used, the child is encouraged to construct conventional symbols (e.g., an oblong paper clip is construed as a rocket ship) but also less conventional ones (e.g., a round button is construed as Darth Vader).

Throughout this step the therapist trains and directs the child in evaluating the symbols used in terms of whether they are more conventional or personal and the degree to which the attributes of the material fit the symbol. To facilitate this evaluation and to teach the child whether and how symbols communicate, the child is invited to ask the therapist to remove particular items in terms of a symbol offered by the child. For example, the child says, "Find all the racing cars, find all the grandfathers." The therapist searches for items that could belong to these symbols, asks the child to evaluate the items collected, and discusses with the child the degree to which his/her referents for the symbol communicated. The child may declare, for example, that the grandfathers were all "cutouts with corners," a referent the child learns has little chance of communicating to others.

Step 6. The child is guided and directed in imagining a situation and event within which the child engages field articulation tasks. The initial fantasy directed by the therapist relies upon the types of fantasies the child revealed in the previous two steps, as well as on the therapist's understanding of the child's unique personality functioning and learning difficulties.

To illustrate, in earlier work a child frequently imaged cutouts as weapons and "bombs exploding." When this step in the program was reached, the therapist asked the child to imagine that he is an expert on a SWAT team that has been called to a school because of a bomb threat. Different parts of the playroom are designated different parts of the school (e.g., cafeteria, principal's office, science room). The therapist arrays a matrix of stacked cutouts in each of these places in the school and asks the child to pretend that only certain stacks are real bombs set to go off and others are "fake" bombs placed there to confuse the SWAT team. Only the stacks with a large, blue square at the bottom, a medium, yellow circle in the middle, and a red diamond on top are real bombs. The child is asked to search each part of the school as quickly as possible. Each time he finds a real bomb, he is to rush it to the "defusing box" (a large cardboard box located "outside the school") where the child dismantles the bombs. With repeated administrations of this directed fantasy, the stacks are made increasingly more complex as are the definitions of "bombs," and the time the child takes to find the bombs is noted as well as the numbers of errors made.

Step 7. After a child engages in a series of directed fantasies within which the child handles field articulation tasks, the treatment process takes on the form of nondirected verbal/play therapy as discussed in Chapter 10. The goal of this step is to focus the child on actively organizing, articulating, and reforming key pathological metaphors with the benefit of efficient cognitive controls and cognitive affective balancing.

Concluding Remarks and a Note About Resistance

With the capacity to articulate flexibly fields of information perceived as they are and construed in terms of symbols and fantasies, the child has available a cognitive tool that should improve the efficiency of learning and adapting and that should serve the nondirected process of verbal/play therapy if the latter is indicated.

As with other programs, the therapist initially trains the child, while engaging the task, to observe behaviors and emotions that compromise the efficiency of field articulation. The behaviors that occur in this program may be more subtle than those observed in previous programs. For example, having been asked to remove small, green triangles, the child may reach for, and remove, a small, green diamond or a medium, green triangle and not recognize the error until it is pointed out by the therapist. Or the child may reach out and touch a small, green diamond, then pick up and correctly remove the designated cutout. These behaviors are brought to the child's attention, bit by bit, until the child shows the ability to recognize spontaneously when field articulation functioning becomes derailed.

Subtle behaviors that signal resistance are also frequently observed when the task complexity increases, for example, from 10 to 20 cutouts or from two sizes to three. At these times, the child may become tense (biting his fingernails) or begin to yawn frequently, or rest his head on his arms, without being aware of the change in affect. Again the child is asked to notice these responses.

As the child develops the capacity to observe and be aware of such behaviors, the therapist suggests connections between these behaviors and the particular ingredient that increased the complexity of the task. And, still later, the therapist encourages the child to relate the current task and behaviors to similar situations and behaviors that occur in school and home. Usually as children learn to generalize from the contemporary experience with a given array to the classroom, they begin spontaneously, to elaborate recent, relevant experiences. For example one child recalled that while trying to read at his seat, his attention shifted and became preoccupied with a messenger who had entered the classroom, and then shifted to a classmate who sneezed several times. As these experiences are detailed, the therapist helps the child see the analogy between actively withholding attention from irrelevant information in the array and task and actively withholding attention from the messenger and classmate.

Also, as children work with those steps which prescribe imaging and fantasies, some, especially adolescents, develop the ability to recognize that particular private thoughts and fantasies that occur in the classroom are irrelevant to the task at hand while others are relevant. For example, one seventh grader, while working on an essay about the French and Indian War became aware that fantasies about Star War movies, which frequently occurred, were not as relevant as recollections and fantasies about conflicts between early colonial settlers and Indians.

Chapter 8
Therapy with the Leveling-Sharpening Cognitive Control

The leveling-sharpening cognitive control concerns the manner in which an individual constructs images of information, holds them over time, and relates them to perceptions of current information. The program described in this chapter is designed to restructure and rehabilitate this cognitive mechanism so that it functions efficiently when external information is handled as it is, as well as when it is transformed with symbols and fantasies within the process of symbolic functioning.

The broad technique of this program calls for the therapist to present the child with a field of information, which the child examines. The information is then screened from the child's view. The therapist introduces a change in the information and removes the screen. The child surveys the information again and, on the basis of the image formed previously, determines whether and how the information changed. If the information changed, the child restores it to its original state.

To benefit from this program, a child should have achieved, in the course of development or with the assistance of programs described previously, stage appropriate efficiency in constructing body schema, regulating body tempos, scanning actively and systematically, and articulating fields of information in terms of relevance.

When compared with the previous program, the therapeutic experiences provided here represent another shift along the developmental hierarchy of cognitive control functioning (see Chapter 2). With therapy in field articulation, the information managed is contained in an existing field, parts of which are defined in terms of relevance for the task at hand. With therapy in leveling-sharpening, there are two fields of information, so to speak, the image of the first display and perceptions of the present display, each one defined in terms of relevance and each connected to the other. The image of the past bears on perceptions of the present, and the present perceptions are related to the image of the past.

The process of leveling-sharpening consists of three part-processes. One concerns whether the organization of the image constructed is global or differentiated; another concerns whether the image is stable or modified and embellished by the requirements of fantasies, and another concerns the efficiency with which the image is fitted with and related to present perceptions. The techniques employed in leveling-sharpening therapy are intended to foster growth and/or to rehabilitate each of these component functions.

PROGRAM 4: *REMEMBER ME*

Purpose and Goal: To develop the capacity to construct increasingly elaborate images of information, to maintain stable images over time, and to relate images with present perceptions; to promote efficient leveling-sharpening functioning when external information is managed as it is and when it is transformed with symbols in the process of symbolic functioning.

Materials: Materials include (a) the same plywood, plastic, or cardboard cutouts, buttons and paper clips used in the program *Find the Shapes*; (b) a gray cardboard screen 2×3 feet, mounted on a stand; (c) a cloth 2×3 feet; (d) 2×3 inch cards on which are drawn silhouettes of persons, animals, and ambiguous designs; (e) keys of various shapes, squares of sandpaper of various grains, squares of cloth of various textures and colors, buttons of various sizes and colors.

Introduction and General Procedure

As noted above, the therapist locates a pattern of information on the table. The child examines the array with the intention of remembering it. The therapist places a screen between the child and the display, or covers the display with a cloth, and changes the display. The screen is removed, the child examines the display again, points out any changes, and restores the display to its original form.

If the child is unable to detect the change, or responds with uncertainty, the therapist points out the change and restores the display to its original configuration. Then the child is presented the same display or another display at the *same level of complexity*. If the child responds correctly, restoring the display to its original form, additional trials are administered, also at the same level of complexity. When the child is able to remember and correctly restore three displays at the same level of complexity, a slightly more complex display is presented, following guidelines discussed below. While the basic method involves introducing changes in information, at appropriate times the therapist could choose to administer a trial in which no change is introduced.

The therapist should not become too concerned if a child requires 10 or 15 trials at one level of complexity before the child can remember the display. In requiring a child repeatedly to construct images of information at one level of complexity, the goal is to foster growth through assimilation of stimuli until the leveling-sharpening mechanism differentiates and accomodates to the complexity of information contained in the display. When a match is achieved between leveling-sharpening and, say, eight pieces of information, the child can move on to remembering 10 or 12 pieces of information.

If this program is followed with a child who has not received therapy in field articulation, it is frequently useful to provide the child with a preliminary phase using a modification of a technique from the program *Find the Shapes* in which the therapist asks for a series of cutouts from a display of cutouts. The therapist displays 30 or 40 cutouts arrayed in rows and columns. The child is asked to remove a series of cutouts in the order named by the therapist (e.g., a large yellow square, two small blue circles, one small red diamond). This task is a bridge to leveling-sharpening therapy since the child must remember the sequence of shapes requested as she surveys the display.

The program consists of seven steps as outlined in Table 8.1. With the first two, the child constructs images of patterns of geometric cutouts, and then of more ambiguous items, which gradually become more complex. To help the child construct stable images of these patterns, the information to be remembered is examined in several ways as indicated (e.g., physically reconstructing the display with another set of cutouts, touching the cutouts). Step 3 requires the child to consider the display from different points of view, each of which organizes the information in different ways. Step 4 provides experiences constructing images and relating them to present perceptions while emotions and fantasies are aroused. With the capacity to use points of view to organize information to be remembered, and to balance emotions and fantasies, the child is ready for Step 5, which requires that the information held in memory be construed as something other than what it is, embedding leveling-sharpening within the process of symbolic functioning. With Step 6, the child integrates gains made by engaging the leveling-sharpening process within elaborate, directed fantasies. At this point, the leveling-sharpening mechanism is available as a tool to serve learning and adapting, and, when indicated, the process of nondirected verbal/play therapy during which

Table 8.1. Steps in Therapy with Leveling-Sharpening: *Remember Me*

Step 1. Child remembers displays of geometric cutouts and compares images with perceptions of current displays
  Part A Therapist increases complexity of displays presented to child
      1. From few cutouts to many cutouts
      2. From one color to many colors
      3. From one shape to four shapes
      4. From one size to three sizes
  Part B Therapist varies mode child uses to examine displays to be remembered
      1. Display reconstructed with another set of cutouts, examined by touch, copied on a sheet of paper, and labeled verbally
      2. Display examined only visually
  Part C Therapist varies changes introduced into displays
      1. From introducing replacements to exchanges
      2. From introducing one change to several
      3. From introducing changes close together to far apart
  Part D Therapist increases delay between first and second displays
      1. From little to more delay
      2. From few to many interpolated tasks during delay
  Part E Child and therapist evaluate leveling-sharpening behavior

Step 2. Child remembers displays of ambiguous objects and compares images with perceptions of current display
  Parts A–E Same as Step 1

Step 3. Child remembers disordered arrays of geometric cutouts and ambiguous objects, imposing organization on the field by assuming multiple points of view
  Part A Therapist locates objects to form random field
  Part B Therapist locates objects to facilitate their organization in terms of points of view
  Part C Therapist trains child to assume points of view, if indicated

Step 4. Child anticipates the pattern cutouts will form
  Parts A, D, and E Same as Step 1

Step 5. Child remembers displays of cutouts surrounded by stimuli that arouse fantasies/emotions
  Parts A–D Same as Step 1

Step 6. Child remembers displays of material construed as something other than what it is
  Child construes and presents material; Therapist remembers it and guesses what the pattern conveys
  Parts A–D Same as Step 1
  Part E Child and therapist evaluate whether symbols constructed are conventional or personal and fit the attributes of the stimuli

Step 7. Child remembers fields of information while enacting a fantasy directed by therapist; then child directs fantasy
  Parts A–E Same as Step 6

Step 8. Child remembers fields of information within nondirected/free play therapy; No restrictions placed on complexity of information or delay

---

the child organizes and resolves key pathological metaphors. The outer-oriented child is administered the seven steps as outlined. The inner-oriented child begins with Step 7 with appropriate modifications and moves toward Step 1.

Introducing the Program to the Child

The Outer-Oriented Child. Present a pattern of cutouts representing a level of complexity which the child should handle easily. Using an analogy of a camera taking pictures is a good way to introduce the task and its purpose. For example, say, "John, we're going to play a game called *Remember Me*. Look at these cutouts. Try to take a picture in your mind of how they are set up so you can remember exactly where each piece belongs." Allow the child to examine the display for about 30 seconds (more if necessary). If the child spontaneously touches or manipulates the objects, permit this without comment.

Then say, "Ready?" Now I'll set up the screen so you can't see the design. I'm going to change it in some way." The therapist sets up the screen, introduces a change, and lowers the screen. "Now look the design over again. Do you notice any change?"

If the child responds correctly (e.g., "This red square was a blue square"), hand the child a blue square and ask the child to restore it to the original display. At this point make a few comments that provide some structure for the therapy process the child will engage (e.g., "You're right. Your mind took a clear picture of the design so when you looked at it again, and checked out the design with the picture in your mind, you noticed the blue square changed. The games we are going to play will help your mind take clearer and clearer pictures, and bigger and bigger pictures, so you can remember more and more"). The therapist could also structure treatment by using an observation from the diagnostic evaluation, or an observation the child shared from school. For example, "Remember when you read the paragraph for me last week you couldn't remember what the paragraph said and you had to keep looking back to answer the questions? With this game your mind will get better and better at remembering things and better and better at using what you remember to figure out what you are looking at."

If the child does not respond correctly to the first display the therapist says, "Your mind took a fuzzy picture of the design so you thought the yellow square changed, but the change happened here. This red square should be a blue one." The therapist restores the blue square to the display and makes comments similar to those noted above, pointing out that the games will help the child to take clearer pictures of things, remember them better, and notice if they change or stay the same. With the next trial, the complexity of the display is reduced.

The Inner-Oriented Child. During the first session or two, observe the child's spontaneous activity. As soon as possible take ingredients from the activity that lend themselves to a leveling-sharpening task. For example, the child moves about the room in a dreamy way, occasionally relating to the therapist, but primarily touching or picking up items and sometimes engaging them in some private play fantasy. The therapist takes four (or six) of these items, places them in a matrix, and says "John, look at these toys you used. Try to remember exactly where they are. I'm going to cover them and change one of them. You try to figure out what changed—the game is called *Remember Me.*" The therapist follows the basic approach, setting up a screen, replacing one of the toys with another, removing the screen and asking the child what has changed.

Another example illustrates behaviors by the child which lend themselves more easily to a leveling-sharpening task. Ignoring the therapist almost completely, one child seemed to be looking for something during the first session, looking underneath form board games, pushing toys to one side as if searching for one particular item. When asked what she was looking for and if there was something the therapist could get for her, she said nothing. The therapist said, "Let's play a *look for* game. Look at these (the therapist arrayed pieces from the form board game) and try to remember where they belong. Now I'll cover them up and take one of them away (the therapist removes an item and then removes the screen). Which one is gone?"

This method is repeated whenever clinical judgment indicates, slowly joining the child in various tasks which involve remembering information and comparing the image with present perceptions. As the alliance builds, and the child interacts more, move to Step 6 and direct a relatively elaborate fantasy which contains leveling-sharpening tasks.

Specific Instructions

Step 1. Four broad guidelines are followed in conducting this step. Part A concerns the complexity of the field to be remembered, Part B the modes the child uses to facilitate constructing an image of the display, Part C the types of changes introduced by the therapist in the display, and Part D the delay imposed on the response which emphasizes holding the image stable over time. Although these guidelines can be followed in combination, they are discussed separately for the sake of clarity.

Increasing the Complexity of the Information to Be Remembered (Part A). With the child severely impaired in leveling-sharpening functioning, the complexity of the displays to be remembered is increased in a stepwise fashion following a particular sequence: (a) patterns of colors are remembered, with shape and size held constant, (b) patterns of shapes are remembered with color and size all constant, (c) patterns of sizes are remembered with color and shape all constant, (d) patterns of color and shapes are remembered with size held constant, (e) patterns of colors and sizes are remembered with shape held constant, (f) patterns of shapes and sizes are remembered with colors held constant, and (g) patterns of colors, shapes, and sizes are remembered.

With each series of trials, the number of cutouts is increased gradually from a few to a larger number appropriate for the child's developmental stage. It may be necessary to begin with only two cutouts and in some cases with a single cutout. When fewer than four cutouts are used, arrange them in a row. When four or more are used, display them in matrices of rows and columns.

Examples of the first guideline, increasing patterns of colors with shape and size held constant, are presented in Figure 8.1, which shows displays of four and nine cutouts of two colors and in Figure 8.2, which shows displays of three colors. A child may require 10 or 15 trials with a display of four cutouts, for example, before performing successfully and therefore ready to proceed to a display of six cutouts and then nine.

After handling eight or nine cutouts with color varied and size and shape held constant, the child moves on to a series of trials with shapes varied and color and size held constant and with the number of cutouts again gradually increased. Figures 8.3 and 8.4 provide examples of displays of four and then nine cutouts, first of two shapes and then of three shapes. When the child is successful, remembering patterns of eight or nine cutouts with shape varied, a series of trials is administered with size varied as illustrated in Figures 8.5 and 8.6, then a series of trials with colors and shape varied and size held constant (see Figures 8.7 and 8.8), then a series with size and color varied and shape held constant (see Figure 8.9), then a series with shape and size varied and color held constant (see Figure 8.10), and finally a series with all three dimensions varied (see Figure 8.11).

By presenting displays repeatedly, which gradually and systematically vary and combine each of the attributes of color, shape, and size, the leveling-sharpening function gradually differentiates, accommodating to and developing the capacity to construct increasingly more complex images of neutral information. The greater the number of cutouts displayed with a particular attribute varied, the more elaborate and differentiated the image the child constructs. When the therapist patiently moves through a carefully planned sequence of displays, children who originally could not remember the pattern of 2 cutouts eventually remember a pattern of 10, with all three attributes varied.

Last, with children who are severely disturbed and limited in leveling-sharpening functioning, it is usually best to begin with displays of black

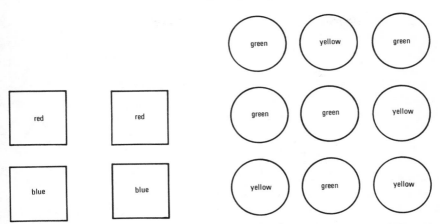

FIGURE 8.1. Colors Varied, Shape and Size Held Constant—Two Colors.
Note: Figures 8.1 through 8.12 are from *A Biodevelopmental Approach to Clinical Child Psychology* by Sebastiano Santostefano, New York: Wiley Publishing Co. Copyright © 1978 by Wiley Publishing Co. Reprinted by permission.

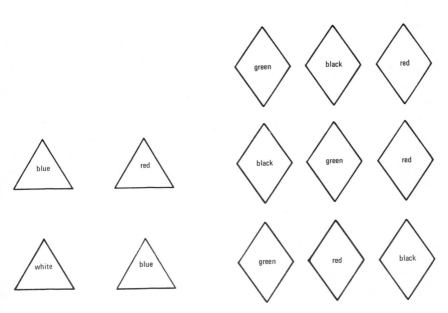

FIGURE 8.2. Colors Varied, Shape and Size Held Constant—Three Colors

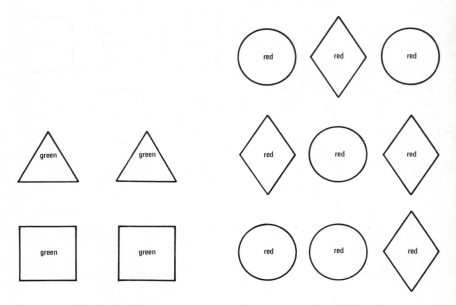

FIGURE 8.3. Shapes Varied, Color and Size Held Constant—A

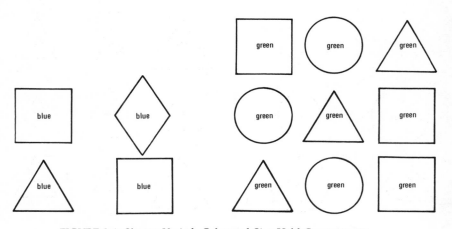

FIGURE 8.4. Shapes Varied, Color and Size Held Constant—B

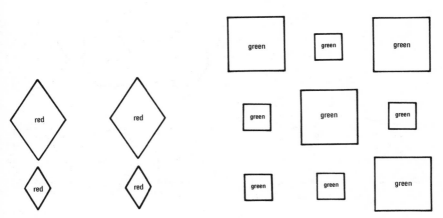

FIGURE 8.5. Size Varied, Shape and Color Held Constant—A

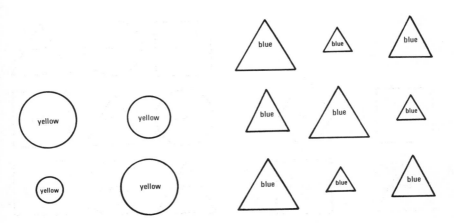

FIGURE 8.6. Size Varied, Shape and Color Held Constant—B

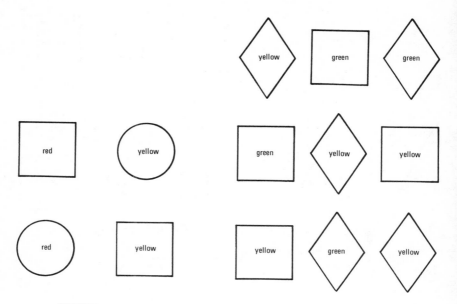

FIGURE 8.7. Colors and Shapes Varied, Size Held Constant—A

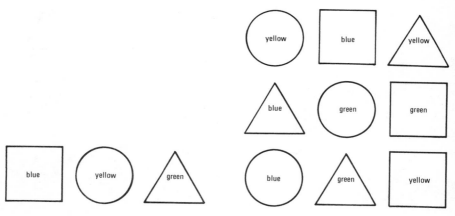

FIGURE 8.8. Colors and Shapes Varied, Size Held Constant—B

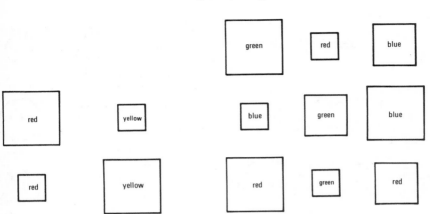

FIGURE 8.9. Size and Color Varied, Shape Held Constant

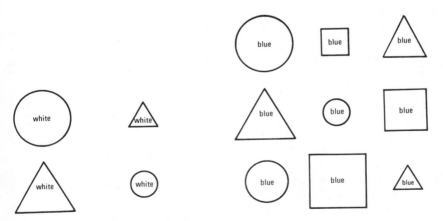

FIGURE 8.10. Shape and Size Varied, Color Held Constant

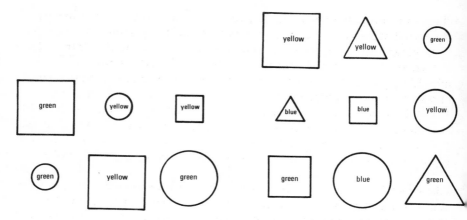

FIGURE 8.11. Shape, Size and Color Varied

and white cutouts and later add chromatic colors, since colors frequently create stress.

Techniques to Aid the Child in Constructing Articulate Images (Part B). When a child has extreme difficulty remembering a display if it is examined only visually, several techniques are used, in the sequence noted or in combination, to help the child construct articulate images: (a) give the child another set of cutouts and ask the child to construct the display systematically from left to right and from top to bottom, (b) ask the child to pass her fingers around the perimeter of each cutout, again in a systematic sequence, while examining the display visually, (c) ask the child to copy the display on a sheet of paper; if colors are being used, the geometric shapes should be colored in with crayon, (d) ask the child to describe and label each of the cutouts in the display systematically (e.g., "a red square at the top corner, then a yellow circle," etc.). Initially the child describes the display aloud, and then covertly.

Once the child is competent constructing a stable, differentiated image by visually scanning the display, and without the need for sensorimotor and verbal rehearsals described above, another technique is used to foster the construction of differentiated images. Administer a series of tasks, at some appropriate level of complexity, and systematically decrease the amount of time the child scans the display before the screen is set up. The therapist points out the purpose of the technique to the child (e.g., "It will help you learn how to take quick pictures with your mind that are clear and don't change"). Usually the time allowed to scan a display is decreased in 5-second increments from 60 seconds to as little as 5 seconds.

Varying the amount of time the child scans an array could be introduced at each level of therapy. For example, after the child develops competence in holding patterns of colors in memory, the therapist administers a series of trials decreasing the amount of time allowed to examine each display. Then, following a series of tasks with varied patterns of shapes to be held in memory, a series of trials is introduced during which the time allowed to examine display is gradually decreased. The same procedure would be followed at the close of each series of tasks as described in Part A.

Guidelines for Introducing Changes in Information Displayed (Part C). Two types of changes are introduced into the display. One, referred to as *replacements*, involves substituting a cutout in the display with another cutout not used in the display. Referring to Figure 8.12, an example would be replacing the red square in the upper-left-hand corner with a red diamond. The other, referred to as *exchanges*, involves taking two or more cutouts within the display and switching their locations. Referring to Figure 8.12, an example would be exchanging the location of the green

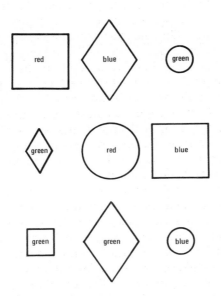

FIGURE 8.12. Display Containing Complex Pattern

circle in the upper righthand corner with the blue circle in the lower righthand corner.

Most children experience replacements as less difficult than exchanges. With the former, only one section of the field to be remembered has been altered with a stimulus that was not a part of the original field. With the latter, two or more sections of the field are altered with information that was part of the original field. Since detecting a new element in a field is usually easier than detecting the rearrangement of existing elements, replacements are introduced in the first phase of treatment. Gradually, as the child demonstrates the ability to construct stable images of the displays presented, exchanges are introduced.

Replacements and exchanges can be simple and more complex, and a simple change can be detected if a global image has been constructed, while a differentiated image is necessary to detect a complex change. By skillfully increasing the complexity of the changes introduced, the therapist fosters the capacity to construct memory images of information that are increasingly more differentiated and stable.

The complexity of changes can be varied systematically by increasing the number of changes introduced and also by introducing changes first in color, then shape, and then size. A change in location of a color is usually easiest to detect, requiring a relatively global image of the pattern of colors in the field. Moreover, detecting a color that was not a part of the original display is a simpler task than detecting a change in a color that was and still is part of the original display.

To facilitate illustrating this guideline, and others discussed below, the display in Figure 8.12 is used which contains a fairly complex pattern that would be administered at advanced levels of therapy. Replacing the center red circle with a yellow circle (a color not part of the field) is a simpler change than replacing it with a green circle (a color which is part of the field). In terms of number of changes, detecting one color, replaced by another which is not part of the field, requires a more global image than would detecting three color changes.

When the child is competent detecting color changes, shape changes are introduced following the same principle. First, introduce a shape that is not part of the display (e.g., replace the small, green diamond, middle left, with a small, green triangle) and, later, a shape that is part of the display (e.g., the same green diamond would be replaced by a small, green square). Similarly, with regard to size changes, replacing a large or small cutout with a medium one is a simpler task (since medium cutouts are not part of the field) than is replacing one size with a large or small cutout (e.g., replacing the small, green diamond on the left with a large, green diamond).

When the child has had sufficient experience constructing images that efficiently detect color, shape, and size changes, exchanges are introduced following similar guidelines. Colors are exchanged first (e.g., the large, blue diamond at the top with the large, green diamond at the bottom), then shapes (e.g., the large, blue diamond with the large, blue square), and then sizes (e.g., the small, green diamond with the large, green diamond).

Changes can also be varied in complexity by manipulating the locations into which they are introduced. The image of a field is usually articulated first at the corners and perimeter and then in the center. Therefore, replacements and exchanges introduced into the periphery of the field are usually detected more easily than ones embedded within the field, and changes located close together are detected more easily than those located far apart. Consider these multiple replacements. The red square is replaced by a yellow square and the blue diamond at the top by a green diamond. In locating the changes side by side that "section" of the field is spotlighted, making more vivid the replacements introduced. With later trials, the blue circle (lower right) is replaced by a small, blue square, and the small, green diamond (center left) by a small, blue diamond. Detecting these changes requires a more articulated image because they are more distant from each other. Along the same line, initially exchanges are located side by side (e.g., the green circle is exchanged with the blue diamond [top row]) and later far apart (e.g., the blue diamond at the top is exchanged with blue circle at the bottom).

Delay Between Examining and Reexamining a Field—Promoting the Stability of Images (Part D). Delay is phased in after the child has had sufficient experience with Parts A, B, and C, showing adequate leveling-sharpening functioning with patterns of colors, shapes, and sizes which are examined only visually and for relatively short periods of time. When introducing the technique, explain to the child that the *Remember Me* game will be played in a different way, that the child is to wait for some period of time before the screen is removed, that the therapist and child will begin to pay special attention to holding images stable over time, and that they will decide together when and how much to increase the delay.

A stopwatch is placed on the table, and child and therapist construct a sheet of paper on which the delay trials are logged, along with the accuracy of the child's response and other relevant behaviors. Usually the child begins with a delay of 10 seconds, the period of time the child has been waiting to this point while the therapist introduced a change. Initially present a display that is less complex than the one with which the child has been working. If the child was dealing with a nine cutout display of two colors, two shapes, and two sizes, the first display could consist of six cutouts with the same attributes and then gradually increase in number. After the child examines the display, the screen is set up and the stop-watch is started. After the delay period, the screen is removed, the child reexamines the display, and the performance is logged. In the next trials, the task complexity remains consistent while the delay period is increased until the child successfully detects changes introduced after a delay of at least two or three minutes. Then, the complexity of the field to be administered is increased and the sequence repeated.

When the delay period is two minutes or more, introduce interpolated activities. Almost any activity will do, but at the start the activity should be neutral (e.g., counting; reading a neutral, brief paragraph; looking at a neutral picture). With older children and adolescents it is useful to include extended delays, presenting a display at the start of the session; and then at the close of the session the child determines whether or not a change was introduced. An even greater period of delay can be employed by presenting a display at the close of a session and asking the child to reexamine the display at the start of the next session.

During the delay period children frequently begin to show significant behaviors (e.g., restlessness, fatigue) and comment spontaneously. These behaviors provide information about a child's personal issues and unique difficulties constructing images of information. The therapist selects aspects of these behaviors for discussion. In the early stages of therapy, these discussions are limited to promoting the child's ability to observe what happens to the child during the delay period, and to the image constructed of the display.

Step 2. Once the child gains some competence with the leveling-sharpening process when dealing with patterns of geometric cutouts, present displays of more ambiguous objects, following the guidelines of Step 1. Various material is used that is easily obtained and not costly (e.g., paper clips of different colors, shapes, sizes, and thicknesses; keys of different shapes, sizes, colors, and design; and ambiguous line drawings on 3×5 inch cards).

Step 3. This step emphasizes how assuming multiple points of view, when examining a field of disordered information, serves to organize the field and to construct and retain a stable, differentiated image of that field.

The displays presented consist of the same materials used in Steps 1 and 2 but are varied in their organization in two interrelated ways. The items are set further apart than the 2 to 3 inches that separated them in the displays presented in Steps 1 and 2; and the items are placed in a random field and not in rows and columns. Further, the items are located to facilitate the child's clustering the field, and therefore an image of it, from a point of view.

To introduce this step, begin with displays of geometric cutouts of several colors, shapes, and sizes, but with a smaller number than was used in Steps 1 and 2. The cutouts are located about 4 to 6 inches from each other and form what at first glance appears to be a field of random or "scattered" items.

Explain to the child that the *Remember Me* game will be played in a different way, that the cutouts to be remembered will look like the example on the table (e.g., "They're all over the place."). Frequently children spontaneously exclaim that it is impossible to remember the sample display. Whether or not the child expresses dismay, the therapist goes on to explain that it *is* more difficult to remember "a bunch of things that are all over the place," and that the job becomes easier if the cutouts are examined and remembered in terms of a point of view (e.g., "If we look at them in a certain way that makes a pattern or design, we can remember them.").

The therapist demonstrates, coaching the child to examine the display in terms of color and to generate a pattern from that point of view (e.g., pointing to the pattern articulated, "You see red goes across and then up. Blue goes down and then up. Yellow bunches in the corner."). The therapist then asks the child to examine the same display in terms of shape and coaches the child to generate a pattern in the field from that point of view. For example, "You see the circles make a point; they go from this one, up here, to this one, and then down to this one over here; and the squares make a line from this one to that one," and so on.

Once the child receives sufficient coaching, present displays that gradually increase in complexity and randomness, following the usual format: after the child examines the display, cover the items, introduce a change, remove the cover, and ask the child to restore the display to its original form. But, with this step, while restoring the display, the child is encouraged to describe how the points of view he/she used organized the field.

Initially the therapist is active suggesting and directing points of view (e.g., "Now with this one, make a design in your mind, bunch these together by looking at the small, green cutouts, and the large, red cutouts, and all the round ones."). In later stages the therapist does not offer possible points of view but encourages the child to experiment with generating his/her own that best organizes the display to be remembered.

The more varied the material used, the more the child is stimulated to use multiple points of view. For example, if cutouts of cloth are arrayed in random patterns, the child is asked to organize the field to be remembered by organizing the items from the points of view of texture, thickness, shape, color, and size. When wooden cutouts are combined with cloth, buttons, and keys, the points of view assumed can now include types of material. At this stage in the therapy the points of view used are limited to physical attributes of the materials in the display. With some children it may be necessary to introduce this step initially using only one point of view over several trials before requiring two or more points of view.

Training the Child to Assume Points of View. Some children have much difficulty or are unable to assume points of view even in terms of relatively concrete attributes. In these cases the therapist takes time to conduct a series of trials during which the child is trained to assume points of view following two guidelines. First, the child assumes a point of view *physically.* To illustrate, locate the display on the table, ask the child to look it over and to indicate "where the red squares are." The child responds, "Over there at the top." Then, ask the child to move to the opposite side of the display and again to indicate where the red squares are. The child responds, "They're right here, at the bottom." At this point the therapist engages in a discussion, pointing out that "where the red squares are depends on where you are." This approach is repeated as often as is required with the child examining the same display from two or more *physical* locations.

When the child readily articulates different patterns in a display when assuming different physical points of view, the therapist begins to train the child in assuming points of view cognitively (e.g., "Do you understand, John, you see the design in different ways depending upon where you stand and where you are looking from? Now stay in your seat, look at all of these, and figure out a design the cutouts make [the child responds]. Now *make your mind walk over* to the other side of the table; while you're imagining yourself over there, figure out a design the yellow circles make.").

Basic training in assuming points of view can also be provided, when indicated, by taking a single object (e.g., a toy car) and engaging a child in discovering that if the object is considered in terms of color, it is red; if it is considered in terms of weight, it is light; if it is considered in terms of composition, it is plastic; if it is considered in terms of what it can do, it rolls on wheels, and so on. With this type of training, the child learns that the particular item remains the same, but the point of view assumed emphasizes a particular quality.

Step 4. This step emphasizes anticipating the pattern or organization a field of information could take. The geometric cutouts are typically used, although other materials such as buttons and keys are also suitable. Explain to the child that the game will now be played in another way called, *Flying Shapes.* To illustrate, set two (or three) squares in a row at the edge of the table and point out that the child will use a ruler to push the shapes onto the floor. Before the child pushes the shapes off the table, the child is asked to draw on paper the location and pattern the shapes will assume when they land on the floor.

If the child seems confused, the therapist actively coaches the child, pointing out that one cannot be absolutely sure exactly what pattern the cutouts will form when they fall, that the location of the cutouts at the edge of the table gives clues, and that "we can picture in our minds where they will be when they are on the floor." The therapist insures the child understands that it is OK to guess and demonstrates as often as needed.

With each task, once the drawing is completed, the therapist pushes the shapes onto the floor, and child and therapist compare the outcome with the anticipated pattern. In later trials the child is invited to push the cutouts onto the floor and encouraged to experiment pushing them with subtle and more vigorous thrusts of the ruler, providing the child with experience anticipating the spread the cutouts will assume as well as the pattern. Through a series of tasks, the number of cutouts, colors, shapes, and size are gradually increased.

The issue with this step is not the accuracy with which the child anticipates the pattern a set of cutouts might assume, but with providing the child repeated experiences constructing images that anticipate the pattern information will take (anticipatory images). Last, only Parts A, D, and E of Step 1 are relevant for this step.

Step 5. With gains in remembering fields of simple and more ambiguous information, and while assuming points of view and anticipating information, the child is ready to engage in leveling-sharpening functioning while experiencing fantasies and emotions.

The first technique used is the same as that described in Step 4 of the program in field articulation. The display of cutouts to be remembered is surrounded by pictures from magazines (or sound recordings are played) that arouse fantasies and emotions (e.g., pictures depicting nurturance, aggression, violence, affiliation among children, authority, violations of rules, loneliness-isolation, persons smiling and enjoying themselves). Stimuli are selected in terms of the child's unique personality difficulties, and which initially are minimally provocative and gradually more provocative.

When introducing this step, explain to the child that the pictures now placed around the display to be remembered, "will make you think of things and make you feel things," that "the game is the same," namely, to remember the display of cutouts, but now the displays are to be remembered "while you get different ideas, memories, and feelings." Also, explain that after the task is completed, the child is free to talk about the pictures and what they aroused.

The complexity of the displays, the mode of examining them, and the types of changes introduced follow the guidelines of Parts A through D of Step 1. Beginning with the first series of tasks, the therapist engages the child in comparing her efficiency with which various displays are remembered when surrounded by different pictures.

Another technique involves the use of delay with interpolated tasks as described in Step 1 above. During the delay between examining and restoring a display, the child looks over, talks about or tells a story about a picture. If a recording is played during the delay, the child describes what she imagines is going on.

With a third technique, a picture is taped on the bottom side of each cutout. When a display is presented, the child not only studies the pattern of the cutouts, but also turns over each one and studies the pictures attached to the bottom, associating some attribute of the cutout with its picture (e.g., "The big, red diamond is a soldier, the big, blue triangle is a policeman."). When the child is ready, the therapist sets up the screen and replaces a cutout, initially with one that is different. When examining the display, the child is asked to identify the changed cutout, turn the cutout over, and recall the picture that was also replaced.

The pictures placed under the cutouts are selected to fit some aspect of the child's therapeutic need for experiencing the leveling-sharpening process while balancing emotions/fantasies. In addition to using pictures cut from magazines, photographs the child is invited to bring in of family members, relatives, and recent events are also taped to the bottom of cutouts.

Step 6. This step relies upon experiences provided with the previous step and embeds leveling-sharpening functioning more formally into the process of symbolic functioning. Wooden and cloth cutouts, buttons, keys, and other materials used in Steps 1 and 2 are used as well as other material that lends itself to being construed in many ways.

To introduce the method, present a display of cutouts, and say, "Now we are going to play *Remember Me* in a different way. Let's pretend these (pointing to the cutouts) are something. What could they be?" If the child does not respond or has difficulty, the therapist suggests, for example, "Let's make believe they are different people, like a teacher, a mother, a father, a sister, a policeman. Which one should we make the mother?" This procedure is followed until the child construes each of the cutouts.

If the child responds, offering, for example, that the cutouts are "animals" or "cars," or "outer-space guys," or "monsters," the therapist engages the child in the same way, asking her to designate each cutout as a particular type of the category construed (e.g., "What kind of monster is this one? Does it have a name? And, how about this one?").

Once the material is construed in some way, with each cutout having an identity, follow the usual procedure and present a series of increasingly more complex displays to be remembered, vary the mode used to examine the displays, the type of changes introduced, and the degree of delay imposed.

Over the series of tasks, encourage the child to construe the material with conventional and less conventional symbols. If a child tends to use conventional referents such as cars and familiar domestic animals, coach the child "to pretend these are something really different, something way out, something nobody would think of." If the child tends to use unconventional referents, the therapist encourages the child "to make these into something that we see everyday, something other kids would think of easily." Similarly, if the child tends to use concrete symbols (e.g., cars) the therapist encourages the child to use more abstract ones (e.g., "strong, sleepy, fast" and vice versa).

In conducting the evaluation process during this step, encourage the child to specify the connection between the vehicle (the particular attribute of the material) and the referent of the symbol constructed. For example, one child designates that "pointy things are strong; curvy things are weak," another child that "pointy things are fast; curvy things slow," and another that "red things are fast cars; yellow things are slow; and blue things are very slow."

In the last phase of this step, which forms a bridge to the next, ask the child to set up a display of material to be remembered by the therapist and while pretending the cutouts are something (e.g., "Pretend in your mind these are something. Don't tell me what you're pretending. After you put them out, I'll try to guess what they are from the design you make and from the place you give to each piece.")

After the child completes the array, the therapist attempts to determine the symbols and fantasized situations the child has in mind. While working with the display, the therapist verbalizes aloud, sharing with the child various possibilities that come to mind (e.g., "Let's see, these green squares could be space ships getting ready to land on a space station, which is this big, blue circle. But, they could also be three cars parked in front of a store."). After producing several possibilities, ask the child to set up the screen, introduce a change, and lower the screen. Then try to determine what changed. Then ask the child to share what she had in mind when constructing the display.

Following this, child and therapist engage in evaluating how and why the symbols the therapist proposed fit the attributes displayed and whether or not they are close to what the child had in mind. As might be expected, some children remain very stimulus-bound when first engaging this task. For example, one child said, "I just put out pointy things around some round things." Other children use highly personal symbols, which have little or no connection with the vehicles employed to convey them. For example, one child said, "This is rain (a wide array of shapes and colors) falling on this frog (a yellow diamond) that's sitting on this rock (a blue circle)." In this case as with all children, this step provides an opportunity to help the child cultivate the capacity to construe with both conventional and personal symbols while engaging in the leveling-sharpening process and to learn to evaluate whether and how a symbol communicates.

Step 7. Experiences with the previous step prepare the child to participate in the directed fantasies phased in at this time and which include leveling-sharpening tasks.

To introduce this step, explain to the child, for example, "Now we're going to pretend that the cutouts are something, but also we're going to pretend that we are in a particular place and you are a certain person. Let's pretend you're a detective and people who own a big house called you to figure out who committed the crime. Make up what the crime was." The therapist uses every opportunity to help the child participate in constructing the fantasy. After the child responds (e.g., "There was a murder."), say, "Now let's pretend all these (the cutouts) are people in a room." Eight cutouts are placed on the floor in a random array (or an ordered array, if indicated). "Let's make up who they are. Who could this green square be?" The child is encouraged and assisted in labeling each square (e.g., the green square is the guy who works in the garden; this white diamond is the butler, etc.); "Now let's say you leave the room for a few minutes, and while you're gone somebody comes in and takes the place of one of these people. You come back and try to figure out who left the room." The child walks to another part of the room, and after a delay returns and determines what has changed.

In this way, the child is engaged in a series of directed fantasies, each one including some activity that requires the leveling-sharpening process. Other directed fantasies include: (a) the scene of a classroom, a teacher (played by the therapist) is asking a student (played by the child) to remember numbers on a blackboard; (b) a marine captain (played by the child) takes roll call; the troops (cutouts) are lined up in rows and columns and each one is given a name and a rank. The captain leaves for several minutes and returns to discover one of the soldiers has been replaced by someone else (or two soldiers have exchanged places in the ranks). The captain names the missing soldiers, or names the soldiers who have exchanged places.

After the therapist directs several fantasies, the child is encouraged more and more to initiate and direct various imagined scenarios within which some of the activity involves remembering information.

Step 8. After the child engages in a series of directed fantasies, which include leveling-sharpening tasks, the treatment process, if indicated, shifts gradually to a nondirected verbal/play format as discussed in Chapter 10. The goal of this phase is to focus the child on organizing, elaborating, and working through key pathological metaphors with the benefit of efficient cognitive controls and cognitive-affective balancing.

Concluding Remarks and a Note About Resistance

With the capacity to construct and retain stable images of fields of information perceived as they are and as they are construed, and to relate these images to present perceptions, the child has available a cognitive tool that should improve the efficiency of learning and adapting and, if indicated, serve a phase of nondirected verbal/play therapy.

As with other programs, the therapist initially trains the child to observe behaviors and emotions that occur while working on the task. However, with this program, these self-observations focus on whether and how these behaviors/emotions influence the clarity of the image constructed of the information to be remembered and/or the efficiency with which the image is related to present perceptions. Once the child who requires therapy in leveling-sharpening is aware of the relations between the complexity of tasks and resistant–intrusive behaviors that occur, he/she has a fair amount of insight into the similarity between what occurs in the office and what occurs in school and home and what can be done to change these maladaptive habits of functioning.

To illustrate, one fifth grader was reexamining a display of cutouts after an imposed delay of several minutes. Suddenly he became flustered, unsure whether the four corners of the matrix should be yellow squares. He began tapping one of the yellow squares on the table, but this behavior was quickly transformed into a more aggressive form as he banged one cutout against another. Then, abruptly, he mumbled with agitation, "This is a s_____ game," stood up and walked away, stretched and yawned. He returned to his seat and rested his head on the table suggesting that they play a form board game. Relying on previous work, the therapist asked the boy to observe what had just taken place and then wondered if something similar happens in school. The child associated to a recent incident when he had been sent to the principal's office for swearing. A reconstruction of the event revealed that he swore during a reading comprehension quiz, when each child was writing answers to questions about a story the teacher had just read to the class. The boy became aware of the parallel between trying to remember the corners of the matrix and trying to remember the story read by the teacher, and between calling the *Remember Me* game "s_____," and swearing in class. At this point the therapist focused the boy's attention on the fact that he had given himself clues that his anger and frustration were mounting when he tapped the cutout on the table and then banged one against the other. And, the therapist engaged the boy in discussing what alternative behaviors are possible once he notices these forecasts of his mounting anger.

Chapter 9
Therapy with Equivalence Range Cognitive Control

The equivalence range cognitive control concerns the manner in which an individual groups information in terms of concepts. As discussed in Chapter 2, the process includes the number and width of categories used, the level of abstraction represented by a category, and whether conventional or personal concepts relate the members of a group. The program described in this chapter is designed to restructure and rehabilitate this mechanism so that it functions efficiently when information is handled as it is, as well as when information is transformed with symbols and fantasies within the process of symbolic functioning (pretending).

With the general technique, the therapist presents an object and the child details its physical and/or functional properties and locates or specifies other objects, each of which share one or more of these properties. Then the child forms groups with the objects so that those placed together share some dimension and qualify as members of a concept. With the therapist's assistance, the child learns when concepts fit the information they embrace and comes to understand the utility of concepts when applied to external information and to information construed in terms of fantasies.

To benefit from this program, a child should have achieved in the course of development, or with the assistance of the programs previously described, stage-appropriate efficiency with cognitive controls that are subordinate to, and integrated within, the process of equivalence range; namely, constructing body schemata, regulating body tempos, scanning systematically, articulating a field of information in terms of relevance, and constructing differentiated, stable images of information that are related to present perceptions.

When compared with the previous program, the experiences provided by equivalence range therapy represent another major shift along the developmental hierarchy of cognitive control functioning (see Chapter 2). With therapy in leveling-sharpening (the previous program), the information managed is contained, for the most part, in images constructed of past information and in the relation between these images and perceptions of present information. Now the therapeutic experiences require that the information perceived, as well as the information held in memory, be related in terms of categories, classes, and concepts.

PROGRAM 5: *WHERE DOES IT BELONG?*

Purpose and Goal: To develop the child's capacity to construct categories of various types of information that are narrow and broad, concrete and abstract, and to learn the utility of these concepts; and to promote efficient equivalence range functioning when external information is engaged as it is and when it is transformed with symbols and fantasies within the process of symbolic functioning (pretending).

Materials: (a) familiar objects and materials of various shapes, sizes, colors, textures, densities, and lengths typically found in the child's home, school, and community; (b) unfamiliar objects varying along the same dimensions not found in the child's home and community. Objects used in homes and farms in the United States before 1940 and from other cultures frequently serve as effective unfamiliar objects; (c) material used in previously described cognitive therapy programs (e.g., geometric cutouts; buttons; keys; pieces of cloth).

Introduction and General Procedure

When administering this program the therapist places an object on the table (referred to as the *starter object*) and asks the child to list its physical and/or functional attributes. Next, the child places these attributes into groups *either physically*, by grouping objects which contain one or more of the attributes listed, *or cognitively* by grouping the attributes that have been recorded on cards. The child evaluates the groups constructed and dissolves the groups. Then, the same objects/attributes are grouped in other ways, using different categories and concepts. At a later phase, the child learns to evaluate and relate these categories and concepts by constructing a model, or "theory," with them. This entire process is repeated with attributes which are construed or imagined.

Now the process of equivalence range will be examined closely. First, each of the other four cognitive controls are orchestrated in a complex interplay that results in conceptual thinking. This complex process, in turn, reminds the therapist to exercise careful, analytic thinking when administering the techniques described here. The therapist should observe, monitor, and understand her own "conceptual style" in order to help the child. If the therapist tends to think in abstract terms, leaping from some data to some conceptual understanding, the therapist may not be sufficiently patient in helping the child cultivate each of the steps required to perform this leap. Last, the therapy program is less structured than the previous program. With each task, the therapist creates a relatively long-term process within which the child gradually cultivates the capacity to perform each of the steps that contribute to conceptual thinking (i.e., comprehensively articulating the attributes of the field of information to be conceptualized, flexibly assigning each attribute the position of relevance and irrelevance, relating attributes to images of information already experienced, and then constructing a category which unifies the information).

For an example, consider a child who is presented a red ball, a yellow poker chip, a 3×5 inch lined index card, a red plastic saucer, and an eraser. When asked to group objects that belong together in some way, the child stands relatively motionless (regulation of body tempo) and actively scans the objects (focal attention), registering the attributes of the ball (red, round, and soft), the poker chip (yellow, round, flat, corregated edges, hard). In terms of the contribution of field articulation, the child perceives a ridge along the perimeter of the ball, and withdraws attention from this attribute, as he squeezes the ball, registering its density in terms of sensorimotor experiences involving other hard and soft objects (body schema). Then the ball is replaced, attention withdrawn from it, and directed to the index card with its blue lines, to the shining surface of the plastic saucer, back to the ball (focal attention and field articulation).

Images of these attributes become a major part of the process as the child determines how the objects belong together. As the child directs attention selectively at the red attribute of the saucer, the perception is related to the image of the red attribute of the ball. At this point, the child sets the ball by the saucer, "They're both red," simultaneously subordinating the softness of the ball, and the hardness of the saucer.

Withdrawing attention from the ball and saucer, the child perceives the index card, relating the perception to an image of the child at school erasing a line on a sheet of paper and to an image of the eraser perceived earlier on the table. The child places the card by the eraser, "You can erase the card." Again, in grouping the items this way, the child subordinates attributes of the eraser (e.g., rectangular, gray, rubber) and the card (e.g., rectangular, white, blue lines).

Compare this example with one of disordered equivalence range functioning. The child groups the eraser, ball, and saucer, saying, "This (eraser) is soft like this (ball), and the ball is red like this (saucer)." With this type of conceptual thinking, a "shifting chain" of concepts ties the objects together rather than a single, stable concept. Or, the child sets the poker chip upright on its rim on the card, saying, "It goes like that on paper," indicating that the objects are "forced" into a group in an unrealistic way. The first example illustrates the interplay of efficiently functioning cognitive controls within the process of categorizing. The second example illustrates how deficits in these controls derail conceptual thinking.

As discussed in Chapters 2 and 3, the equivalence range control is unique in involving language, beliefs, and concepts within its process. In the early phases of therapy, or in the early phases of each step, a child, especially a young child or one who has limited language ability, may not be able to construct a label/concept/explanation which unifies the objects in the group. The therapist should not insist on labels. Rather, she should wait for developmental advances to take place that enable the child to construct labels or explanations. This position is in accord with numerous studies which make clear that by the end of the first year of life infants construct groups of objects, clearly reflecting a common denominator, long before the child shows a verbal label for the dimension being used.

Unlike the other therapy programs, there are no criteria that define when a child successfully completes a task. With equivalence range therapy, the therapist evaluates whether, for example, a child needs 1, 10, or 15 sessions to cultivate the capacity to articulate comprehensively the attributes reflected by a starter object. As another example, one child may require only a few sessions to cultivate the capacity to regroup a set of material in new ways, while another child may require many sessions.

The program of equivalence range therapy consists of eight steps as outlined in Table 9.1. The first two steps provide "basic training," so to speak. The child articulates attributes of neutral, familiar, and then less familiar starter objects, locates objects made available, each of which contains one or more of the attributes listed, and then groups the objects. This process is repeated as often as indicated, using a series of starter objects.

With Step 3, once objects are grouped, the groups are dissolved, and the same objects are grouped again, now from other points of view. In this way, the child experiences reversing the original concepts, cultivates an understanding of how the point of view one holds influences the way in which information is conceptualized, and learns that the same information can be conceptualized in different ways. In the next step the child conceptualizes information which is not present (distal), as well as probable or hypothetical.

Then, the child conceptualizes while balancing emotions and fantasies aroused by the material (Step 5). Following this, the program embeds conceptual thinking within the process of symbolic functioning (pretending) by requiring the child to categorize objects and attributes construed as something else (Step 6), and then by requiring the child to categorize information while participating in directed fantasies (Step 7). At this point the child is equipped to use equivalence range functioning as a tool in

Table 9.1. Steps in Therapy with the Equivalence Range Cognitive Control: *Where Does It Belong?*

Step 1. Child conceptualizes neutral, present information: familiar objects used as stimuli

Part A Child conceptualizes information in terms of physical properties
1. Therapist presents neutral, simple stimulus (starter object)
2. Child lists physical properties of starter object
3. Therapist guides child as needed to discover and evaluate attributes
4. Child locates objects (response objects) that contain at least one physical attribute of the starter object
5. Child places response object into groups, each defining a dimension
6. Child and therapist evaluate each group in terms of the fit between objects and dimension of group
7. Therapist presents a series of starter objects increasingly more complex and less familiar; Child repeats (2) through (6) above; Therapist encourages groups that contain increasingly more objects

Part B Child conceptualizes familiar information in terms of functional properties (usages)
1–7 same as Part A with usages of objects focused

Part C Child conceptualizes information in terms of physical and functional properties
1–7 same as Part A

Part D Child builds conceptual model that organizes several groups already constructed

Step 2. Child conceptualizes neutral present information: unfamiliar objects used as stimuli

Parts A–D Same as Step 1

Step 3. Child conceptualizes present information from multiple points of view: familiar and unfamiliar objects used as stimuli

Part A Child groups and regroups the same response objects in terms of physical and functional properties, comparing the points of view which guided each grouping

Parts A–D Same as in Step 1
1. Child articulates points of view guiding location of objects in groups
2. Child trained in assuming points of view if indicated
3. Child rates and compares groups and points of view (e.g., narrow-broad; concrete-abstract)
4. Child builds conceptual model organizing groups as rated

Step 4. Child conceptualizes information that is absent: familiar and ambiguous objects used as stimuli

Part A Child conceptualizes information that exists in daily environment (e.g., home; school)

Part B Child conceptualizes information that exists but is not a part of the child's daily environments
1–7 of Step 1 and 1–4 of Step 3

Step 5. Child conceptualizes present and absent information that arouses fantasies/emotions

Follow methods of Step 4. Therapist uses starter objects that increasingly provoke fantasies/emotions

(continued)

Table 9.1. (*continued*)

Step 6. Child conceptualizes information construed as something other than what it is
Part A Therapist guides child with techniques of free sort, directed sort, directed pretend uses, and directed linguistic symbols
1. Child and therapist take turns in constructing groups of material construed as someting else and the other guesses the dimension guiding the group
2. Child and therapist evaluate whether symbols constructed are conventional or personal and how they fit attributes

Step 7. Child conceptualizes information while enacting a fantasy directed by therapist

Step 8. Child conceptualizes information within a nondirected/freeplay format

learning and, if indicated, when engaging in nondirected verbal/play therapy designed to help the child elaborate and reform key pathological metaphors that contribute to his/her maladaptive functioning.

The outer-oriented child begins with Step 1, cultivating the equivalence range function without the interference of fantasies against which cognition is defended or with which cognition is incompetent. Gradually the child moves to Step 8 as outlined. The inner-oriented child begins with Step 8, with modifications indicated, cultivating the equivalence range function with information from the prefered personal world and without interference from the requirements of the external world against which cognition is defended and with which cognition is relatively incompetent. Gradually the inner-oriented child moves to Step 1.

Introducing the Program to the Child

The examples describe young children who are especially deficient in equivalence range functioning. Older children and children less deficient may not require the degree of direction illustrated.

The Outer-Oriented Child. Place a red rubber ball on the table and say, "John, we're going to play a game called *Where Does It Belong?*. Look at this ball and feel it. We want to find other things it belongs to." The child spontaneously comments that the ball belongs to a toy box and his mother doesn't like toys laying around. The therapist says, "That's *where* it belongs. Where we keep it. We want to figure out how this belongs to other things; how it's the same as other things. To do that we have to first find out what is special about the ball. Tell me what the ball is made of." "It is hard; you can bounce it on the wall (grinning), and you can bounce it off someone's head."

The therapist responds, "Bouncing is what you can do with the ball. Hard *is* one thing the ball is made of. What else?" The boy responds, "It's red." The therapist says, "Good. What else?" The boy responds, "It's small." To help John discover that this attribute requires further differentiating, the therapist (following techniques discussed below) asks John to place a marble and soccer ball next to the red ball. Discovering that the red ball is large when next to the marble, and small when next to the soccer ball, John decides to call the ball "medium-small." In a similar way, John is given squares and other shapes until he articulates the attribute "round." The therapist says, "That's right; it's round. Round is something special about the ball. It stays round no matter what you put it next to. Medium-small is special, too, but not as special because it doesn't stay medium-small when we put other things next to it."

Next John locates objects in the room and in the "game box" provided by the therapist that have "at least one of the special things the ball has—red, round, or medium-small." John rummages through the game box, places objects on the table, and with each the therapist asks John to point out the attribute. After John locates six to eight objects, the therapist proceeds with the remaining techniques of Step 1, Part A.

The Inner-Oriented Child. Use the first session or two to observe the objects in the playroom the child tends to use in spontaneous activity. These objects and others the child brings to the session are used to introduce the program. One child came to the session wearing many buttons and badges on his shirt (baseball players, rock group performers, "Star Wars" figures). The child does not comment when asked about them although he frequently takes one off and manipulates it. The therapist asks the child for a button he is holding and engages the child in detailing the attributes of the button following the procedure discussed above. A number of such interventions may be required over several sessions before the child begins selecting objects from the box.

Another child, during her dreamlike wanderings through the playroom, manipulates an animal puppet for a moment, and then changes its location, placing it next to a human puppet. In this case, the therapist takes both of the objects and asks the child to detail the attributes that belong to both of them.

The therapist repeats this procedure as often as is clinically indicated, slowly engaging the child in the task of detailing physical and functional attributes. As the alliance builds, the therapist moves more formally into Step 7, asking the child to group the objects within some fantasy into which the therapist has been invited.

Specific Instructions

Step 1. In Part A place a neutral, relatively simple object on the table. One of the geometric cutouts used in other programs is frequently an effective initial starter object. Ask the child, "What makes this (a green wooden square)? What is it made of?'' If the child articulates a functional attribute, point out, "That's one thing you can do with it. Right now we want to figure out what are some of the things that this is made of." Occasionally a child will spontaneously articulate drive-dominated attributes (e.g., "You can crack someone's head open with it," "You can eat it like a Cookie Monster."). At this time, point out only "that is what you can do with it." The instructions for Part B discuss how these "functional" attributes are handled.

Print each attribute the child articulates on a 5 × 8 inch card, if the child is able to read. If a child cannot read, use simple designs (e.g., a circle to connote round; red crayon mark to connote red, and a drawing of stick figure holding a huge weight to connote heavy). These cards are then used as the anchor points for a later step.

Guiding the Child to Discover and Evaluate Physical Attributes. The therpaist guides the child in discovering physical attributes and evaluating their appropriateness using several techniques: (a) manipulate the starter object and, if necessary another object, in ways that suggest a physical attribute (e.g., lift the starter object in the palm of the hand, "hefting it," or place the starter object in one hand and another object in the other hand to convey weight; pass your fingers along the perimeter of the object to convey some unique shape; tap the object against a table to convey density); (b) verbally direct the child to explore a particular attribute (e.g., "Jimmy, pass your finger over the top; do you notice anything?"); (c) provide a label for one attribute as a way of encouraging the child to discover others (e.g., "Mary, right here in this part it's blue; this edge is round").

After the child has articulated at least three or four physical properties of the starter object ask the child to look through the "game box" to find objects (response objects) that have one or more of the attributes articulated. The game box should be filled with many different "odds and ends" (e.g., washers, bolts, clothes pins, shoelaces of various lengths and colors, sea shells, buttons of various colors and sizes, nuts and bolts, corks, pieces of colored sponge, cotton balls, wooden sticks, metal rods, small springs, paper clips, old brushes, pieces of ribbon, twine and wire, wooden blocks, pieces of styrofoam). The more items in the box the more the child is enabled to locate possible response objects. Also, the smaller the items the better, since small objects lend themselves more easily to being grouped. With older children and adolescents, the box should contain at least 100 items.

Place the cards, on which the attributes of the starter object were recorded, on the table and ask the child to place each item under the card listing the attribute the object shares. Once the child locates at least six to eight objects, ask the child to place the response objects into groups, "Put into a bunch the things that belong together for some reason."

Initially the child, especially the young child, will cluster the objects in terms of the attribute shared with the starter object (e.g., two objects are clustered that have the color green, two objects that are square, etc.). In all cases, ask the child, "How do these belong together? What's the same about them?" Accept these groupings and engage the child in evaluating each whether or not the groups appear "reasonable" or "correct" (e.g., "That's right. These go together because they are all green. These go together because this one is made out of wood and this one has some wood on the handle").

On occasion, even at the start of therapy with simple starter objects, a child constructs an inappropriate group. The therapist guides the child, using the techniques described above, in discovering why a particular object does not belong (e.g., the child places a square, wooden brush with a square sponge and says, "They're wood." The therapist taps the brush against the table and then the sponge and asked the child to do the same, saying, "What about that? Are they both wood?") After the child has articulated the physical properties of the first starter object, selected, grouped, and conceptualized some number of response objects, place another starter object on the table. If a child manages the first trial with ease, the next starter object could be somewhat more complex (e.g., a marble containing the attributes: sphere, glass, smooth, yellow, blue, white, and red) or considerably more complex (e.g., a wooden ruler, flat on one side, concave on the other; a metal strip on one edge; black, red, and white lettering; and circular designs on each end). If the child shows limitations during the first trial, a second equally simple starter object is used for the next trial (e.g., a red ball).

The therapist continues administering additional trials using a series of starter objects each one slightly more complex than the last. The number of trials required, and the complexity of the starter objects, are determined by the child's age, developmental stage, and degree of impairment in conceptual thinking. With each trial the therapist encourages the child to locate a few more response objects than were located in the previous trial. Some children spontaneously increase the number of response objects from trial to trial; others become fixed on some number. In the latter cases, it is usually helpful if the therapist joins the child in rummaging through the box, modeling and verbalizing the search for possibilities. "Let's see. Could this be one we could put there? Does it have something like that (the starter object)?"

Following the same procedure for Part B, ask the child to articulate functional attributes of the starter object. Say, "Now we are going to play the game *Where Does It Belong?* in a different way. This time, let's figure out all the things you can do with this."

Initially, use some of the same starter objects from Part A. If the child worked with a wooden cube, for example, the child now deals with the same cube in terms of its functions, although simple and few in number (e.g., can be used as a game piece, or to hold paper down, or to hold a window up).

In addition to "static" objects from Part A, starter objects for these trials should also include items which inherently stimulate usages (e.g., door hinge, a sponge, a shoe lace, a wooden clothes pin, a coat hanger, a pair of scissors, an egg beater). With each starter object the child follows the same seven steps of Part A: lists functions, locates response objects that perform one of the same functions, groups the response objects, and evaluates the groups.

From task to task, the child is trained to evaluate the fit between the functions articulated and the unique attributes of the object, whether the proposed function is neutral and related to external information or highly personal and related to internal information. For example, articulating the functions of a stick as a starter object, the child proposes, "You can use it like a ruler to draw a straight line, and you can build a house with it." The first use is evaluated as closely fitting the attributes of the stick. With the second, help the child discover that the stick cannot be used to build the walls of a regular house, but could to trim a window or to build a toy house.

To illustrate further, if the child says, "You can poke somebody's eye out," the child is helped to evaluate that an eye could be poked out with many different objects (e.g., a finger, a book, a pencil)—"almost anything, except things like feathers, so poking eyes out is not a very special thing that belongs to a stick." This example illustrates that the dynamic issues involved in such responses are avoided at this phase in therapy in favor of training the child to evaluate the proposed function cognitively in terms of the properties in question.

Part C provides therapy in conceptualizing information when physical and functional attributes are considered simultaneously. The starter objects, although still familiar to the child, are now more complex and contain properties that stimulate both physical and functional attributes (e.g., coat hanger, egg beater, a drinking cup, a hammer, padlock with key, a working flashlight).

With each starter object, ask the child to note both what the object is made of and the different ways you can use it. Each physical and functional property is recorded on a card and each card is set on a table as a reminder. Following the 7 steps of Part A, the child locates objects from the game box that contain one of the physical or functional properties or some combination, then places these objects into groups, labeling and evaluating each. Over a series of trials use starter objects that are gradually more complex, and ask the child to locate an increasingly larger number of response objects.

Since including both physical and functional properties permits more abstract and broad categories (e.g., "tools," "toys"), the therapist help the child articulate categories that are broader and more abstract than those of previous steps within what is expected for the child's age and developmental stage.

Part D provides the child with preliminary experiences "building a conceptual model" and constructing some "superordinate understanding" of how several groups can belong together. With the general procedure, the therapist selects groups of objects the child already constructed, places them on the table, and guides the child in developing a model with them.

To illustrate, assume that during the course of Step 1, the child grouped objects and formed categories listed in Level 1 of Figure 9.1: a saw and yellow paint can were grouped because they both contained yellow; a screwdriver with a green handle and a small wire cutter were grouped because they both contained green; washers and a paint roller were grouped as round; a hammer and file as long; a screwdriver and paint brush because each had a wooden handle; and tweezers, scissors, and a piece of wire because they are metal things.

The therapist places the groups on the table saying, "Jimmy, these are different groups you made before. Remember, you put the saw and paint can together? Do you remember why? Right, they both have yellow. Do you remember why you put the screwdriver and wire cutter together? Right, they both have green handles." The therapist reviews each group arrayed. If the child does not recall the category, the therapist reminds the child of the reason given previously for the group. Each category name is printed on a card and placed above the respective items.

After this review, the child is instructed to construct a second level of concepts that could unite two or more first level groups and concepts. In our example, the therapist says, "Jimmy, this bunch is yellow things and this bunch is green things. If we put both of these bunches together what do they both have to do with?" Child responds. "That's right. They both have to do with color." Continue guiding the child as needed until the child articulates the other Level 2 concepts of "how they are shaped" and "what they're made of" as shown in Figure 9.1. Print each of the Level 2 concepts on a card and place the cards on the table above the groups that fall within the concepts.

Next, the child is guided in constructing a subordinate concept. For example, "Jimmy, these groups have to do with the color of things, these groups with the shapes of things, and these with what the things are made out of. Now, let's think of a way all these things, and all these groups, can belong to one family—one group." The therapist guides the child in constructing a superordinate concept (e.g., "They all have to do with fixing things"). This Level 3 concept is also printed on a card and placed above all the groups.

The number of conceptual levels required at this stage should be rela-

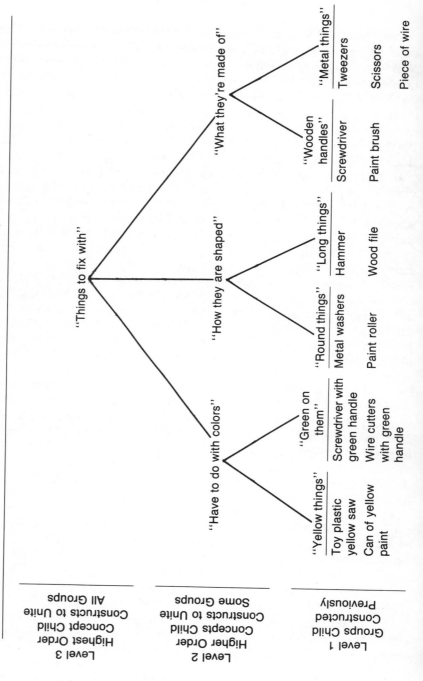

FIGURE 9.1. Sample Conceptual Pyramid for Step 1, Part D

"Things to fix with"

"Have to do with colors"

"How they are shaped"

"What they're made of"

"Yellow things"
Toy plastic yellow saw
Can of yellow paint

"Green on them"
Screwdriver with green handle
Wire cutters with green handle

"Round things"
Metal washers
Paint roller

"Long things"
Hammer
Wood file

"Wooden handles"
Screwdriver
Paint brush

"Metal things"
Tweezers
Scissors
Piece of wire

Level 3
Highest Order
Concept Child
Constructs to Unite
All Groups

Level 2
Higher Order
Concepts Child
Constructs to Unite
Some Groups

Level 1
Groups Child
Constructed
Previously

tively simple, but, of course, as complex as is appropriate given the child's cognitive status. At least two or three such pyramids should be constructed before moving on to the next step. Some adolescents are capable, even at this early stage of therapy, of constructing three pyramids and then uniting these three pyramids within a superordinate, fourth level of abstraction.

As illustrated by the example, the models constructed with most children at this step in therapy should make use of simple physical and functional attributes. In constructing Level 2 and Level 3 categories, a child may make use of concepts that are too global or that rely on interpretations that are too personal. For example, "all these are happy things," "these have to do with war and these have to do with peace." Though at first glance such concepts appear "creative," they should be examined carefully to determine if excessive liberties are being taken when imposing these concepts, and whether the items contained within the group provide an appropriate referrent. In general, initially guide the child in constructing higher order concepts that are more closely tied to the "data base." When the child demonstrates the ability to articulate the physical and functional properties being used to form higher order concepts, the breadth and abstraction of the higher order concepts can be increased.

The example given also illustrates that initially the therapist locates the groups selected to construct a model in a way that gives the child clues as to how several groups can be clustered together. In setting the yellow group and the green group next to each other, the therapist facilitates the child's constructing the higher order category of color uniting these groups. If the yellow group were located to the far left and the green group to the far right, it would be more difficult for the child to arrive at this possible higher order concept. Initially, then, the therapist locates groups close together so as to suggest possible higher order categories. Later in therapy the groups are arrayed randomly, requiring more vigorous conceptualizing on the part of the child.

Step 2. This step requires starter objects that are unfamiliar to the child and introduces new, important ingredients in the treatment process. When asked to list physical and functional attributes of an unfamiliar object, most children tend to dismiss it outright, or explore it only briefly. Unfamiliar objects are not unlike unfamiliar information, that is, information not readily assimilated into preexisting schemata and understanding. Therefore, by using unfamiliar starter objects, the child is provided therapeutic experiences in conceptualizing the unfamiliar and unknown which, in turn, requires accommodating preexisting schemata to the unfamiliar material.

A large number of objects, relatively unfamiliar to the child, are required to serve either as starter or response objects. Gadgets used on farms and in kitchens before the 1940s are ideal, as well as objects the therapist may have collected from other cultures and countries. Novelty shops and "flea markets" are usually excellent sources for this material. The therapist should not presume that an object is familiar to a child, and, of course, the therapist should keep in mind that an object familiar to one child may be unfamiliar to another (e.g., a wire rug beater; an allen wrench; a washboard). Before beginning the therapist establishes whether the objects are unfamiliar by showing each to the child and asking, "What is this? Have you ever seen it before?"

Once materials are gathered, follow the steps outlined in Parts A through D of Step 1. As might be expected, when more ambiguous and/or less familiar objects are used, evaluating the fit between the category and the physical and functional properties of objects in the group takes on special significance. Now the child is more likely to propose a physical property that is not sufficiently articulate (e.g., "They all have bumps on them," or a function, "You can do things with all of them, like you can lean them on this.").

Step 3. This step requires the child to assume multiple points of view while conceptualizing the information. The familiar and unfamiliar objects used in Steps 1 and 2 are used here in combination.

In the first part of this step, present a starter object and follow the procedure of Step 1, Part C: Ask the child to list both physical and functional attributes of the starter object, locate relevant response objects, place the response objects into groups and then label the groups. The items that form a group and the reasons why the items belong together are printed on 5×8 inch cards, each group recorded on a separate card. The cards are set aside for the moment.

Next, instruct the child to dissolve the groups. For example, "Johnny, let's leave all of the things you used in these groups on the table, but let's mix them up." The therapist moves items, asking the child to join in. When the items are arrayed more or less randomly the therapist says, "Look over all of these things again. Make new groups with them. Try to find other ways these things can belong together for some reason." After the child has formed another set of groups, the items of each and the concept the child assigns are printed on a 5×8 inch card.

At this point engage the child in comparing the groups and concepts. Move the objects just sorted to one side, and array the two sets of cards on the table, the cards of each sort in a single row. Select an item and discuss where it was located in each sort in order to cultivate the child's understanding of how points of view influence the way an item is conceptualized. For example, say, "Johnny, the first time you put the screwdriver in this group because it was long and skinny like everything else in that bunch." Point to the card describing that group and review the group. "The second time you put the screwdriver in this group because a part of it is made of metal, like the other things in that group." Point to the card describing the group and review the group. "The first time you were noticing the screwdriver one way, by its shape; the second time you were noticing it another way, by what it is made of. Do you see? The way we look at things (for older children—the point of view we use) makes us see a thing in a certain way."

Select other items and proceed in the same way, cultivating, bit by bit, the child's understanding that different points of view guided the location of an item in different groups. In these comparisons, emphasize that the object or piece of information does not change when imposing different points of view on it, but the membership assigned to the item changes in keeping with the feature the point of view has made salient. For example, "Johnny, notice the screwdriver stays a screwdriver wherever you put it, but here it belongs to a long, skinny group because that's what you picked out of it when you looked at it that way. Here it belongs to a metal group because that's what you picked out when you looked at it that way. Do you see? The same thing can be understood in different ways and belong to different groups."

With older children and adolescents, train the child to rate each group constructed in each sort in terms of width and level of abstraction. The purpose of rating is to cultivate the child's understanding that all categories are not the same in terms of the understanding they bring and that the understanding a category provides is a function of various dimensions such as the width of a category and the level of abstraction. The complexity of the ratings the therapist introduces would vary, of course, in terms of a child's cognitive ability. The therapist should invent appropriate rating scales.

To illustrate, consider the following three-point rating scales the author and colleagues have used with children as young as eight to nine years old. In terms of category width, a rating of 1 defines a narrow group, a 3 a broad group, and a 2 falls between. In terms of level of abstraction, a rating of 1 defines a concrete group, a 3 an abstract group, and 2 falls between. With the therapist's help, the child reviews each group (listed on a card) of each sort and writes the ratings assigned on the card. Examples: items grouped in terms of identities (three red poker chips placed together because they are the same thing) would be rated as reflecting a more narrow category than items grouped in terms of the color red. The former group limits membership to things that are identical. The latter defines membership in broader terms since items that are different in some way, but colored red, can belong. Items placed in a group labeled "tools" would be rated as more abstract than a group called "fixing things," since some tools perform functions in addition to fixing. And, the category "fixing things" would be rated as more abstract than the category "metal things," which represents a more concrete attribute.

It should be noted that category width and level of abstraction are relatively independent considerations. For example, a narrow group of items (e.g., aluminum nails) can be conceptualized in more concrete terms ("nails to hook two boards together") and in more abstract terms ("You can hang a lot of different things on them."). Of course, there are no absolute criteria for defining these ratings, but criteria should be used that fit a child's conceptual abilities at this stage in therapy. Once each group of each of the two sorts is rated, the ratings are used to help the child compare whether one group and another within the same sort was guided by a narrow or broad, or by a concrete or abstract point of view. The child also compares the first and second sorts in the same way.

After the child gains experience comparing at least two sorts, instruct the child to dissolve the groups of the second sort and to group the same items again in another way, if objects permit. If the items do not permit a third sort, another starter object is introduced (or two starter objects are used simultaneously). Ask the child to collect a larger number of response objects and guide the child through three or four successive sorts of the same material which are subjected to the same comparisons and ratings. With adolescents, a conceptual pyramid can be constructed, as outlined above, which unites groups as much as possible from each of the three or four sorts, generating as many levels and concepts as the child is capable.

Training in Assuming Points of View. Once they have grouped a set of objects, some children and adolescents have extreme difficulty viewing the same objects in a new way and are unable to form appreciably different groups with the material. In these cases, the child is trained to assume points of view that initially are concrete and physical and later more abstract and cognitive. The techniques are integrated with those already described designed to help a child discover the physical and functional attributes of material (see Step 1).

1. To develop physical points of view, set an item on the table and ask the child to stand about 6 feet away, to look at the object, and to describe its physical and functional attributes. Then ask the child to move 180 degrees and to examine and describe the same object. If the object is complex enough, the child is asked to view it and describe it from each of four vantage points (360, 90, 180, 270 degrees). Coach the child in comparing observations made from each physical point of view, emphasizing that "the way in which you look at it makes you see different things." Whenever necessary, instruct the child to walk up and touch the object when

viewed from a particular angle or to observe the therapist manipulating the object in some way to stimulate discovering salient attributes.

2. To develop cognitive points of view, set an item on the table and explain to the child, for example, "Now instead of walking around and looking at something from different angles, we are going to let our minds walk around and look at things from different angles." Assume the therapist presents a glass sculpture; which is translucent and the outer surface is square; a circle of carved wood forms the base; inside is filled with clear fluid and contains eliptical flower petals made of red, yellow, and blue glass. Initially, the therapist proposes a concrete point of view, "Look at this for color. What belongs to this when you look at it for color?" The child responds with the therapist assuring that all colors are named. "Look at this for shape. What belongs to this when you look at it for shape?" The child responds with the therapist again insuring that all contours and shapes are articulated. "Now look at this from the point of view of what it's made of," and so on. Gradually, the therapist centers discussions on how "the angle we use; the way we look at something" makes us notice certain details about the same object but the object itself stays the same.

3. As the child gains confidence in viewing the same item from several points of view that are more or less concrete, the therapist follows the same procedure, now suggesting more abstract points of view, (e.g., "Look at this as something you would find in a store. What could you say about it? Look at this as something about art. What can you say about it? Look at this as something you use in an office. What can you say about it?").

Step 4. This step provides experiences that emphasize conceptualizing physically distant or hypothetical information. Ask the child to note all of the physical and functional attributes of a starter object, and, if appropriate, the child or the therapist prints each attribute at the top of a sheet of paper. Then ask the child to picture her bedroom at home (or kitchen, or den) and to think about things located there which contain one or more of the properties listed. When the child names an object, the name is printed on a 3×5 inch card, which is placed on the sheet of paper containing the title of the attribute the item named shares with the starter object.

Initially, the therapist designates particular rooms in the child's home, school, or in a relative's home the child frequents, to help the child cultivate the capacity to use as much information "out there" as possible. For example, a child may list only a yellow bread box in the kitchen in response to a yellow poker chip presented as a starter object. The therapist asks the child to focus attention on the kitchen (the walls, cupboards, utensils), describe what she recalls, and determine whether other objects share some property with the yellow poker chip. The child now lists dishes and a clock on the wall "because they are round, like that, and a waste basket "because it's plastic, too."

After generating a number of items, each recorded on a card, the child groups the cards, conceptualizing, evaluating, and rating the groups following the procedure outlined in Step 3. If an object does not belong to a group in which it is located, ask the child to picture the object in her mind again and relocate the object if appropriate. The groups formed are recorded. Then the groups are dissolved and the same cards are used to form new groups. Following the procedures of Step 3 as many new sorts are constructed and compared as the objects listed permit.

Stimulated by a starter object, the child next lists items and information that exist but which are not part of the child's daily environments. These items are grouped, conceptualized, and evaluated and then regrouped. The goal is to provide the child with experiences conceptualizing information that is somewhat more hypothetical than that contained in her daily environments. Initially the therapist may need to suggest locations. For example, if the child has not been to a railroad station, or has on only one occasion, say, "Think about railroad stations. Think of everything you have heard or read about them. List all the things you might find there that have the same things as this (starter object)." With adolescents, the settings or events suggested could be more distant and hypothetical (e.g., periods in history, "Think of when the settlers landed in Jamestown," "Think of imperial China.").

Step 5. This step provides experiences conceptualizing information while fantasies and emotions are aroused. The starter object presented, and the response objects made available, are real items or pictures of items that are likely to arouse fantasies and emotions. Examples: various types of knives; baby bottles; nipples for baby bottles; rubber and plastic figures of humans, animals, insects, monsters, and mythical figures; toy racing cars; small pictures such as a wounded soldier, an airplane about to crash, a policeman, a school principal, a child swinging a baseball bat, can be pasted on 3×5 inch cards.

In the first part of this step, present a starter object, ask the child to list its physical and functional attributes, to select objects and/or pictures as response objects, and to then group, conceptualize, evaluate, and regroup them following the same procedures. In the second part of this step, beginning with a starter object, the child lists response objects that are absent, or located in distant environments or in hypothetical worlds. Each response item is listed on a card and the cards are grouped, evaluated, and regrouped following the same procedure.

In advanced stages of this step, especially with older children and adolescents, the therapist designates a domain to be conceptualized within which the child is known to experience considerable stress. For example, if an adolescent has had considerable difficulty with science courses, the therapist could suggest, "Let's list all the things that belong to biology." Each detail listed is written on a card and the cards subjected to the same grouping and regrouping procedure. As another example, if one child or a member of a child's family has experienced surgery, the therapist could ask the child to list "all the things that belong to having an operation."

With this step, the therapist has the opportunity to bring to the child's attention how fantasies/emotions influence the types, widths, and degree of abstraction of groups constructed with materials that arouse aggressive fantasies, for example, versus those from materials that arouse fantasies about nurture or discipline.

Step 6. The child categorizes attributes which are construed and therefore gains experience conceptualizing within symbolic functioning. Several techniques are used to cultivate this capacity.

Free Sort. A wide array of material is located on the table. For example, eight washers of different diameters, some of rubber, others of metal and others of cork; six metal screws of different lengths and pitches. Say, "Let's pretend these are all something. Make believe these things are something. What could they be?" The child responds, "People." (or racing cars, or animals). The therapist accepts the child's designation and continues, "OK, let's make groups of people (or animals or cars). Put all the people that are the same in some way in one group. Then put all of the people that are the same in another way in another group. Make as many groups as makes sense to you." With each group constructed, ask, "What's the same about these people? How do they belong together?"

Although ambiguous items are used which lend themselves to being construed in many ways, the therapist engages the child in evaluating conceptual thinking within symbolic functioning. At this step the evaluation process emphasizes the relation between an actual attribute and the way it is construed and between what was pretended and the symbol assigned to the group. For example, a child calls a group of long metal screws, "angry lions, because they are the biggest," and does not articulate a referent for angry. Another child construes a group of screws as "angry lions because the grooves of the screws are big and wide like a lion's mouth growling."

Directed Sort. The goal with this technique is to engage the child in construing items and pretend that they could be like the starter object. Therefore, care should be taken not to convey to the child that items should be selected that have a close physical resemblance to the starter object.

Locate a wide array of objects on the table, present a teaspoon, for example, and ask the child to locate within the array, "all the things that could be like this." Some of the items the child chooses might have properties close to the starter object (e.g., a tablespoon, a ladle). Others might have properties less similar (e.g., a spatula) and still others might have properties that are quite dissimilar (e.g., a wooden dowel 8 inches long).

The technique of direct sort provides opportunities to cultivate the child's ability to construe information in terms of both personal and conventional symbols. If a child is stimulus-bound, the therapist encourages the child to include items into a group that are very much unlike the starter object. "You're right, the stick doesn't look at all like the spoon; but we could pretend it is a spoon." If a child has a tendency to construe items in highly personal terms, the therapist accepts this pretending but emphasizes when and how the items selected for a group depart appreciably from the properties of the starter object.

Directed Pretend Uses. With a variation of the directed sort technique, the child is presented with a wide array of material and the therapist suggests that some function be performed with or to the starter object. For example, "Let's pretend this (a stick) is a girl (boy). Give her different things to eat for supper. Pick something out from here to feed her." The child brings a wooden cube up to the stick. "What are you feeding her? What are you pretending that is?" The child responds, "A sandwich." "Now feed it something else." As another example, the therapist could say, "Let's pretend this is a horse (wooden cube). Let's pretend different people get a ride on the horse. Pick something out from here (items on display) and pretend it is riding the horse." Again, the therapist requests the identity of each item the child places on the cube.

Directed Linguistic Symbols. With another variation, the therapist sets a wide variety of items on the table and says, "Now, I am going to say a make-believe word and you pick out all the things that belong to it. Whatever you pretend the word I say means, pick out things that would belong to that word. Ready? Pick all of the *Zips* and put them in a group here. What things can you pretend are *Zips*? Now, put all of the *Wams* here," and so on. The therapist engages the child in articulating what physical and functional attributes are construed by the child and in locating particular items belonging to a group, labeled by the therapist with a linguistic symbol.

When the child is capable of construing information fairly easily, child and therapist take turns constructing groups of material which are construed as something else and the other guesses the dimensions unique to the group. The same familiar and ambiguous materials used earlier are used here. The therapist says, "John, I'm going to put these things into groups. Watch me." The therapist located three wooden cubes in a row and places a metal screw on each. "Guess what I'm pretending these are." The child responds, "Cowboys racing their horses." The therapist replies, "That was close. I'm pretending they are cars and the drivers in a race. Now you take a turn. You make up a group, and I'll try to guess what you're pretending."

Begin with a single group, and, when appropriate, increase the number of groups, the number of items in a group, as well as the mixture of familiar and less familiar items included in groups. When engaging the child in evaluating these groups, emphasize when and how the items are used, their positions, attributes, and so on, and communicate to the other person the symbol constructed.

Step 7. This step extends the previous activities within an elaborate directed fantasy, within which the child assumes a pretend role, discards the role, assumes her own identity, then assumes another pretend role, and so on. A directed fantasy could take an entire session or several sessions. With the general method, a wide array of materials are placed on the table. The therapist directs the child to imagine a particular scene and situation and to perform some activity within it, emphasizing categorizing.

The following is an illustration. The therapist says, "Johnny, pretend you are a sheriff, and you just brought six crooks who tried to rob a bank into the police station. You put each one of them in a cell. Here they are." The therapist points to six blocks of different sizes and colors located on the floor at different points in the room. It may help the reader to view each of these blocks as starter objects. The therapist continues, "Some of these guys are bigger and stronger than others. You have to put each one in a different cell, give each one some furniture they can use in the cell, and give each one some food to eat. Then lock the doors of each cell with the right lock. Pick some things out from here and put them in each of the cells. Give them some supper to eat and some furniture to use and then put a lock on the cell door that belongs there." After the child performs the therapist engages the child in evaluating the material located within each group.

Step 8. When indicated, the treatment process takes on a more nondirected format, following the guidelines discussed in Chapter 10. The therapist gradually relinquishes directing fantasies and follows the themes and fantasies a child constructs, in the service of working through and resolving the child's key pathological metaphors.

Concluding Remarks and
a Note About Resistance

When dealing with the tasks described in this chapter, children with significant deficits in equivalence range functioning regularly show thinking that is affect-dominated or concrete and stimulus-bound, both types equally unrealistic in terms of the information at hand. As examples of the former, when the therapist passed his fingers over the edge of a square to guide the child in articulating an attribute, the child perceived that the therapist, "cut his finger," rather than perceiving the realistic property of squareness. And, when another child was dealing with possible uses of a red wooden cube offered, "It can crack your head if someone threw it at you."

Examples of concrete, unrealistic thinking occur without evidence of overriding anxiety, aggressive tensions, or fears of injury. Consider examples of physical properties articulated by children when dealing with each of the following starter objects: a red checker piece ("It's heavy and clean"); a hammer ("It's got an end on the handle"); and, in forming a group, a child slipped a pipe cleaner into the key hold of a lock and gave as an explanation of the group, "It goes in there like that." While these examples do not reveal, in one sense, very bizarre thinking, they illustrate that distinguishing attributes of information are not being conceptualized.

The broad strategy used to deal with both types of unrealistic thinking is *to remain focused on the perceptual and conceptual qualities of the objects being managed*. Help the child discover the obvious physical and/or functional attributes being missed, that more realistic relationships are possible, and teach the child why the attributes or relationships she articulated are unrealistic. In no case do we recommend that the therapist pursue possible dynamic issues suggested by a moment of disordered thinking, whether drive-dominated ("It can crack your head open") or less so (a pipe cleaner slipped into a key hole), until the child develops efficient equivalence range functioning as outlined above. Then the child is helped to develop an understanding of fantasies and motivations which influence conceptual thinking.

To illustrate this strategy with the child who declared the cube could crack your head open, the therapist acknowledged this, pointed out that the same was the case with a hammer, a cup, a stone, and many other items, and added, "Let's see if we can find something the block of wood can do with these things (in the game box); something that only the block of wood can do." With the child who slipped a pipe cleaner into the key hole of a lock, the therapist demonstrated that a pin and toothpick can also be slipped into the key hole and added, "We can put a lot of things in there. Let's see if we can find a way that makes the pipe cleaner do something with the lock that a pin or a toothpick can't do." The therapist inserted her finger in the loop of the lock, raised it, and asked the child if that gave her any ideas. The child passed the pipe cleaner through the loop and raised the lock.

As with other programs, resistance typically occurs whenever the complexity of the task increases, creating "conflict" between the child's conceptual abilities and the task demands (e.g., the child is asked to increase the number of response objects; or to construct a conceptual pyramid). This conflict, as discussed in Chapter 3, results in affects/behaviors characteristically used by the child to lower stress by avoiding the task. To manage, the therapist follows the guidelines of negotiation discussed in Chapter 4 along with the same broad strategy employed with other programs: the child is helped to observe the unique behaviors/affects; connects these behaviors to the particular quality of complexity introduced into the task; relates these behaviors and task complexities to similar events and requirements at school and home; and develops new responses.

The following example illustrates that resistant behaviors during this more advanced program may sometimes take on nonaggressive qualities. A 12-year-old girl frequently offered "to help" the therapist (e.g., returning response objects into the game box, washing the table top). These behaviors gradually showed themselves as serving resistance by avoiding the tasks whenever they became more complex. For example, the child would spontaneously offer to "straighten out all the items in the game box" and, on several occasions, she arrived with a large shopping bag filled with odds and ends, which she offered to the therapist for their work. However, each time she spent most of the session taking out each item, showing it to the therapist, making comments, and carefully placing it in the game box. With assistance the child gradually came to recognize that her "clean-up mood" occurred when the tasks became more complex and served to avoid the task.

Chapter 10
Restructuring Pathological Cognitive Orientations and Metaphors

RESTRUCTURING PATHOLOGICAL ORIENTATIONS

Four types of pathological cognitive orientations have been identified in Chapter 3. Techniques used to structure outer and inner orientations were illustrated in Chapters 5–9 and therefore will be treated only briefly here. In this chapter, techniques used to deal with the other two types of pathological orientations are examined—cognitive pathology in aggressive disorders and excessive shifts in cognitive orientation. The material presented assumes the reader is familiar with the treatment programs described in previous chapters and with rationale and concepts presented in Chapters 2 and 3, especially the concept of cognitive autonomy. The numbers of treatment steps noted refer to numbers assigned as listed in the tables of preceding chapters.

Outer Orientation

Outer-oriented children maintain a pervasive, rigid, outer cognitive orientation, which limits the accessibility of symbolic functioning and pretending as a way to discover new information. Frequently they do not experience stress while learning unless pressed to complete new assignments that contain more complex demands than daily, usual work. They tend to be sticklers for detail and routine (e.g., recopying a theme several times because, "the words didn't come out just right on the page") and often reveal rituals (e.g., becoming very uneasy if circumstances do not permit them to line up window shades).

Course of Treatment. Because this child's cognitive orientation is incompetent with, or defended against, symbolizing information and pretending, treatment begins with neutral tasks from Step 1 to Step 3 becoming increasingly more complex, ambiguous, random, and requiring different points of view. In the middle phase, treatment continues with tasks from Steps 4 to 6, which require the child to respond cognitively in the face of task-irrelevant stimulation that arouses fantasies/emotions and while engaged in symbolic functioning, first using conventional (secondary process) and later personal (primary process) symbols. In the final phase, freed from defensive, rigid uses of external information and capable of permitting fantasies/emotions to participate in cognitive functioning, the child deals with cognitive tasks embedded within fantasies directed initially by the therapist and gradually by the child. Here the child is helped to connect symbols/fantasies to present and past experiences, to learn how these personal definitions, which were previously segregated from awareness, influence maladaptations, and to develop alternative actions.

Clinical Example. John was described as a loner and "mopey." While managing marginally in the first grades, he seemed almost unable to learn in the third grade, which he was now repeating. At school he frequently rearranged his desk; at home he spent much time lining up, counting, and pasting stickers in a scrapbook. He was referred for CCT by his therapist because during a year of nondirected therapy, John steadfastly maintained control over himself and the treatment process by repeatedly initiating tic-tac-toe games. Without results, the therapist had introduced interpretations and activities in the belief that trust would be established, resistance dissolved, and conflicts managed by John's obsessional activity would emerge.

John's program began with displays of geometric cutouts to be remembered (leveling-sharpening program) arranged in orderly rows and columns, and gradually increasing in number, colors, shapes, sizes, and eventually consisting of more ambiguous items arranged randomly. During interpolated delays, John and the therapist initially engaged in games of tic-tac-toe. John was enthused by the challenge of remembering displays of highly structured material and seemed relieved that he had "something to do in the meetings" and that the therapist did not "bug" him with questions.

Next, following Steps 4 and 5, John pushed cutouts from the edge of the table after drawing patterns he anticipated the cutouts would form. Because John associated that his cat leaped suddenly from various perches, "like the shapes," the therapist suggested the tasks be called "the cat game." Then John was engaged in remembering displays of cutouts surrounded by pictures (e.g., wounded soldier; car wreck), or while listening to recordings (e.g., machine guns; exploding bombs), which John had identified stirred up fantasies and emotions he found both exciting and stressful. After showing ability to remember displays while balancing fantasies/effects, he dealt with displays of emotionally arousing material. Various knives were among the items used because, on several occasions, John had quietly carved his initials and other designs in school furniture, resulting in reprimands by the principal and punishment by parents (his sticker collection was taken away for two weeks).

Then when engaging tasks that required him to symbolize geometric cutouts and wooden cubes arrayed in patterns to be remembered, at first, John construed the items with conventional, neutral symbols (e.g., cars, animals), then with more personal symbols (e.g., leaves blown by heavy wind; pieces of a vase that had crashed to the floor), and finally with highly personal primary process symbols that reflected aspects of the pathological metaphors against which his cognition had been defended (e.g., pieces of bodies blown apart by a bomb). Throughout, John evaluated the degree to which a symbol communicated and fitted its referent (e.g., a large diamond was someone's leg; a small square an ear, following an explosion).

When introducing the first directed fantasy in the final phase, the therapist relied upon these earlier observations and transference phenomena (e.g., John experienced the therapist as furious with him when he had accidently knocked over a vase in the waiting room). The therapist asked John to pretend a bomb scare had been reported in a building in John's hometown and he was a member of a special team trained to locate and diffuse bombs. The therapist located cutouts on the floor, which John imagined as specific pieces of furniture in the lobby of the building. John memorized the display, left, and returned. If the location of a cutout changed from its original position, the bomb was located under it. Subsequent fantasies gradually depicted more explicit violence, borrowing John's earlier fantasies. Displays of cutouts were imaged as persons with specific identities who were in a building just before a bomb exploded. When John reexamined the display, he determined who had been killed (missing cutouts) or "blown to the other side of the room" (cutouts changed location).

In the course of this work John gradually shared that when he had experienced the therapist as angry with him he imagined the therapist would "tear him apart," that he rearranged his desk instead of working because he feared the teacher would tear him apart once she observed the paper. He recalled with anguish beatings he had received from his father (acknowledged by father) and father's temper outbursts, and he evaluated expectations of being beaten by others in terms of the context at hand.

Inner Orientation

Inner-oriented children maintain a pervasive, rigid inner orientation, limiting the extent to which pretending participates in perceptions of reality and guides experimental actions in the environment. Frequently these children invest most of their mental activity in a fantasy world and become stressed especially when others block the ease with which they can slip into fantasy (e.g., parents remove the stereo set or super hero comic books; a teacher increasingly reminds the child he is staring out the window, tuned out). In extreme cases these children make use of hallucinated persons (as imaginary friends) and events as part of their fantasy world (e.g., a 14-year-old girl attending a public school revealed she was visited in her bedroom every night by a man who sometimes "smiled" and sometimes "stared in a mean way"). The fantasy to which the child retreats is viewed as both a defense and solution; that is, the fantasy is used as an escape from the demands of reality and pathological metaphors (e.g., the girl who hallucinated a man also entertained a continuous romantic fantasy world which provided protection from both school requirements and ongoing battles between her parents, as well as from her own aggressive-sexual conflicts).

Course of Treatment. Treatment begins by elaborating and organizing the child's preferred fantasy and representing aspects of this fantasy (e.g., persons, mythical figures, objects) with concrete items to be used in later tasks (Steps 7 and 6). Once the fantasy has solid referents in physical objects and attributes, these items are presented in cognitive control tasks (Steps 5 and 4) with which the child construes task-relevant information, first with highly personal and later with more conventional symbols, and develops an appreciation for those qualities of symbolic functioning that communicate to others. Then the child performs the cognitive control response with information perceived as it is but surrounded by task-irrelevant distractions that arouse fantasies/emotions. Once the child is efficient in perceiving and responding to the requirements of external stimuli, while simultaneously balancing fantasies/emotions, the child performs cognitive control responses with neutral, increasingly complex external information, without the participation of symbolizing and pretending (Steps 3–1). In the final phase, freed from the defensive, rigid uses of fantasy and capable of flexibly integrating external stimuli and fantasy in cognitive functioning, the child deals with cognitive tasks embedded within fantasies directed initially by the therapist and gradually by the child. Throughout this process, the child is helped to connect symbols and fantasies to present and past experiences, to learn how symbols fit the requirements of both reality and fantasy, how rehearsals in fantasy serve acting in reality, how the requirements of reality, previously segregated from awareness, influence maladaptations, and what alternative behaviors are possible.

Clinical Example. Jane was described as frequently lost in fantasy, and having no friends. After sitting for 30 minutes before a math exam, she had written only a 4-letter expletive in the margin. Although managing the first school grades, she steadily became more withdrawn and "peculiar."

Jane arrived for the first sessions with a tape recorder. Removing its cover, she interacted with the examiner through the recorder, fingering wires and gears. On occasion she spoke to her dog, Cuddles, who was not present. The therapist slowly joined Jane, peering into the recorder, talking with Cuddles, touching and inquiring about certain parts of the recorder, and engaging the recorder in conversation. Jane began to specify parts of the recorder (gears, wires of different colors) as various animate and inanimate objects. Gradually, the therapist specified concrete items as referents for the persons and things Jane noted in her fantasy (e.g., a particular red wire became the road from Jane's house to her school).

The therapist invited Jane to replicate, on the floor of the playroom, the world that had been created within the tape recorder so, "We can play it better and see it better." Pictures of buildings were cut out of magazines and geometric cutouts were used to designate various buildings, rods, telephone poles, and streets were defined with tape. Jane and the therapist walked on the streets at different tempos (tempo regulation program), visiting stores where items were purchased with no particular restriction as to how the material purchased was construed (e.g., paper strips as candy bars). Focal attention tasks were introduced next to engage Jane formerly in the process of symbolic functioning. For example, she scanned two rods to determine which was bigger, at first construing them with personal symbols (as big and little bowls of porridge) and later with more conventional ones (as pencils), evaluating the fit between a symbol and the attributes construed. When field articulation tasks were phased in, she surveyed rows of a few geometric cutouts and gradually of a larger number strung across the length of the room, fantasying that she was inspecting items on a store counter to select the ones designated. Again the items were construed initially in personal terms (e.g., cakes and cookies) and later in more conventional terms (e.g., as fruits and vegetables each matching the colors and contours of the cutouts to some degree). Still later Jane handled more complex field articulation tasks, with cutouts now perceived as they are and while the displays were surrounded by pictures that for Jane aroused particularly stressful fantasies/emotions (e.g., an infant nursing). When Jane showed efficiency performing while balancing fantasies/emotions, she handled a long series of more complex field articulation tasks consisting of neutral stimuli (e.g., cutouts, paper clips, buttons) without engaging in fantasy.

When ushering in the final phase of directed fantasy, the therapist relied upon earlier observations. Jane had often centered on the issue of relative size (e.g., small and large switches; short and long wires), and when symbolizing information, typically offered constructions illustrated by a small, blue circle construed as "a stomach monster that eats forever." In the transference she sometimes perceived the "stomach monster" in the therapist's belly, playfully patting it and saying, "The little thing is eating forever." In the first fantasy directed, the therapist asked Jane to pretend that an array of single cutouts, and stacks of two or three, were mountains of ice cream of certain combinations of flavors and to feed dishes of ice cream, designated by the therapist, either to a baby doll or to herself (a field articulation task). Jane elaborated and directed that the baby regularly ate big mountains of ice cream (stacks of cutouts) while Jane ate "only a little bit" (single cutouts). With the benefit of cognitive gains achieved, she gradually cultivated awareness of her global view that her baby sister "gets everything," while Jane gets "nothing," examined events involving her sister and parents in more specific and realistic terms, and attempted to modify behaviors she brought to these relationships, as well as to teachers who Jane regularly complained always favored the work of other children.

Cognitive Control Dysfunctions in Aggressive Disorders

From the view of CCT, one main reason for the child's habitual lack of control over physical aggression is the fact that the autonomy cognition should maintain between reality stimuli (especially those suggesting aggression) and fantasies (especially those concerned with aggression) collapses abruptly. With this collapse a specific detail in reality is centered (e.g., someone's eyes; position of the hands) and fused with the requirements of aggressive fantasies, resulting in "exaggerated apperceptions" of imminent danger to one's integrity and/or safety (e.g., "The glare in his eyes—like he was ready to kill," "The way he held his hands; He was going to swing"). Sometimes cognitive autonomy collapses in response to an inanimate object, which is suddenly used in an aggressive way (e.g., "I saw the brick on the ground and the next thing I knew it was flying." "His shirt was hanging out; I just pulled and tore it.").

Goals. Develop an appreciation of standards of objects and persons and whether one's actions meet them, the capacity to recognize and maintain cognitive autonomy from external stimuli that are likely to be construed in aggressive terms, and the capacity to pretend, expressing aggression in play acting rather than in concrete terms.

Course of Treatment. Having selected the appropriate program, begin with the neutral tasks of Steps 1 through 3, giving special attention to developing the child's capacity, while responding with the cognitive control, to manage more ambiguous information, and to shift points of view. The aggressive child needs a particularly solid base in flexibly shifting points of view in preparation for the next steps, which involve fantasies/emotions and symbolizing.

When the child is ready to process neutral tasks surrounded by task-irrelevant, emotionally arousing distractions, extra care is taken to guide the child in selecting a wide range of stimuli which provoke degrees of aggressive fantasies/tensions from none to moderate to very intense. The more fitted the material to the child's unique make-up the more effective this phase of treatment. For example, because a child indicated that particular boxers and boxing matches were especially potent triggers of aggressive tensions, tasks were eventually surrounded by boxing pictures from sports magazines (Step 4). Along the same lines, when construing neutral material (Step 5), the child is guided in using the same aggressively potent categories and in evaluating the fit between a symbol and the attributes of its referent. For example, the child noted above imaged various forks to be remembered as specific professional fighters, fitting the attributes of each (e.g., a thin, small fork was a particular very fast, light weight; a big, thick fork was a slow, heavy weight; etc.). The fantasies directed by the therapist in the last phase rely upon these same ingredients.

Special Techniques. One technique regularly employed with aggressive children blends methods used to manage resistance with those used in directed fantasy (see Chapter 3). Each time the child aggresses against material or the therapist, the aggressive response is made part of the response required by the cognitive task with which the child is working. By repeating this technique over many tasks, aggression is modified and transformed into more indirect, attenuated, delayed, and symbolic behaviors.

Another technique, *Fantasy/Reality Chairs,* is used especially with aggressive disorders at that step in a program when the child construes information. With this technique, intended to cultivate flexibility in cognitive autonomy, the child produces aggressive imagery in response to a stimulus, abruptly suspends the imaging process, engages the same information as it is, and then shifts again into the mode of imaging, and so on. The therapist places two chairs side by side and attaches a sign, ''fantasy chair,'' to the back of one and ''reality chair'' to the back of other (or with younger children ''make believe chair'' and ''real chair'') and says, ''With this game you shift back and forth between making believe with something and thinking about the same thing without making believe. When you sit in this chair (pointing) you make believe; when you sit in this chair you don't make believe." The therapist explains further that the child begins in one chair, engages the task as defined by that chair, and then *without* notice, upon the therapist's request, shifts to the other chair continuing to engage the same material as defined by that chair.

A focal attention task can serve as an illustration. Assume the child first sits in the reality chair. The therapist presents keys placed 6 feet apart and asks the child to describe each one in detail and then to point to the one that contains a particular set of multiple attributes (e.g., the one with more teeth, a thinner stem, and fewer designs engraved on the head). As the child describes each key, the therapist taps the fantasy chair. The child immediately gets up from the reality chair, sits in the fantasy chair, and *at the same time* changes the response process, now imaging the keys as something else as designated by the therapist (e.g., pistols to determine which one can shoot farther). Then again, while the child is imaging the keys, the therapist taps the other chair without warning; the child shifts, suspends making believe, and engages the keys as they are.

An illustration of the technique with aggressive stimuli: the child is presented two pictures, each depicting crowds in a riot, one in a street with buildings burning, and the other in a large lobby with furniture toppled and scattered about. When in the reality chair, the child counts the people (or police) to determine which picture has the larger number. When in the fantasy chair, the child images what's going on and makes up a story about each—what led up to it, what's happening now, how it ends. With practice, children learn to shift quickly and eventually continue with a fantasy whenever sitting in the fantasy chair. This technique is also used with directed fantasies to cultivate flexibility in the child's cognitive autonomy and to help the child learn the difficulties he/she experiences when attempting to subordinate and suspend an aggressive fantasy in order to perceive details in reality accurately.

Clinical Example. At home Harry frequently exploded in anger "over little things," was easily frustrated and bored while doing school work, and rarely completed chores. At school, he showed a very short attention span, restlessness, angry outbursts, and poor academic performance. Parents were finally pushed to seek assistance for him when he hurled a book at a student.

Emphasis of Initial Phase. In presenting tasks that gradually increase in complexity, point out aggressive fantasies and behaviors that are reactions to specific increases in task complexity in order to help the child observe and become aware of habitual cognitive strategies used to manage emerging aggression tensions; integrate aggressive behaviors within the task as relatively brief, segmented aspects of the response required.

Illustration: While engaged in tempo regulation tasks, Harry frequently bolted out of the room. The therapist asked Harry to leave the room and walk down the corridor at various tempos (fast, regular, and slow), timing him and asking him to image an animal associated with the tempo, following the guidelines of that program. When dealing with focal attention tasks, Harry abruptly broke a wooden rod used in a scanning task. The therapist placed wire coat hangers next to each rod and asked Harry to twist the coat hanger next to the rod that he selected in response to the task requirement (e.g., biggest, thinnest). The therapist also pointed out, "As soon as we moved the rods 10 feet apart, so the game is harder, you broke the rod to get out of doing it." At another time, with a field articulation task, Harry suddenly screamed "This is f_____ boring!" (a common complaint) and with an open hand "karate chopped" the cutouts off the table. In seconds the behavior escalated, as he karate chopped various toys. The therapist restrained Harry and pointed out that a familiar pattern was happening. He becomes bored and then fights everything when the work becomes complicated. With subsequent tasks Harry was invited to karate chop particular series of cutouts from the display.

Emphasis of Middle Phase. Integrate repetitive aggressive behaviors within a cognitive task, but now sustain the behavior and task for longer periods within the child's metaphor. The first metaphors emphasize macroactions as well as some fantasy, and gradually emphasize differentiated fantasies with actions subordinated. The task and metaphors require increasing degrees of delay and displacement of aggressive actions.

Illustration: As Harry showed gains with field articulation, the next time he regressed, the therapist sustained the metaphor of a karate fighter within the task. He asked Harry to pretend he was "Congo the karate fighter" and "chop" each cutout, which now were construed as persons or as bars of metal or wood of different thicknesses. Harry followed the suggestion with exuberance, pounding each item and yelling, "Yuh!"

Each time Harry regressed while dealing with tasks, other action metaphors were introduced followed by fantasy metaphors with actions subordinated. The therapist suggested competition be staged between two fighters to see who remembered the most complicated sequence of cutouts. As Harry enacted the part of each fighter, the therapist suggested that someone important needed to set the standards for these matches. Harry introduced the "King of Karate" to keep records and determine the conditions and winner of each match. Instead of enacting this character with his whole body, Harry designated a puppet as king. With each trial, the number of cutouts to be chopped increased and the order became more complex. Further, the king (directed by the therapist) required the fighters to perform specific, increasingly elaborate body movements, before striking a cutout, and designated edges of the cutouts which, if struck, demolished the victim and brought extra points. Gradually arenas were staged and tickets sold to imaginary fans who witnessed the battles.

In addition to illustrating the technique of embedding aggressive behavior into cognitive tasks and metaphor, this theme illustrates how cognitive control of aggression is achieved by transforming action metaphors into fantasy metaphors that attenuate and delay activity. Harry's karate chops gradually diminished in vigor without comment by the therapist. Eventually a melodramatic ''Yuh'' was accompanied by a moderate physical tap against the edge of the cutout.

Emphasis of Final Phase. As the child effectively integrates and regulates cognitive activity, aggressive actions, and fantasies, introduce interpretations that rely upon previous metaphors used with the cognitive-aggressive games. Interpretations should address both the complexity of information being processed and the aggressive components.

Illustration: When Harry reached the final step engaging in directed fantasies, the therapist relied upon the same metaphor and encouraged Harry, for example, to assign identities to other fighters and label particular karate moves. Harry named one fighter, ''Chink the Chopper.'' Chink broke rules, could not wait his turn, used foul language, and set fires. Chink was replaced by Tony, who, in turn, became an actual peer in Harry's class whose behavior qualified for the part. In this way the metaphor was transformed from the world of private symbols to the world of social convention, real persons, and events. Initially, Harry talked about his difficulties with aggression through discussions of Tony's escapades which served as a displacement. Gradually Harry examined his own thoughts and behaviors directly. Moreover, he eventually recognized that Chink the karate fighter, Tony the karate fighter, and Tony, the classmate, were different lenses, each one bringing some issue about himself into view.

Excessive Shifts in Orientation

These children habitually shift abruptly between outer and inner orientations, maintaining a segregation between the two sources of knowledge. In retreating to fantasies to escape the demands and stress of outer information, or in retreating to external information to escape the demands of fantasies, these children block the influence of metaphors on action and prevent the assimilation of actions that could restructure metaphors. Since these shifts represent exaggerations of cognitive autonomy, the details to which cognition shifts are usually irrelevant to the context at hand and hold no obvious connection with the information immediately preceding it.

Goals. Rehabilitate the tendency to employ exaggerated degrees of cognitive autonomy as a defense and develop the child's ability to *sustain* the two-fold process of dealing with information as it is and when construing it in terms of fantasies/metaphors that arouse stress/anxiety.

Course of Treatment. Begin with Steps 1–3 of the program selected which present neutral tasks that do not require the process of imaging/fantasy. While administering these tasks, whenever the child shifts from an outer to an inner orientation, elaborate and categorize the issue *to which* cognition retreated, then the issue *from which* cognition retreated, and then, with a series of expanding symbols or metaphors, join the two issues to bring new information into view and to guide new actions in the environment. The same principle is followed when tasks are introduced later that require construing information. Now the child is more likely to shift from the inner orientation required by the task to an outer detail. Again the issues to which and from which cognition retreats are noted, elaborated, and joined with symbols.

Criteria guide which shifts in orientation are selected for formal intervention. When working with tasks, the child usually reveals issues in reality, as well as metaphors, that are major sources of stress and unsuccessful adaptation. These issues are usually accompanied by brief but significant bursts of intense anxiety and agitation. An abrupt shift from such an issue to the opposite orientation, and to a detail that is *unrelated* to the anteceding issue, qualify for formal intervention. Also, when engaged in extreme shifts, the child frequently turns attention to the same detail. This perseverative quality indicates the issue is cast in a category that has "hardened" and signals the need for intervention. Since the therapist is relatively unfamiliar with details in the patient's current situation and private metaphors, cognitive shifts are allowed to sustain, during the first phase of treatment, as an understanding is gained of issues being segregated. Later the therapist intervenes more quickly.

Clinical Example. Tom, a 14-year-old, fluctuated between spending hours wearing stereo earphones or "keeping busy" (e.g., constantly categorizing his collection of rock records). In school he was sometimes "spaced out" and sometimes frantically working on assignments, which were usually poorly organized and rarely completed.

Emphasis of Initial Phase. As neutral tasks increase in complexity, make a mental note of the issue *from which* the child retreats and aid the child in elaborating and "loosening" the issue *to which* he/she retreats. With each elaboration, impose a new symbol on the issue, providing a different view and facilitating future elaborations. Fit the degree of emotionality introduced by symbols with the patient's psychology. As the internal issue is elaborated and reformulated with new symbols, return the child to the issue *from which* cognition retreated and loosen and elaborate that issue.

Illustration: Beginning with a program of equivalence range tasks, Tom examined starter objects, listing and categorizing their attributes. Initially starter objects were neutral (e.g., a marble cube) and later invited fantasies (e.g., a jackknife; a picture of teenagers walking hand in hand).

While categorizing the attributes of a jackknife, Tom abruptly stopped, became agitated, and complained he could not concentrate. Thoughts about biology class were racing through his mind, a topic to which Tom had retreated on other occasions and which had been loosened and elaborated. For example, when Tom detailed that he could not get started with experiments and papers due, the therapist symbolized, "Biology class is like being stuck in mud." When Tom listed he would be "damned" if he completes an extra assignment, and that he always arrives late for class, the therapist symbolized, "Biology class is holding yourself back from doing something." When Tom listed his lab partner "p_____ me off" and the teacher's style irritates him, the therapist symbolized, "Biology class is getting furious at people."

When Tom retreated to the biology class, this time while listing the physical attributes of a knife, he was asked again to list details of the class. In addition to repeating details, he added that he frequently looks at frogs immersed in a large jar of formaldehyde, sometimes poking them to see if they are alive or dead. Yesterday the teacher reprimanded him for standing there again, "dreaming" instead of working.

Because Tom had elaborated the issue of biology class to a fair degree, the therapist returned Tom to the starter object (knife), and to the card on which he had listed the last attribute (sharp) from which he retreated, and asked him to recall what was on his mind when he wrote "sharp" and just before his thoughts jumped to the biology class. Tom exclaimed, "Kill! I was going to write kill." Then he added, "I had a dream about killing." To elaborate this issue Tom was asked to list and group details of the dream, following the technique of equivalence range therapy. Over several such analyses it emerged that Tom experienced a recurring dream in which he repeatedly stabbed some animal or person, lifting the eyelid with each stab to see if the "thing" was dead or alive. While listing details of the dream, Tom initially was in a near panic state, vigorously scratching his thighs, and gradually displayed more efficient cognitive-affective balance while detailing and grouping the biology class and the dream.

Emphasis of Middle Phase. Relying on the child's ability to elaborate issues to and from which cognition retreats, without regressing or resisting, the therapist introduces symbols/metaphors which *integrate elements from inner and outer issues.* Initially the symbols are concrete, global, and neutral, and later more abstract, differentiated, and emotional. Imposing a series of expanding metaphors increases the extent to which inner and outer details are integrated and teaches the child how each new integration, with its metaphor, brings the issues into view in a different way, resulting in new information.

Illustration: As the biology lab and dream were detailed and categorized, the therapist integrated one concrete detail from each pointing out that Tom's attention jumped from the knife (and dream of killing) to biology (dead frogs), that the dream occurs repeatedly and he repeatedly looks at the frogs, and thus the dream and frogs are the same because his mind returns to each "over and over again," a relatively neutral, concrete metaphor joining the two domains. As therapy continued successive metaphors embraced new details especially ones concerning sadism Tom witnessed and sadist metaphors Tom entertained while listening to rock music (e.g., watching a Boy Scout use his knife to taunt a cat he had tied; fantasies in which Tom imagined himself as a Gestapo torturer).

Emphasis of Final Phase. As the child shows some ability to associate from one issue to a *related* issue in the other domain, gradually relinquish giving directions and follow the child's lead, examining and integrating current topics with metaphors. In this phase the process resembles issue-oriented psychotherapy where child and therapist remain focused on a topic each has agreed to examine.

Illustration: While engaged in a directed fantasy, which included equivalence range tasks and the motif of prisoners of war, Tom anxiously noted that his father fell and had gone to the emergency room where a cast was placed on his ankle. His thoughts went to a history assignment concerning World War II. With no guidance from the therapist, Tom began to relate aspects of the assignment (describing the invasion of Normandy) to his rage towards father and fantasies Tom had indulged in which he tortures father. Here Tom showed a cognitive orientation that related, rather than segregated, external details with metaphor, and was able to explore again how, whether, and when his rage was appropriate, on the one hand, and on the other, that his fantasy did not break his father's ankle.

RESTRUCTURING PATHOLOGICAL METAPHORS

This section describes observations from a nondirected phase of treatment conducted after a directed CCT program. (For other clinical examples of restructuring metaphors in nondirected treatment see Santostefano, 1984; in press a; in press b.) The case is intended to illustrate how children repeat and restructure pathological metaphors with the benefit of stage-adequate cognitive functioning. The discussion assumes the reader's familiarity with the concept of metaphor and related issues discussed in Chapters 2–4.

Narrative descriptions of treatment sessions were recorded and subsequently examined to determine what pathological metaphors were repeated, whether with each repetition the metaphor was restructured following the developmental progression from action to language, whether with each restructuring the child internalized standards (superego) represented by imagined ideals, whether the metaphor spiraled to a higher developmental level as new coding capacities emerged, and whether the child's reformed concepts of self and others resulted in less pathological behavior.

The metaphor was viewed as having been restructured whenever major changes occurred in the theme, the roles assigned to child and therapist (e.g., a shift from mythical to human figures), and the behavioral mode dominating the play (e.g., action to fantasy). The child initiated and authored the configurations of play; the therapist initiated behaviors within the child's metaphor, in the service of providing the child with interventions to assimilate that could restructure the metaphor.

Clinical Illustration

Mary was referred at the age of 5 years because during preschool she regularly pushed children, took away their toys, and on occasion angrily bit or struck them. She stubbornly refused to engage in classroom activities, and moved about in a frantic pace, showing a very short attention span and a marked inability to sustain work for even a few minutes. At home she was impossible to manage, frequently taking toys from her siblings, exclaiming that no one liked her, defacing property (she painted the hallway wallpaper) and sometimes withdrawing to her room. Mary was adopted at the age of three years and removed from a foster home because of physical abuse. Her course of directed treatment consisted of programs in body ego–tempo regulation, focal attention, and aspects of field articulation. When she showed stage-adequate cognitive control functioning and the capacity to participate efficiently in directed fantasy, a phase of nondirected therapy was conducted for a year, two sessions per week.

Metaphor: I am Vulnerable and Need Protection. When the treatment took on a nondirected format, Mary spent a few sessions in diffuse aggressive activity, toppling dolls and other material off the shelves and shooting darts at the ceiling, walls, windows, and sometimes at the therapist, shouting repeatedly, "I shoot you in the eye—you're dead—you can't see." Each time the therapist fell to the floor melodramatically and held his hands over his eyes pleading (e.g., "I can't see! You have to help me see so I can help you.").

Gradually Mary stopped her diffuse aggressive activity and busied herself collecting a wide variety of objects, (e.g., pieces of paper, wooden blocks, paper clips, sticks) which she called "money," eventually filling a box. The therapist offered papers from his desk and credit cards from his wallet. Mary accepted these, and the two spent several sessions spreading the "money" on the floor carefully arranging and counting it. Mary elaborated the meaning of this activity. She stuffed the material in her shirt, behind her belt, or in her pockets pretending that with "all the money in the world I get anything—no one can hurt me." The therapist helped Mary "pad herself" with money (e.g., in her shoes, socks, taped to her shirt), enacting that the more money she has the safer she would be.

Metaphor: Balla the Good Force Battles Bocco the Evil Force. Mary shifted the activity when she handed the therapist a mask announcing, "You're Bocco the bad guy" and she "Balla the good guy." She prescribed that the two engage in fighting using bottacas (long pillow-like clubs with handle grips). During numerous battles, Mary elaborated that Bocco's sword was better (it had a "special green point") and he was very mean and wanted to "hurt her." On occasion Mary wore the mask and played the role of Bocco. When Mary sometimes bordered on regressing, flailing wildly and screaming, "Die Bocco!" the therapist introduced tempo regulation tasks used during the structured CCT program and directed, for example, that Bocco and Balla fight on a sidewalk (tape was placed on the floor to form a path) and that sometimes they fought in slow motion "sunk in water," and sometimes fast.

Metaphor: Balla Obtains Special Protection to Battle Bocco. As the battles ensued, with Mary emphasizing Bocco's strength and the power of his magic "point," the therapist, when assigned the role of Balla began to arm himself with "special things to make me extra strong against the magic point." Mary assimilated this intervention and for several weeks, collected various objects and located them on her person (e.g., she placed several dart guns, plastic darts, and an assortment of Tinker Toys® in a belt she borrowed from the therapist; she wore a necklace of large wooden beads around her neck, and she stuffed rods and cutouts, used previously in structured tasks, in her pockets). At times, when loaded down with this material, Mary spontaneously climbed on the table, raised her arms and exclaimed, "I'm Balla the Strongest. Wow, no one can hurt me now." The therapist echoed the exclamation and enacted awe over Balla's strength. During this phase Bocco did not appear nor were battles fought.

Metaphor: Bocco Is Crazy and Tortures Balla. Handing the mask to the therapist, Mary reintroduced Bocco, prescribing a series of activities over a number of weeks in which Bocco enacted increasingly more sadism. For example, "crazy" Bocco tied Balla and put him in a dark corner or under the table. While Balla was tied Bocco poked at him and yelled at him. When Mary assumed Bocco's role, she tied up the therapist as Balla, had him lie on the floor, and whipped him with a belt or rope. Sometimes Mary crossed the boundary between play acting and acting on impulse, showing little or no evidence of pretending. The therapist yelled, "You're hurting me," and demonstrated how someone can "play" whipping another person. When the therapist played Bocco, he emphasized pretending to whip, vigorously waving his arms, but insuring that the belt only touched Mary.

Metaphor: An Ego Ideal, Mr. T Comes to Balla's Aid, Overpowers, and Reforms Bocco. When playing the role of Balla being tortured, the therapist enacted, "Somebody help! I need somebody who can really get Bocco!" When playing the role of Bocco torturing, the therapist enacted, "Is somebody coming to save you? I hope not!"

Mary introduced "Mr. T" (a favorite television character of hers) and assumed the role. Mr. T, armed with toy pistols, sticks, rods, cutouts, and paper "badges" taped to his shirt, repeatedly broke into the room as the therapist "whipped" an imaginary figure, overpowered the therapist, and marched him off to jail (under the table). Mr. T sometimes arrived with his "gang," a group of highly disciplined fighters, armed with special weapons, and TV cameras so that "they know what's going on that's bad and they can go everywhere to stop bad people." After Bocco is repeatedly defeated and jailed, Mr. T decides to kill him "once and for all since you won't stop whipping." Bocco, who had already expressed awe of Mr. T and his squad, pleaded for a chance to join the squad and prove his worth. Mr. T agrees, civilizes and trains Bocco, and assigns him a place in the squad, now with the name "Sala" (a new identity).

Metaphor: Mimi, a Doll, Is Punished and Rescued. Mary shifted the motif to a girl doll, "Mimi," (a significant change since until now all characters were males) who is spanked by human dolls, then beaten, whipped, and sometimes placed in a shoe box, which Mary carefully and elaborately tied with a long string. Sometimes while lying tied in bed Mimi startled upon hearing footsteps, "The witch is coming!" Mary elaborated an imaginary "green witch" who was meanest of all and kept Mimi captive. Another doll (a hand puppet of an elderly male figure) repeatedly came to Mimi's rescue and took her away by car, boat, or airplane.

Metaphor: I Enjoy Competitive Games and Academics and Recall Traumatic Experiences. Mary phased out Mimi and initiated formboard games (e.g., "Candyland," "Chutes and Ladders,") engaging the therapist with an intense competitive spirit. She also "played office," arranging a table with paper, pencils, and talking to fictitious persons who telephoned. During this play she frequently referred to her adopted mother who was an executive in a business firm. She brought school books to the sessions, proudly showing the therapist her newly acquired reading skill. Gradually she initiated comments about her current situations and past experiences (e.g., "Do you know my parents aren't my real parents?" "When I was a baby I used to live in a small place, not like the big house I live in now." "The lady before was a witch." "The small place had green wallpaper everywhere." "All these guys kept coming to the house." "My mother is tall; my first mother was fat."). She also discussed events occurring at home and school. At these times details were examined and discussed and she gained some awareness that her chronic view of "no one likes me" was not always supported, that the view is correct in terms of her foster mother and friends, and that Mary sometimes behaved in ways that should result in parents, siblings, teachers, and peers not liking her.

Critique. Aided by cognitive tools developed previously, Mary was able, during a phase of nondirected therapy, to sustain effort in pretending and symbolic functioning so as to define, express, and eventually resolve particular pathological issues which had been interfering with her functioning and development. These issues were organized in a series of metaphors, which represented the past and prescribed behaviors initially coded in the action mode. Mythical symbolic characters and events were enacted by her total body and that of the therapist's and by using all available space in the room. The same issues were then organized in a metaphor that represented and prescribed behaviors coded in the fantasy mode as humanlike symbolic characters were enacted by dolls and materials within the microspace of a tabletop. As interventions by the therapist were assimilated into these action and fantasy metaphors, pathological issues were restructured and resolved in the unconscious, resulting in prescriptions of more sublimated behavior. At the same time, the issues also surfaced into consciousness as memories, attitudes, and beliefs, coded and expressed in the language mode and became available for reflection and discussion.

The first metaphor Mary constructed defined her body/self as vulnerable and in need of protection. The therapist communicated his understanding and availability in the action mode by providing credit cards and papers from his desk. Having guaranteed the therapist's availability, Mary then expressed her conflicts in terms of a good force (her wish for competence and growth) battling a bad force attempting to hurt it (representations of early caretakers and negotiations).

When the good force acquired special protection and strength to continue the battle, Mary organized her key pathological metaphor: A bad force, Bocco, is a sadistic monster with a special green pointed sword who tortures the good force (Balla). Mary usually enacted this issue symbolically though sometimes in terms that were concrete and nearly autobiographical. This metaphor clearly represented abuse she had experienced during her first three years. According to the adoption agency, Mary, on occasion, had been shut up in a closet, tied, and beaten, sometimes by her foster mother (who incidently made heavy use of the color green, e.g., her apartment was wallpapered in green) and sometimes by one of her boyfriends.

Mary's key pathological metaphor represented the earliest developmental issues defining her body/self as vulnerable and despised and others as untrustworthy and attackers, or as indiscriminant targets of her aggression, which was coded in oral (biting) and anal (opposition) terms. This metaphor construed present stimulation, even the classroom, as potentially dangerous and prescribed that Mary constantly flee or aggress, resulting in behaviors characteristic of her at home and school.

To help Mary restructure this metaphor, the therapist intervened always in the child's metaphoric mode of action. He assisted the good force in obtaining special resources (guns, darts, sticks), elaborating the qualities and intentions of the good and evil forces, and then directed that an ally, feared by the bad force because of its power to invoke standards, could rescue the good force from its plight. Mary assimilated these interventions and introduced ego ideals in the metaphor of Mr. T and his squad who overpowered and eventually reformed the bad force. As Sala, the new identity of the bad force, the pathological representations and prescriptions were now civilized and responded to rules (superego).

Having assimilated these interventions, restructuring the action metaphor, Mary repeated the same issues now in the fantasy mode, assisted by microactions. Using only the surface of the table, she manipulated dolls, strings, and boxes. While the metaphor again represented and pre-scribed, for example, imminent danger and abuse by others, it now em-phasized escape to freedom. Rather than mythical creatures, the characters were identified as humans. Even the green witch, who was Bocco reincar-nated, was more human-like. This transformation indicated that the issues were being cast in more conventional symbols and steadily surfacing to consciousness.

Freed from the pathological metaphor, Mary's representations of self/other spiraled to the phallic stage defining her body/self as less vulnerable and more adequate and others as competitors. Her aggression was now coded in terms of competitiveness and pride in academic achievement, transformed from biting and pushing to intensity in winning and suc-ceeding. Further, the foundation for her sexual identity was put into place. In play, she identified and imitated her adopted mother as a successful executive. Significantly, at the same time she began using self-reflection and self-report, spontaneously discussing present and past reality events that related to her difficulties.

How did the restructuring of metaphors in the treatment situation relate to Mary's behavior at school and home? Teachers reported that Mary's punching and biting dropped out, she cultivated a few friends, and en-gaged her school work with intense competitiveness, so much so that teachers hoped the intensity would eventually attenuate. Parents reported she stopped defacing property, was less oppositional with them and sib-lings, and no longer withdrew in angry silence. Most importantly for mother, on occasion Mary spontaneously hopped on her lap, hugged her, and playfully commented, ''It's my turn,''—referring to her infant step-sibling who was born about the time Mary entered a nondirected phase of treatment.

These observations suggest the value of the proposed concept of meta-phor as a guide in nondirected treatment. Ideally, self-statements, beliefs, opinions, forming metaphors about oneself, others, and experiences, should have deep and widespread roots within the fantasy mode where the same issues are cast in images, and also within the developmentally earlier mode of actions and gestures. Without these roots, integrating the three modes, self-statements and beliefs, float detached as intellectualiza-tions having little power to steer behavior, fantasies are deprived of the benefits of rehearsal and fulfillment in reality experiences, and actions are robot-like lacking the breadth, psychological economy, and comprehen-sion provided by language and fantasy.

Chapter 11
Related Research and Critique

As discussed in the first chapter, CCT is designed and conducted in terms of a developmental-interactional model which places cognition *within* personality. Briefly, a person experiences and "controls" a continuous flow of changing stimulation, occurring in both internal and external environments, with a set of cognitive mechanisms, which shift flexibly in the autonomy they maintain between reality and fantasy, mediating and coordinating these two sources of information.

Of the concepts from this model that are especially relevant to the methods and rationale of CCT, three are pivotal: (a) the notion that cognitive functioning consists of a set of processes that characterize the manner in which all individuals deal with information from early childhood through adolescence and that these "cognitive controls" form the substructure of other cognitive activities involved in academics and intelligence; (b) the relation between cognitive controls and learning; and (c) changes that occur in cognitive orientation and autonomy in response to changes in stimulation. Considerable research with these and other concepts is detailed elsewhere (Santostefano, 1978; Santostefano & Rieder, 1984). The highlights presented here derive from these sources unless otherwise noted.

SUMMARY OF RESEARCH WITH THE CONCEPT OF COGNITIVE CONTROLS

Construct Validity of Cognitive Controls and Their Relationship with Intelligence and Sex

Seven independent factor analytic studies by the author and studies by others (e.g., Wertlieb, 1979) demonstrate that when various groups of children and adolescents (normals, outpatient and inpatient psychiatric populations, learning disabled, brain damaged, orphaned) are administered a wide range of tasks they manage them with a particular set of cognitive functions that fit the definitions of cognitive controls presented earlier: body ego–tempo regulation, focal attention, field articulation, leveling-sharpening, equivalence range. These results, along with those of studies which relate measures of cognitive controls to measures from other cognitive tests (e.g., Benton Visual Retention Test, Continuous Performance Test) provide considerable support for the validity of the construct of cognitive controls. Studies also demonstrate that cognitive control functioning underlies a child's academic skills and the manner in which a child deals with, for example, Piagetian tasks of conservation, while other studies show that cognitive control functioning is relatively independent of intelligence and sex. Boys and girls of high or low intelligence, for example, could make habitual use of narrow scanning or sharpening as cognitive strategies.

Developmental Changes and Reliability in Cognitive Control Functioning

When longitudinal assessments of cognitive controls were obtained, from children ages 4 to 11 years, and in cross-sectional studies of children through adolescence, maturational changes were observed as outlined in Chapter 2. For example, scanning (focal attention) is characteristically narrow and passive with young children and gradually becomes more broad and active with age. While the organization of cognitive controls change throughout development, individual differences in cognitive control functioning are stable over several years. For example, if a 5-year-old child is the most narrow scanner in a group of 5-year-olds, although that child's scanning becomes progressively more broad with age, when assessed at the age of 10 years, the same child is again the most narrow scanner in a group of 10-year-olds.

Cognitive Controls and Learning Disabilities

Studies demonstrate that dysfunctional cognitive controls underlie learning disabilities and poor classroom performance as judged independently by teachers. For example, children who characteristically "level" rather than sharpen information are rated as showing poor knowledge of classroom routine, forgetting assignments, and needing frequent reminders. As another example, children low in field articulation are rated as distractible and requiring extra effort on the part of the teacher to focus their attention on relevant projects.

Two studies explored whether cognitive control functioning predicts learning disabilities. In both studies the entire kindergarten population attending a public school was evaluated (about 180 children in each group). On the basis of dysfunctions in cognitive controls (determined by a discriminant function analysis), predictions were made as to the probability that a child would show difficulty in learning by the third and fourth grade. Several years later interviews were conducted with teachers who had no knowledge of a child's kindergarten test performance. A high relationship was observed between predictions based on cognitive control assessments obtained in kindergarten and academic failure and learning disabilities observed in the third and fourth grades.

Cognitive Control Functioning and the Environment

A study by Garrity (1972) illustrates how the structuring of cognitive controls is influenced by, and accommodates to, the environment's pace and complexity of stimulation. Assessing black and white children from various socioeconomic status (SES) levels, Garrity correlated cognitive control measures developed by the author with assessments of social deprivation. Following Deutsch's Social Deprivation Index Scale, children and parents were interviewed to obtain information about (a) physical make-up and organization of the home, (b) number of children under 18 in the home, (c) extent of dinner conversation, (d) cultural experiences the child anticipated for the coming weekend, and (e) parent's educational aspirations for the child. Children who constructed global, fluid images of information and compared these inefficiently with present perceptions (the leveling-sharpening control) were associated significantly with disorganized homes and a low degree of social stimulation.

Changes in Cognitive Control Orientation with Changes in Stimulation

Several studies explored the concept that cognitive controls shift the degree of autonomy maintained from external and internal stimuli in order to maintain affects and the complexity of information at a level that serves successful adaptation. Among the hypotheses explored were (a) if the situation permits the individual to engage information actively, the cognitive orientation maintained emphasizes perceiving and working on external stimuli; (b) if the situation restricts the individual's participation, the orientation maintained emphasizes perceiving and working on fantasies which construe the situation; (c) if the environment is unusual given the individual's history, cognitive orientation seeks and/or avoids information so that emotions prescribed by fantasies construing the event do not interfere with successful adaptation; and (d) a cognitive orientation is judged successful on two interrelated counts: whether requirements of stimuli and fantasy are coordinated to foster mastery and learning, and whether the type and intensity of affect prescribed serve rather than restrict adaptation.

Two studies evaluated individuals when dealing with two molar situations, one usual and the other unusual, the latter presumably arousing fantasies and affects. Guthrie (1967; see also Santostefano, 1978) measured the leveling-sharpening control of novice parachutists in their homes and again at an airport before executing a parachute jump. The latter situation was construed by all subjects as jeopardizing survival. Also, the situation clearly required that subjects actively engage and use available external information. When compared with parachutists not scheduled to jump, experimentals showed a significant progressive shift (from home measures) toward increased sharpening when at the airport. The finding was interpreted as a change in cognitive orientation which balanced fantasies of annihilation (accompanied by fear/anxiety) so as to limit the extent to which they interfered with perceiving external stimuli, an orientation necessary for executing a successful jump.

The second study (Santostefano, 1978; Shapiro, 1972) assessed the leveling-sharpening mechanism and several personality/affective variables in an unusual situation that limited active participation. Boys 8–11 years old were assessed in their homes, again in a hospital hours before undergoing surgery for hernia repair, and again at home 30 days after discharge. The comparison groups were children evaluated at a dentist's office during their first visit for dental repair, or only at home, at three comparable points in time. Among the personality dimensions measured were: castration anxiety, fantasied aggression, fantasies representing body barriers and penetration, and behavioral signs of emotional upset. The surgical group shifted most toward leveling information when in the hospital environment. Moreover, children who shifted most toward leveling produced *fewer* images while in the hospital that represented body barriers (i.e., the inner world became more accessible), and they produced *more* fantasies which depicted castration anxiety and aggression in concrete literal terms. They were also rated by their mothers as adjusting best after surgery.

Viewed according to the model outlined in Chapter 2, these results suggested that the hospital group construed hernia surgery in terms of mutilation fantasies, and the hospital setting limited the extent to which these children could engage external information. Accordingly, when in the hospital the cognitive orientation assumed by the leveling-sharpening mechanism avoided the requirements of external stimuli, turned inward, and addressed fantasized castration and aggression, a shift associated with more adaptive, post-operative adjustment.

Other studies used molecular environments defined as test stimuli. The fantasies activated by these stimuli were inferred from differences observed between populations which shared some key variable relative to the stimuli.

In the parachute study described above, one test of a neutral "house" scene was always administered immediately after either a test depicting a parachutist in free fall (the chute was not yet deployed) or a parachutist in slow descent (the chute was fully deployed). A significant test sequence effect was observed. Individuals administered the House Test after the Free Fall Test, sharpened more with the House Test than did individuals administered the House Test after the Slow Descent Test. Given results discussed earlier, the following interpretation is possible. The two parachute scenes represented different "environments," activating different fantasies and associated affects. The requirements of a free fall scene for novice parachutists at an airport represented a level of stress and danger which prescribed a shift to an outer orientation and accurate perceptions of external stimuli (i.e., the same shift observed in response to the molar environment of the airport).

Santostefano and Rieder (1984) assigned psychiatrically hospitalized children to high or low aggression groups on the basis of their performance with an action test of aggression. The two groups were compared with two tests of the leveling-sharpening control: a house scene representing nonaggressive test stimuli and a scene of two cowboys in a fist fight, a stimulus which usually arouses fantasies of violence. High aggression children were significantly more efficient in maintaining images of aggressive stimuli in memory and comparing them with present perceptions (sharpened), while low aggression children leveled aggression stimuli and sharpened nonaggressive stimuli. This difference was interpreted in terms of the hypothesis that the requirements of aggressive fantasies of high aggression children (which included low anxiety about aggression) were concordant with those of aggressive stimuli, prescribing an orientation that called for the ready assimilation of aggressive test stimuli. Conversely, the requirements of aggressive fantasies of low aggression children (which included high anxiety and conflict with aggression) were discordant with those of aggressive test stimuli, prescribing an orientation that avoided (leveled) their attributes.

With another study, hospitalized emotionally disturbed children, also designated as high or low in aggression, were administered multiple tests of focal attention (large sheets on which were printed, in random arrays, drawings of one type of stimulus: geometric shapes; neutral objects [e.g., chair]; oral objects [e.g., bottle of milk]; aggressive objects [e.g., pistol]).

With each form the child scanned and marked, as quickly as possible, for 30 seconds, particular stimuli (e.g., circles and crosses; chairs and shoes). The location and sequence of markings were recorded. The scanning of high aggressive children was most narrow when surveying aggressive stimuli. If related to the previous study, this finding suggests that although aggressive children sharpen aggressive test stimuli (hold images stable in memory and compare these efficiently with perceptions of present aggressive stimuli), at the same time when scanning, they tend to center on a few aggressive stimuli (myoptic perception).

STUDIES OF CCT

The author and colleagues have examined the functioning and test findings of children and adults treated with the CCT method and, whenever possible, obtained follow-up data. We have been especially interested in persons who were first treated only with a nondirected, verbal/play format without appreciable results, and then treated along the lines of CCT. A discussion of these individual cases is reserved for a future communication. Several formal studies of CCT have been conducted involving control groups and are summarized below. Details are available in a previous publication (Santostefano, 1978) or as otherwise noted. Sketches of CCT with an autistic child and a blind child are also provided to illustrate the method with severely impaired children.

CCT with Retarded Children: I

This study evaluated whether a short-term course of CCT in focal attention and field articulation would advance the efficiency with which retarded children scanned and articulated relevant/irrelevant information and also result in a greater degree of cognitive plasticity (i.e., a greater capacity to assimilate guidance and stimulation provided by others). The treatment group consisted of 31 children attending a day care program (17 boys, 14 girls; age range, 3.5–7.8 yrs.; mean age, 5.6 yrs., mean I.Q., 54). A comparison group consisted of 32 children selected from other day care centers participating in the same state-wide program (17 boys, 15 girls; mean I.Q., 51; mean age, 5.2 yrs.). Mothers conducted the treatment program at home with their respective child for a period of 16 weeks, five sessions per week, each 30–60 minutes. Mothers were provided a special manual of instructions, materials, and weekly supervision.

Pre- and post-treatment evaluations consisted of five tests, which could be administered by pantomime, required only nonverbal responses, and used only white, black, and grey material: (a) Maze Trail test, (b) Picture

Discrimination and Matching test, (c) Buttons test (segregating a pile of buttons into designated containers), (d) Object Sort test (grouping wooden cutouts according to commonalities, and (e) Arm Movement Imitation test (imitating movements performed by the examiner). To assess cognitive plasticity (whether the child shifted from one level of cognitive efficiency to a higher one after being provided coaching), the examiner physically guided the child through a successful response whenever the child's first response fell below a predetermined level. When the item was readministered, if coaching resulted in improved performance, a "gain score" of 1 was assigned, if no improvement was observed the score was 0.

At pretest the groups did not differ in I.Q., age, or in their performance with each of the tests. At posttesting, the treatment group showed performance that was statistically better with all tests except the Arm Movement Imitation test. In terms of cognitive plasticity, at pretest the groups showed no difference in their need for, or capacity to assimilate, coaching provided by the examiner. Each group required coaching for an average number of nine test items, and each improved their test performance with about 45% of the items for which coaching was received. In posttesting, the CCT group showed significantly less need for coaching and a greater capacity to assimilate demonstration. The CCT group required coaching for an average of five test items versus nine test items by the comparison group, and improved in test performance 63% of the time as a result of coaching versus 45% by the comparison group.

Although treatment was conducted by nonprofessionals, the results suggested CCT in focal attention and field articulation, with retardates, generalized to more efficient perceptual-cognitive functioning and promoted a greater capacity to assimilate stimulation provided by others.

CCT with Retarded Children: II

This study compared the effects of CCT in body ego–tempo regulation with CCT in focal attention–field articulation. We explained to parents of retarded children attending the same day care program, that CCT in focal attention, when conducted at home, appeared to promote cognitive growth, that we had every reason to believe CCT in body ego also promoted cognitive growth, and that learning whether these programs promoted cognitive growth in different areas would help professionals better prescribe CCT for a child. We also explained that if a mother elected the program, mother-child pairs would be randomly assigned to a treatment group. Of the 33 mothers who enlisted, 11 were assigned to one of three treatment groups. However at some point along the way, 11 mothers elected to drop out finding the requirement of conducting daily sessions too demanding. The groups for which complete data were available are as follows: (a) CCT in focal attention (16 weeks): four boys and four girls, age range 3.6–8.2 years; mean age 5.6 years; mean I.Q. 51; (b) CCT in body ego (16 weeks): five boys, three girls; age range 4.3–6.7 years; mean age 5.6 years; mean I.Q. 52; (c) CCT in body ego (8 weeks) followed by CCT in focal attention (8 weeks): five boys, one girl; age range 4.3–8.0 years; mean 5.6 years; mean I.Q. 47.

The parents were given special manuals of instruction, materials, and weekly supervision. The children were administered a series of tests before and after therapy including several used in the previous study and others. The tests, in the sequence listed, were conceptualized as requiring cognitive activity representing body experiences (proximal) to activity representing conceptual experiences (distal): (a) Maze-Trail test; (same as above), (b) Object Discrimination and Matching test (the child matched each of 24, three-dimensional cutouts with 8 standards displayed), (c) Buttons test (same as above), (d) Picture Discrimination and Matching test (same as above), (e) Circles and Cross test (the child scanned various geometric shapes printed on a sheet of paper and marked only circles and crosses), (f) Object Sort test (same as above). Again the items were readministered with coaching whenever indicated and a gain score computed.

The results were evaluated with the Mann-Whitney U-test. At pretest the three groups did not differ in age, I.Q., and test performance. To evaluate the effects of therapy, difference scores were computed for each child, with each test, between pre- and post-therapy measures. An examination of these difference scores suggested that CCT in body ego versus focal attention–field articulation had different effects. Body ego therapy improved performance most with the Maze test. Therapy in body ego followed by focal attention (Group 3) resulted in the most improvement in discriminating and matching three-dimensional objects (with body ego therapy showing a greater influence than focal attention). Focal attention therapy alone had an increasingly greater effect in improving a child's discriminating and matching pictures of familiar objects, scanning and marking geometric shapes mixed among others, and grouping objects according to common attributes. In terms of cognitive plasticity, the three groups did not differ at the start of treatment. After treatment, the group receiving body ego CCT followed by focal attention CCT (Group 3) showed the greatest gain in the capacity to assimilate stimulation provided by coaching.

Although the observations were obtained from retarded children and the therapy provided by nonprofessionals, the results suggest that CCT programs have different effects on cognitive processes and skills, encouraging further study of this issue.

Group CCT with Kindergarteners in Public School

Gunnoe (1975; see also Santostefano, 1978) and the author collaborated in a study comparing CCT and academic skill tutoring. "Freshman" kindergarteners were administered a battery of tests (cognitive and academic skills). On the basis of these results and teacher observations during the first weeks of school, children were selected who showed significant cognitive dysfunctions and who appeared to be at risk negotiating classroom demands. The parents of these children were contacted and asked to volunteer having their child randomly assigned to either a group CCT program or an academic tutoring program that would be conducted in the school, one hour, four times per week, by the same two teachers. We explained that we believed both group programs, supplementing the child's regular kindergarten program, should be beneficial and that we were interested in learning more about the relative effectiveness of each. Three groups were formed: (a) CCT: 9 boys, 2 girls, mean I.Q. 119; (b) Tutoring: 8 boys, 2 girls, mean I.Q. 116; (c) no treatment: 9 boys, 13 girls, mean I.Q. 123. The treatment programs were conducted for a period of 15 weeks. Before and after treatment, each child was administered a battery of cognitive control tests and the California Test of Mental Maturity (CTMM). Each child was also reevaluated with the same procedures one year later.

At pretest, the two treatment groups did not differ from each other in test performance, but each group showed significant lags in cognitive functioning and academic skills when compared with the no-treatment groups, as might be expected since the children were selected for treatment because of their dysfunctions.

To evaluate the effects of treatment, the test scores were combined into a composite score and examined by means of a multivariate analysis of covariance with pre-therapy scores serving as baselines. The pretest difference between the two treatment groups and the comparison group were no longer observed, indicating that both treatment groups "caught up" to the controls in terms of cognitive functioning and academic skills. However, CCT and tutoring did not have differential effects on the composite test score. Further, an analysis of scores obtained one year later produced the same results. Both groups sustained the gains achieved, showing no difference when compared to the control group. And again the two treatment groups did not differ from each other.

However, when the rate of change observed with individual test scores was examined by means of quadratic trend analysis, noteworthy differences were observed between the CCT and tutoring groups. Quadratic analyses examined the rate of change from times one to two and compared this rate with change observed from times two to three, providing an opportunity to explore whether the rate of change was influenced differently by each treatment approach.

While the treatment groups showed no difference at the start with a measure of fine motor delay, the CCT group improved sharply at time two and slightly more at time three. The tutoring group showed moderate improvement at time two and again at time three. The difference between rates of change was statistically significant. CCT was also associated with greater rates of change with two other cognitive measures: scanning information actively (focal attention) and withholding attention from irrelevant information (field articulation). In addition, the rate of change shown by the CCT group with the CTMM Verbal Concepts Test reached statistical significance. Though lagging significantly behind the tutoring group at pretreatment, with a test that measures drawing inferences from statements and understanding the meaning of words, the CCT group showed a greater rate of growth immediately after treatment, closing the gap between them. This gain sustained 1 year later.

In summary, although CCT and tutoring had about the same general effect on cognitive functioning and academic skills, CCT was associated more with a greater rate of change and growth. This study, and the previous one contrasting two CCT programs, emphasize the need to compare CCT with alternative treatment methods. Among the issues requiring attention in such studies are the skill and commitment of the therapists. In the study reported, although the same teachers conducted the CCT and tutoring programs, they had prior training in "tutoring" but no training in conducting group CCT, except for weekly supervision.

CCT with Children Hospitalized in a Psychiatric Facility

Donahue, Rokous, and Santostefano (1984 a) explored the effectiveness of CCT with children hospitalized in a psychiatric facility because of severe personality disorders and cognitive dysfunctions. The children were among about 200 admissions into a 40-bed facility, over a four year period, and who had been administered psychological tests on admission and at discharge after a course of CCT (experimental group) or on admission and at discharge, but who had not received a course of CCT (control group). Except for CCT, the hospital program of each child in each group was essentially the same: they attended a psychoeducation program on hospital grounds (9:00 a.m. to 2:30 p.m., 5 days a week), participated in after-school recreational activities, and received the same milieu program.

CCT consisted of 2 to 4 one-hour weekly sessions conducted by psychology interns, postdoctoral fellows, and psychiatric residents with weekly supervision provided by staff psychologists. Although the therapists varied, and their skill with CCT was relatively underdeveloped, a comparison of the groups provided an opportunity to evaluate the method. Children were recommended for CCT whenever testing on admission showed severe cognitive control dysfunctions, and those most impaired were assigned whenever a therapist was available.

The CCT group consisted of 12 boys and 6 girls (age range: 6.2–15.0 years) and the control group, 9 boys and 7 girls (age range: 8.0–15.0 years). The two groups did not differ statistically in mean age at pretesting (CCT mean was 12.0 years; control mean was 12.6 years), in total days of hospitalization (CCT mean was 428 days; control mean was 416 days), and in average family income (CCT mean was $26,000; control mean was $19,500). Four additional months separated pre- and posttesting of the two groups (CCT mean was 14.5 months; control mean was 10.0 months). The CCT group received an average of 102 treatment sessions over an average period of 10 months.

At pretest the children were administered cognitive control tests (Santostefano, 1978) assessing scanning, field articulation, leveling-sharpening, and conceptualizing. In addition, the admitting psychiatrist routinely rated the severity of a child's presenting symptoms from severe to moderate following guidelines provided by the Group for Advancement of Psychiatry. At posttest the same procedures were readministered and again a staff psychiatrist routinely rated severity of symptoms, without knowledge of a child's test performance or necessarily that the child participated in a course of CCT.

To evaluate the effects of CCT, 19 cognitive test scores were compared with the Mann-Whitney U test. At pretest the control group showed more advanced cognitive functioning on all scores, 8 reaching statistical significance, an expected result since children were assigned to CCT because they showed major lags in cognitive functioning. However, at posttest all of the differences were less in magnitude, and only one reached statistical significance, indicating the CCT group "caught up" with the control group.

In addition, at posttest, the CCT group showed *more efficient* equivalence range functioning, which reached statistical significance in spite of the fact that at pretest the control group showed more efficiency. The measure in question derives from the Object Sort test, which assesses conceptual thinking. In a free sort format, the child places 46 familiar objects into groups and explains how the objects located in each group belong together. The Mean Breadth score produced by this test takes into account three aspects of the performance: (a) the average number of objects the child locates within each realistic group, (b) the average level of abstraction the child imposes on all groups when explaining how the items belong together, and (c) the total number of realistic groups the child constructs. When these values are set in a ratio, they reflect the category width or breadth the child tends to impose on information when free to conceptualize in his/her preferred way. Although lagging initially in category width, at posttesting the CCT group showed an average category width that was significantly broader and more abstract than that of the control group.

Symptom ratings by a psychiatrist provided another source of data about the possible effects of CCT. The CCT group was rated as showing less severe symptoms at discharge, a difference which approached statistical significance ($p = .10$).

These findings suggest that a course of CCT with severely disturbed, hospitalized children was associated with overall cognitive growth, growth in conceptual thinking in particular, and with a decrease in severity of symptoms. The interpretation seems tenable since both groups represented severe psychological illnesses, received the same hospital care, with the exception of CCT, and since cognitive lags revealed at pretesting by the CCT group were diminished at posttesting and no longer statistically different. The one possible contaminating factor concerns the difference in the duration of time separating pre- and posttesting. It could be argued that the gains made by the CCT group were a function of the four additional months of hospitalization they received. But, this possibility should be considered in terms of the more severe impairments the CCT group showed at the start. It seems unlikely that the few additional months separating the evaluations alone resulted in the cognitive growth which took place, especially in conceptual thinking, or in the reduction of symptom severity.

CCT with Outpatient Children

Donahue, Rokous & Santostefano (1984 b) also explored the effect of CCT with children treated in a community outpatient facility because of learning disabilities and adjustment problems. The group consisted of 26 children (16 boys, 10 girls) for whom cognitive control test scores were available before and after a course of CCT. Their ages ranged from 5 to 17 years, with a mean age of 11.6 years. As a group they received an average of 78 sessions (conducted one or two times per week) over an average period of 14 months. Because a comparison group was not available, and the age range of the groups spanned kindergarten to high school, we decided to use the average age of the group (11 years) as the index of comparison. We reasoned that a comparison of the group's mean score on each test with the mean score associated with normal 11-year-olds would provide an opportunity to probe the effectiveness of CCT. The tests administered before and after treatment assessed scanning, articulating relevant and irrelevant information, comparing images of past information with present perceptions, and categorizing and conceptualizing information. Before treatment, the group means of each of nine scores fell significantly below the means associated with 11-year-old typical learners (Santostefano, 1978). After treatment, eight of the nine scores were no longer significantly different from norms, suggesting that as a group these children and adolescents achieved noteworthy cognitive gains.

CCT with an Autistic Child

Mike's history showed severe atypical and retarded development and at one point he was evaluated for possible blindness because of his vacant stare. He participated in a day care program from the age of 5 to 6, when independent evaluations by a clinical psychologist and psychiatrist showed that he had not yet formed speech patterns (he wailed in a high-pitched voice) and gave no evidence he was aware of objects, persons, sounds, or events around him. His main activity consisted of running along the walls of a room, moving his hands ritualistically. It was decided to continue Mike's day care program and to provide him with two sessions per day of individual CCT in focal attention. The main question asked was whether CCT in focal attention would break through his autism and cognitive withdrawal.

Following the guidelines noted in Chapter 4 (see section on Special Considerations for Seriously Disturbed Children) and Chapter 6, the therapist began treatment by placing a single, white square in the center of a table and devoted her efforts to helping Mike stand in front of the table, reach out, grasp the cutout, and release it in a box. At the end of the second month, Mike was able to perform this response purposefully and without coaching. (Incidentally, at the same time it was noticed that he was creating more disturbance in classroom, behavior suggesting that he was beginning to perceive the environment.)

At this point the therapist presented a white square and a black square, directing Mike to remove the square that she touched, leaving the other one on the table. Over the next 5 months the displays gradually increased in complexity, eventually consisting of 25 cutouts, all white, three shapes, and randomly arrayed, and Mike removed, for example, all the squares, or circles, as designated by the therapist.

During these 7 months, Mike used various strategies to resist the demands of therapy and escape from the information of the "outside world" which persistently intruded upon his autistic withdrawal. For example, during the fourth month of treatment, he cried whenever he was seated at the table. Sometimes he placed his head on the therapist's shoulder and sobbed, or looked at her with a "pathetic" expression, seeming to make an appeal that therapy be abandoned. That he was attempting to stop therapy was clearly supported by the observation that as soon as he was told he could get up, the tears were gone and he quickly began running about the room jabbering. During these episodes of resistance the therapist hugged Mike, stroked the cutouts, but gently persisted. Later Mike teased the therapist, suggesting a higher form of resistance. For example, laughing mischievously, he removed incorrect cutouts after having shown he could identify the correct ones, or he removed a correct cutout but would not release it, shaking his wrist as if the form was glued to his hand. At the same time, Mike began to reciprocate purposely the therapist's smiling and laughing.

Observations made by day care staff suggested that Mike's growth in focal attention–field articulation, and in negotiating, generalized from the tasks to the environment. Staff noticed he seemed to be "looking at" children, teachers, and events in the classroom. Once when the therapist entered the classroom, a child spontaneously hugged her, while Mike obviously watched. After looking back and forth from the child to the therapist, he suddenly covered his eyes with his hands, apparently attempting to block out the incident because it was too painful for him. When he looked up again and found the child still hugging the therapist, his face puckered, tears fell, and he walked over, offering his cheek to the therapist for a kiss. During the sixth month of treatment, Mike got up from his cot during nap time, walked over to a shelf, surveyed the row of shoes several times, and picked out his pair.

Using Mike's observations during the previous year as a baseline, Mike's behavior during this seven month period clearly suggested that the CCT program promoted growth in focal attention and dissolved his autistic withdrawal to some degree. Treatment was terminated because circumstances beyond the control of the center required that Mike be relocated in a distant facility.

CCT with a Blind Child

One therapist (Kimball, 1969) used aspects of the field articulation program to treat a blind child. The child was asked to examine by touch each display of cutouts presented, and then to remove the cutouts designated by the therapist. The displays were systematically varied in terms of number of cutouts, sizes, and shapes, and the child was asked to remove the cutouts with increasing speed. After 6 months (twice a week), the therapist felt that treatment had generalized and transferred to other situations. For example, the child now showed that he could discriminate sizes and shapes of various everyday material, and he understood number concepts. His language had improved noticeably, although the degree of blind mannerisms did not change.

SELECTED WORK BY OTHERS
AND A CRITIQUE OF CCT

The revolution created in psychotherapy by advances in cognitive psychology (Mahoney, 1977) has resulted in numerous publications, some polarizing cognitive and psychodynamic therapies (e.g., Szasz, 1967), others constructively comparing them (e.g., Feather & Rhoades, 1972), and an increasing number searching for useful integrations (e.g., Marmor & Woods, 1980; Wachtel, 1977). Since space does not permit discussion of this vast literature, we conclude by examining CCT in terms of selected issues emphasized by reviewers (e.g., Arnkoff & Glass, 1982; Glass & Arnkoff, 1982; Kendall & Hollon, 1979; Mahoney, 1980; Mahoney & Arnkoff, 1978), providing the reader with guidelines to compare techniques and rationale proposed here with those of others.

Defining Cognition

Because different cognitive behaviors have been the focus in cognitive approaches to therapy (see Chapter 1), reviewers vigorously remind us to define cognition with conceptual consistency:

What aspects of cognition are involved—the development of attention, the encoding and construction of percepts, the retrieval and construction of memories, categorization, inference, problem-solving, language, or what? . . . the investigator must employ particular techniques designed to tap each of these aspects of the human cognitive system. Otherwise, "cognition" like the "motive" and "instinct" constructs that dismayed earlier generations of psychologists, becomes just another catchall label, frequently bandied about by those who keep up with new trends, but actually void of any specific meaning. (Kihlstrom & Nasby, 1981, p. 291)

In this spirit we recapitulate that CCT defines cognition, within personality functioning and development, as discrete, hierarchically ordered, mobile processes (cognitive controls) that range from physical to mental and from nonverbal to verbal behaviors which produce (copy) information. In addition, these processes are involved in symbolic functioning, mediating between external stimulation and fantasy/metaphor through the autonomy maintained from each source of stimulation. At one time cognition is autonomous from fantasy and oriented more toward prescriptions from reality, at another oriented more toward those of metaphor, and at another oriented toward some combination from each. The development of these cognitive processes, and of flexible cognitive autonomy, are defined as occurring during the first three years of life. The definition of cognition held by CCT, then, clearly emphasizes cognition as *process* which takes place in a context consisting of both reality and fantasy requirements.

This definition differs appreciably from those proposed by the better-known cognitive therapies. Rational emotive therapy (RET) (Ellis, 1970), self-instruction therapy (SI) (Meichenbaum, 1977), and Beck's cognitive therapy (BCT) (Beck, 1976) define cognition almost exclusively as verbal behaviors (e.g., beliefs, the statements a person makes to herself) and accordingly emphasize cognitive *content* rather than process (e.g., Arnkoff & Glass, 1982, p. 3). Moreover, while acknowledging the importance of fantasy life, these approaches do not systematically conceptualize the means by which cognition mediates between reality and fantasy or the developmental origins of beliefs and self-statements.

Defining Maladaptive Cognition: The Behavior to Be Restructured

It follows that CCT defines maladaptive cognition in two ways: as measureable, developmental lags or dysfunctions in cognitive control processes, and as a pervasive, rigid cognitive orientation or excessive, rapid shifts in orientation. Research findings (see above and Santostefano, 1978; 1984) illustrate that the presence of these two types of maladaptive cognition is associated with unsuccessful learning and psychopathology, and their absence with successful learning and adaptations to changing stressful stimulation.

A longitudinal study by others (Wolf & Gardner, 1979) conducted without any discernable interest in psychotherapy produced results that strongly support those of the author—the concept of rigid cognitive orientations and the rationale of CCT. Wolf and Gardner observed children, beginning at the age of 12 months, in free play and dealing with structured tasks, and concluded that between 12 and 24 months, children develop one of two "styles" of activity which they term "patterning" and "dramatizing." Patterners show a tendency to engage material in terms of external attributes and resist symbolizing (e.g., refusing to treat a toy block as if it were a cup). In contrast, dramatists take considerable liberties with external attributes of material and prefer symbolizing (e.g., using a toy block as a cup or even as a moving vehicle). These two styles of symbolic play are identical to the outer and inner cognitive orientations described by the author.

Wolf and Gardner also concluded that from 24 to 36 months a child gradually integrates aspects of the other style, resulting in a balance between patterning and dramatizing. Again, this conclusion converges with the rationale of CCT, that by the age of three years a normal child achieves flexible cognitive autonomy, at one moment transforming information in terms of highly personal symbols/metaphors, and at another engaging information as it is.

These investigators include observations in their report that related to cognitive pathology. They note that while most individuals acquire skill in both styles, " . . . traces of these contrasting modes can still be observed . . . for instance (in elementary school children) we find a significant minority who can still be characterized as strong patterners or strong dramatists. . . . It is possible that there exist individuals who remain throughout their lives capable of only one approach to material . . . " (pp. 134 and 137). These observations converge with the author's proposal that rigid outer or inner cognitive orientations contribute to cognitive/personality disorders, but the author takes the position that, rather than characterizing a minority, pathological cognitive orientations may be more pervasive and implicated in various psychological difficulties than heretofore realized.

Wolf and Gardner do not discuss factors that might relate to a child's failure to develop an integration of both styles (i.e., flexible cognitive autonomy) between 12 and 36 months. From reconstructed histories in clinical practice, the author has developed several speculations about experiential factors that could interfere with the emergence of flexible cognitive autonomy. For example, if a child's testing of aggression and physically experimenting with material is sharply limited, from 12 to 36 months, by caretakers (e.g., parents conflicted about their own aggression) or by environmental accidents (e.g., the need for a body cast), the child solidifies a rigid inner cognitive orientation, ignoring the attributes of external stimuli and prefering symbolizing which gradually develops into an elaborate fantasy life. If caretakers do not pretend, especially with humor, or if caretakers are excessive in requiring the child to respond to external stimuli in terms of order, cleanliness, and detail, the child internalizes these standards and develops a preference for an external orientation.

Another study of pretend behavior in the first years of life (Fein & Apsel, 1979) adds further support to the conclusion that by the age of 3 years normal children develop competence with a two-fold process—engaging material as it is and in highly symbolic ways. While Fein and Apsel refer to this development as an apparent paradox, the rationale of CCT views this two-fold capacity as the emergence of flexible cognitive autonomy, a tool that serves adaptation and learning throughout the life span.

In defining maladaptive cognition as specific dysfunctions in cognitive control processes and orientation, judged according to normative expectations, CCT differs from RET, SI, and BCT, which define maladaptive cognition as irrational beliefs or negative self talk. Moreover, these approaches predetermine which beliefs are irrational and which self-statements are negative, sometimes proposing a "correct list" of irrational beliefs without a theoretical or empirical basis (e.g., Arnkoff & Glass, 1982).

Fitting the Treatment Method to the Definition of Maladaptive Cognition

Guided by its definition of maladaptive cognition, CCT begins with a directed format to restructure dysfunctional cognitive control processes. A person is presented a series of graded tasks which require the malfunctioning process and around which patient and therapist negotiate. The tasks also initially call for nonverbal cognitive functioning in order to rehabilitate deeper cognitive structures that underlie verbalizing. At the same time, the tasks are administered in a sequence designed to rehabilitate the pathological cognitive orientation, either requiring or prohibiting the participation of symbolic functioning and then gradually requiring the reverse. The last step, involving directed fantasy, cultivates flexible cognitive autonomy from reality and fantasy stimulation, a skill achieved by the normal 3-year-old. In its nondirected format, CCT emphasizes restructuring pathological metaphors that contribute to maladaptions, linking conscious thoughts, affects, and daydreams to action, connecting fantasy to reality, and making unconscious structures available to consciousness.

In contrast, following their definition of maladaptive cognition, RET, SI, and BCT employ methods designed to replace irrational beliefs with rational ones and to modify the content of what a person says to himself. These techniques implicitly assume that the individual can perceive reality stimuli accurately, as well as represent them, and that the person knows when he is engaged in one or the other mode.

The Issue of Change—Can Regressive Behavior Be Adaptive?

Arnkoff and Glass (1982), in particular, stress that workers conceptualize change and failure to change, and raise the related question (as did Lazarus, 1980) whether only accurate perceptions of reality, or assumptions about life, are adaptive (i.e., the issue of regression in adaptation). With its emphasis on process, CCT's view of change in cognitive structures relies upon the writings of Rappaport (Gill, 1967), Holt (1976), and Piaget (1977). Detailed elsewhere (Santostefano, 1978, and Santostefano, 1985, Chapter 3), a person's actions (physical, perceptual, and conceptual) on stimuli feedback to the structure that gave rise to the action. A discrepancy between the action and the existing structure induces a state of disequilibrium, and the existing structure reorganizes to fit the stimulation, restoring equilibrium. This process of action, feedback, disequilibrium, assimilation, equilibrium, action, feedback, and so on, is a continuous one and results in progressive structuring and a hierarchy of more differentiated behavioral structures.

Accordingly, a cognitive control mechanism changes when its process actively engages and assimilates the stimulation of graded tasks, each task presenting stimulation slightly more complex than the last. Cognitive orientations change when the individual internalizes ideals/models which invite symbolizing to influence perception and when the intensity and type of affect prescribed by fantasies/metaphor construing the stimuli are fitted to the person's emotional/personality development and adaptive intention.

Why cognitive controls fail to change is discussed in Chapter 3. Briefly, pathological cognitive processes structured in the first three years of life to fit the pace and complexity of stimulation at that time, become rigidified and persist, serving primarily to avoid stress associated with the requirements of increasingly more complex external and/or internal information.

Further, CCT holds the view that both regressive cognitive changes (i.e., behaviors characteristic of earlier developmental stages), as well as progressive ones, serve successful adaptation. Studies cited earlier provide empirical support that both progression and regression in cognitive control processes serve successful adaptations to environmental changes (e.g., airport, hospital, test stimuli) and associated fantasies.

In contrast, other approaches to cognitive therapy cited earlier view cognitive change in terms of replacing beliefs and self-statements with others judged by the therapist to be less maladaptive. As Arnkoff and Glass point out, the method of replacing beliefs and thoughts fails to take into account the purpose and function served by a belief and presumes that an unrealistic belief is automatically "bad" when in a particular context and personality even a delusion may be adaptive.

The Use of Active Intervention to Produce Change

Employing directed tasks in therapy is the hallmark of all behavioral-cognitive therapies, but is still alien to psychodynamic therapy with its heritage in Freud's nondirected approach to treatment. In spite of Freud's own use of direction (e.g., giving the patient the task of focusing on the situation that gives rise to a symptom), early proposals by Ferenzi, who directed patients to engage in particular fantasies (see Santostefano, 1978), were sharply criticized by psychoanalysts. However, most recently, psychoanalytic therapists have articulated a clear rationale for the use of active intervention (e.g., Wachtel's [1977] integration of psychoanalytic and behavior therapy; Weiner's [1975] use of structured tasks, such as Wechsler items, during which the patient free associates).

CCT takes the position that some children, adolescents, and adults do not have the cognitive tools required to scan experiences freely, relate observations to early memories, and conceptualize, and that these tools are best forged by asking the patient to deal with carefully graded, directed tasks. In addition to active intervention, CCT shares the use of desensitization, self-observation, and modeling with other cognitive-behavioral approaches.

Transference and Resistance

For years, the writings of cognitive-behavioral therapists have been conspicuously devoid of concepts and techniques for managing resistance. However, a recent volume (Wachtel, 1982) makes clear that therapists from many persuasions now recognize the importance of this topic. CCT ascribes to the psychoanalytic position that to promote change a patient must relive maladaptive behaviors and affects in the office (not experience them hypothetically) and then successfully resolve the phenomena of transference/resistance. To accomplish this CCT proposes a set of techniques, based upon a model of negotiation, which differ from techniques traditionally used in psychodynamic therapy with individuals who are less cognitively impaired. While the child negotiates tasks and therapist, the therapist helps the child develop the capacity of self-observation and awareness of *how* he thinks and behaves, an aspect of CCT that converges with the increasing interest in metacognition.

Formal Assessments—Fitting Treatment to a Person's Unique Pathology

CCT is highly prescriptive in fitting a program to a child's unique cognitive pathology. Particular treatment tasks and sequences in method are prescribed for particular dysfunctional cognitive controls and cognitive orientations. Moreover, CCT prescribes whether the child's developmental stage requires the therapist to intervene primarily with action, or fantasy, or language metaphors, and cautions against premature use of verbal interventions.

Of the alternative approaches to cognitive therapy, the proposal by Kendall to treat impulsive, aggressive children (e.g., Kendall, 1981, 1984; Kendall & Hollon, 1979; Kendall & Wilcox, 1984) is most related to the issue of fitting treatment methods to the child's preferred mode of behaving. Kendall employs a series of tasks, similar to those of CCT, beginning with nonstressful, psychoeducation material (e.g., the child selects a geometric cutout that should come next in a sequence of cutouts), then shifts to representations of interpersonal situations (e.g., examining pictures of children, the child identifies emotions and offers explanations for these feelings), and finally involves the child and therapist alternating role-playing in hypothetical situations. However, in contrast to CCT, Kendall's approach emphasizes the self-instruction technique throughout as the main therapeutic intervention. For example, with a psychoeducational task, the child is trained to think aloud (e.g., "Let's see, what am I supposed to do? How can I figure out which design comes next?"). The question for future study is whether a severely impulsive, cognitively disabled child, of the type considered in this volume, is equipped to make use of self-talk, at the start, as a way of controlling his aggressive behavior and gathering information relevant to solving the task. CCT advocates that at the start the *nonverbal* impulsive, aggressive responses of the child are *integrated within the response required by the task*, then transformed into symbolic, fantasy behaviors, and only later verbally described, examined, and rehearsed in discussions with the therapist. (Similarities and differences between the techniques of CCT and those of other approaches are discussed in Santostefano, 1978, 1984.)

The Use of Directed Fantasy and Play

CCT appears to make more explicit and systematic use of directed symbolizing in its structured format, and of fantasy and pretend play in its unstructured format, than do other cognitive therapies employed with children (see Kendall & Hollon, 1979).

The technique of directed fantasy resembles the technique of guided affective imagery (GAI) (Leuner, Horn, & Klessmann, 1983) but also differs from it in several important ways. With GAI, intended for children "beyond play" but not ready for adult psychoanalysis, the child relaxes physically and remains immobile. The therapist describes a motif from a list typically used (e.g., you are climbing a mountain; you are entering a house to explore its contents). Guided by questions from the therapist, presented in measured steps from neutral to emotional, the child elaborates the fantasy, including characters, happenings, defensive maneuvers, and solutions. The clinical examples presented by these workers make clear that GAI requires the child to be able to sit still, symbolize, fantasize, and scan and articulate mental pictures. Moreover, the focus is exclusively on the content of the fantasy the child produces.

In contrast, with the directed fantasy technique of CCT, the child initially *enacts* the prescribed fantasy, and performs a particular cognitive process by engaging a task embedded within the fantasy. The therapist's interventions emphasize cultivating a fit between a symbol or fantasy and the material to which they refer and the capacity to shift flexibly between symbolizing information and dealing with information as it is. In the author's opinion, GAI, as presented, would suit inner-oriented children who are not cognitively impaired or handicapped by impulsivity.

In its nondirected phase, CCT proposes that pretend play follow a progression of behavioral transformations, from action to fantasy to language metaphors to restructured pathological metaphors. CCT also proposes that the therapist's interventions follow the same progression. (The concept of alternative coding systems that represent past experiences and prescribe present behavior is related to other proposals; see Santostefano, 1984; in press a, especially those of Horowitz, 1978, and Paivio, 1971). These technical proposals elaborate and modify the psychoanalytic conception that play offers a child temporary escape from reality and the opportunity to release tension and express unacceptable impulses. Therapeutic play as a progression of metaphoric modes is viewed as providing a child with an opportunity to *join* fantasy and reality (not to escape from reality), restructure the prescriptions of pathological metaphor, transform these prescriptions into more conventional terms, and establish roots among action, fantasy, and language behaviors, providing thoughts, words, and insights with power to steer behavior. The view of play presented here departs more from that of Piaget who, though proposing that play represents a transformation of reality, also proposes that play represents cognitive immaturity and enables the child to escape from the pressing demands of the adult world (Golomb, 1979). For CCT, pretend play with its use of symbolic functioning represents the height of cognitive maturity.

The Relation Between Cognition and Affect

The most common position on the relation between cognition and affect among prevailing cognitive therapies has been that cognition precedes and causes affects whether appropriate or inappropriate and therefore holds that cognition and affect are two independent but related systems. Detailed in Chapter 2 and elsewhere (Santostefano, in press a), CCT conceptualizes cognition and affect as inseparable. The child performs different cognitive actions on different types of information that vary in the degree to which they prescribe emotions. Affects are an integrated part of the way in which information is construed, a view held by contextualist-interactionist theories of cognition.

The method of CCT outlined in this volume represents one way in which psychodynamically-oriented psychotherapy and cognitive behavior therapy can be integrated to treat children. This integration is in keeping with promptings by other psychodynamic therapists (e.g., Freud, 1965;

Wachtel, 1977; Weiner, 1975) that technique be adopted to a person's level of ego development, responds to the prevailing use of verbal intervention by other cognitive therapies, and agrees with Meichenbaum (1977) that saying the right thing may not be enough.

As discussed throughout, the broad goal of CCT is to provide the child with cognitive controls that produce information efficiently, and then, with the benefit of this capacity, to develop the child's power and freedom either to deal with information as it is or to symbolize and transform it with personal metaphors—power and freedom achieved by the normal 3-year-old. If we consider Aristotle's view that mastery in metaphor is a sign of originality and genius (Billow, 1977) then in one sense, the goal of CCT is to enable the child to recover and rehabilitate the originality and genius of which he/she is capable. With the power of efficient cognitive controls and symbolic functioning, all children could be artists, continuously constructing and reforming representations of past victories and defeats with developmental battles and coordinating the prescriptions of these metaphors with opportunities and limitations of everyday environments, resulting in pleasure in learning and coping, and freedom from pathological pain.

References

Anthony, E. J. (1956). The significance of Jean Piaget for child psychiatry. *British Journal of Medical Psychology, 29,* 20–34.

Arieti, S. (1970). The role of cognition in the development of inner reality. In J. Hellmuth (Ed.), *Cognitive studies* (Vol. 1, pp. 91–110). New York: Brunner/Mazel.

Arnkoff, D. B., & Glass, C. R. (1982). Clinical cognitive constructs: Examination, evaluation, and elaboration. In P. C. Kendall (Ed.), *Advances in cognitive-behavioral research and therapy* (Vol. 1, pp. 1–34). New York: Academic Press.

Barten, S. S. (1979). Development of gesture. In N. R. Smith & M. B. Franklin (Eds.), *Symbolic functioning in childhood* (pp. 139–152). Hillsdale, NJ: Lawrence Erlbaum.

Beck, A. (1976). *Cognitive therapy and the emotional disorders.* New York: International Universities Press.

Bedrosian, R. C., & Beck, A. T. (1980). Principles of cognitive therapy. In M. J. Mahoney (Ed.), *Psychotherapy process: Current issues and future direction* (pp. 127–152). New York: Plenum Press.

Benjamin, J. D. (1961). The innate and experiential in development. In H. W. Brosin (Ed.), *Lectures in experimental psychiatry* (pp. 19–42). Pittsburgh: University of Pittsburgh Press.

Billow, R. M. (1977). Metaphor: A review of the psychological literature. *Psychological Bulletin, 84,* 81–92.

Bruner, J. S., & Klein, G. S. (1960). The functions of perception: New look retrospect. In B. Kaplan & S. Wapner (Eds.), *Perspectives in psychological theory* (pp. 61–77). New York: International Universities Press.

Bruner, J., & Postman, L. (1948). An approach to social perception. In W. Dennis (Ed.), *Current trends in social psychology* (pp. 71–118). Pittsburgh: University of Pittsburgh Press.

Cacioppo, J. T., & Petty, R. E. (1981). Social psychological procedures for cognitive response assessment: The thought listing technique. In T. V. Merluzzi, C. R. Glass, & M. Genest (Eds.), *Cognitive assessment* (pp. 309–342). New York: Guilford Press.

Craine, J. F. (1982). Principles of cognitive rehabilitation. In L. E. Trexler (Ed.), *Cognitive rehabilitation: Conceptualization and intervention* (pp. 83–98). New York: Plenum Press.

Decarie, T. G. (1965). *Intelligence and affectivity in early childhood.* New York: International Universities Press.

Dember, W. N. (1974). Motivation and the cognitive revolution. *American Psychologist, 29,* 161–168.

Donahue, P., Rokous, B., & Santostefano, S. (1984a). *Cognitive control therapy with children hospitalized in a psychiatric facility.* Unpublished manuscript.

Donahue, P., Rokous, B., & Santostefano, S. (1984b). *Cognitive control therapy with outpatient children and adolescents.* Unpublished manuscript.

Ellis, A. (1970). *The essence of rational psychotherapy: A comprehensive approach.* New York: Institute for Rational Living.

235

Emery, G., Hollon, S. D., & Bedrosian, R. C. (1981). *New directions in cognitive therapy*. New York: Guilford Press.

Erdelyi, M. H. (1974). A new look at the new look: Perceptual defense and vigilence. *Psychological Review, 81*, 1–25.

Feather, B. W., & Rhoads, J. M. (1972). Psychodynamic behavior therapy: I. Theoretical aspects. *Archives of General Psychiatry, 26*, 496–502.

Fein, G. G., & Apsel, N. (1979). Some preliminary observations on knowing and pretending. In N. R. Smith & M. B. Franklin (Eds.), *Symbolic functioning in childhood* (pp. 87–99). Hillsdale, NJ: Lawrence Erlbaum.

French, T. (1933). Interrelations between psychoanalysis and the experimental work of Pavlov. *Psychiatry, 12*, 1165–1203.

Freud, A. (1965). *Normality and pathology in childhood*. New York: International Universities Press.

Freud, S. (1958). Remembering, repeating, and working-through (Further recommendations on the technique of psychoanalysis: II. In *Standard edition of complete works* (Vol. 12). London: Hogarth. (Original work published 1914).

Gardner, R. W., Holzman, P. S., Klein, G. S., Linton, H. B., & Spence, D. P. (1959). Cognitive control: A study of individual consistencies in cognitive behavior. *Psychological Issues, 1* (4).

Garrity, C. (1972). *Academic success of children from different social class and cultural groups*. Unpublished doctoral dissertation, University of Denver.

Gill, M. (Ed.). (1967). *The collected papers of David Rapaport*. New York: Basic Books.

Glass, C. R., & Arnkoff, D. B. (1982). Think cognitively: Selected issues in cognitive assessment and therapy. In P. C. Kendall (Ed.), *Advances in cognitive-behavioral research and therapy* (Vol 1, pp. 36–75). New York: Academic Press.

Goldfried, M. R. (1980). Psychotherapy as coping skills training. In M. J. Mahoney (Ed.), *Psychotherapy process: Current issues and future directions* (pp. 89–119). New York: Plenum Press.

Golomb, C. (1979). Pretense play: A cognitive perspective. In N. R. Smith & M. B. Franklin (Eds.), *Symbolic functioning in childhood* (pp. 101–116). Hillsdale, NJ: Lawrence Erlbaum.

Gruber, H. E., Hammond, K. R., & Jesser, R. (Eds.). (1957). *Contemporary approaches to cognition*. Cambridge, MA: Harvard University Press.

Guidano, V. F., & Liotti, G. (1983). *Cognitive processes and emotional disorders: A structural approach to psychotherapy*. New York: Guilford Press.

Gunnoe, C. (1975). *The evaluation of a structure-based and a skilled-based intervention program for at risk four and five-year old children*. Unpublished doctoral dissertation. Harvard University.

Guthrie, G. D. (1967). Changes in cognitive functioning under stress: A study of plasticity in cognitive controls. (Doctoral dissertation, Clark University, 1967). *Dissertation Abstracts International, 28*, 2125B.

Holt, R. R. (1964). The emergence of cognitive psychology. *Journal of American Psychoanalytic Association, 12*, 650–665.

Holt, R. R. (1976). Drive or wish? A reconsideration of the psychoanalytic theory of motivation. *Psychological Issues, 9* (36), 158–198.

Horowitz, M. J. (1978). *Image formation and cognition* (2nd ed.). New York: Appleton-Century-Crofts.

Kagan, J. (1981). *The second year: The emergence of self-awareness*. Cambridge, MA: Harvard University Press.

Kendall, P. C. (1981). Cognitive-behavioral interventions with children. In B. Lahey & A. E. Kardin (Eds.), *Advances in child clinical psychology* (pp. 53–87). New York: Plenum Press.

Kendall, P. C. (1984). Social cognition and problem solving: A developmental and child-clinical interface. In B. Gholson & T. Rosenthal (Eds.), *Applications of cognitive-developmental theory* (pp. 115–148). New York: Academic Press.

Kendall, P. C., & Hollon, S. D. (1979). *Cognitive-behavioral intervention: Theory, research and procedures.* New York: Academic Press.

Kendall, P. C., & Wilcox, L. E. (1980). Cognitive-behavioral treatment of impulsivity: Concrete versus conceptual training in non-self-controlled problem children. *Journal of Consulting and Clinical Psychology, 48,* 80–91.

Kihlstrom, J. F., & Nasby, W. (1981). Cognitive tasks in clinical assessment: An exercise in applied psychology. In P. C. Kendall & S. D. Hollon (Eds.), *Assessment strategies for cognitive-behavioral interventions* (pp. 287–317). New York: Academic Press.

Klein, G. S. (1951). The personal world through perception. In R. R. Blake & G. V. Ramsey (Eds.), *Perception: An approach to personality* (pp. 328–355). New York: Ronald Press.

Klein, G. S. (1954). Need and regulation. In M. R. Jones (Ed.), *Nebraska symposium on motivation* (Vol. 2, pp. 224–274). Lincoln: University of Nebraska Press.

Klein, G. S. (1970). *Perception, motives and personality.* New York: Knopf.

Klein, G. S., & Schlesinger, H. J. (1949). Where is the perceiver in perceptual theory? *Journal of Personality, 18,* 32–47.

Kogan, N. (1976). *Cognitive styles in infancy and early childhood.* Hillsdale, NJ: Lawrence Erlbaum.

Lazarus, R. S. (1980). Cognitive behavior therapy as psychodynamics revisited. In M. J. Mahoney (Ed.), *Psychotherapy process: Current issues and future directions* (pp. 121–126). New York: Plenum Press.

Leuner, H., Horn, G., & Klessmann, E. (1983). *Guided affective imagery with children and adolescents.* New York: Plenum Press.

Magnusson, D. (1981). *Toward a psychology of situations.* Hillsdale, NJ: Lawrence Erlbaum.

Mahoney, M. J. (1977). Reflections on the cognitive learning trend in psychotherapy. *American Psychologist, 32,* 5–13.

Mahoney, M. J. (Ed.). (1980). *Psychotherapy process: Current issues and future directions.* New York: Plenum Press.

Mahoney, M. J., & Arnkoff, D. B. (1978). Cognitive and self-control therapies. In S. Garfield & A. Bergin (Eds.), *Handbook of psychotherapy and behavior change* (2nd ed., pp. 689–722). New York: Wiley.

Marmor, M., & Woods, S. M. (Eds.). (1980). *The interface between psychodynamic and behavioral therapies.* New York: Plenum Press.

Meichenbaum, D. (1977). *Cognitive-behavior modification: An integrative approach.* New York: Plenum Press.

Mounoud, P. (1982). Revolutionary periods in early development. In T. G. Bever (Ed.), *Regressions in mental development* (pp. 119–132). Hillsdale, NJ: Lawrence Erlbaum.

Ortony, A. (1975). Why metaphors are necessary and not just nice. *Educational Review, 25,* 45–53.

Ortony, A. (Ed.). (1979). *Metaphor and thought.* New York: Cambridge University Press.

Ortony, A., Reynolds, R. E., & Arter, J. A. (1978). Metaphors: Theoretical and empirical research. *Psychological Bulletin, 85,* 919–943.

Paivio, A. (1971). *Imagery and verbal processes.* New York: Holt.

Piaget, J. (1977). The role of action in the development of thinking. In W. F. Overton & J. M. Gallagher (Eds.), *Knowledge and development* (Vol. 1, pp. 17–42). New York: Plenum Press.

Rees, K. (1978). The child's understanding of the past. *Psychoanalytic Study of the Child, 33,* 237–259.

Reese, H. W., & Overton, W. F. (1970). Models of development and theories of development. In L. R. Goulet & P. B. Baltes (Eds.), *Life-span developmental psychology* (pp. 116–149). New York: Academic Press.

Ritvo, S. (1978). The psychoanalytic process in childhood. *Psychoanalytic Study of the Child, 33,* 295–305.

Sander, L. W. (1962). Issues in early mother-child interaction. *Journal of American Academy of Child Psychiatry, 1*, 141–166.

Sander, L. W. (1964). Adaptive relationships in early mother-child interaction. *Journal of American Academy of Child Psychiatry, 3*, 231–264.

Sander, L. W. (1976). Infant and caretaking environment. In E. J. Anthony (Ed.), *Explorations in child psychiatry*. New York: Plenum Press.

Santostefano, S. (1967). *Training in attention and concentration: A program of cognitive development for children*. Philadelphia: Educational Research Associates.

Santostefano, S. (1969a, December). *Clinical education and psychoanalytic cognitive theory: A structure-oriented approach to assessing and treating cognitive disabilities in children*. Paper presented at the meeting of the American Association of the Advancement of Science, Chicago, IL.

Santostefano, S. (1969b). Cognitive controls versus cognitive styles: An approach to diagnosing and treating cognitive disabilities in children. *Seminars in Psychiatry, 1*, 291–317.

Santostefano, S. (1977a). Action, fantasy, and language: Developmental levels of ego organization in communicating drives and affects. In N. Freedman & S. Grand (Eds.), *Communicative structures and psychic structures* (pp. 331–354). New York: Plenum Press.

Santostefano, S. (1977b). New views of motivation and cognition in psychoanalytic theory: The horse (id) and rider (ego) revisited. *McLean Hospital Journal, 2*, 48–64.

Santostefano, S. (1978). *A biodevelopmental approach to clinical child psychology: Cognitive controls and cognitive control therapy*. New York: Wiley.

Santostefano, S. (1980). Cognition in personality and the treatment process: A psychoanalytic view. *Psychoanalytic Study of the Child, 35*, 41–66.

Santostefano, S. (1984). Cognitive control therapy with children: Rationale and technique. *Psychotherapy, 21*, 76–91.

Santostefano, S. (in press a). Cognitive controls, metaphors and contexts: An approach to cognition and emotion. In D. Bearison & H. Zimiles (Eds.), *Thinking and emotions*.

Santostefano, S. (in press b). Metaphor: An integration of action, fantasy, and language in development. *Imagination, Cognition, and Personality*.

Santostefano, S., & Rieder, C. (1984). Cognitive controls and aggression in children: The concept of cognitive-affective balance. *Journal of Consulting and Clinical Psychology, 52*, 46–56.

Shapiro, I. F. (1972). Cognitive controls and adaptation in children (Doctoral dissertation, Boston College, 1972). *Dissertation Abstracts International, 33*, 1780B.

Smith, N. R., & Franklin, M. B. (Eds.). (1979). *Symbolic functioning in childhood*. Hillsdale, NJ: Lawrence Erlbaum.

Sollod, R. N., & Wachtell, P. L. (1980). A structural and transactional approach to cognition in clinical problems. In M. J. Mahoney (Ed.), *Psychotherapy process: Current issues and future directions* (pp. 1–27). New York: Plenum Press.

Szasz, T. S. (1967). Behavior therapy and psychoanalysis. *Medical Opinion Review, 2*, 24–29.

Wachtel, P. L. (1977). *Psychoanalysis and behavior therapy: Toward an integration*. New York: Basic Books.

Wachtel, P. L. (Ed.). (1982). *Resistance: Psychodynamic and behavioral approaches*. New York: Plenum Press.

Weiner, M. L. (1975). *The cognitive unconscious: A Piagetian approach to psychotherapy*. New York: International Psychological Press.

Wertlieb, D. L. (1979). *Cognitive organization, regulations of aggression and learning disorders in boys*. Unpublished doctoral dissertation, Boston University.

Winner, E., Wapner, W., Cicone, M., & Gardner, H. (1979). Measures of metaphor. *New Directions for Child Development, 6*, 67–75.

Wolf, D., & Gardner, H. (1979). Style and sequence in early symbolic play. In N. R. Smith & M. B. Franklin (Eds.), *Symbolic functioning in childhood* (pp. 117–138). Hillsdale, NJ: Lawrence Erlbaum.

Wolff, P. H. (1960). The developmental psychologies of Jean Piaget and psychoanalysis. *Psychological Issues* (5). New York: International Universities Press.

Zimmerman, B. J. (1983). Social learning theory: A contextualist account of cognitive functioning. In C. J. Brainerd (Ed.), *Recent advances in cognitive-developmental theory* (pp. 1–50). New York: Springer-Verlag.

Author Index

Subject Index

243

Cognitive rigidity (*continued*)
    tion, Cognitive control therapy
    programs
Cognitive revolution, xiii, xiv, 6
Cognitive structuring, 5, 226
  in adaptation to environments,
    metaphor, emotions, 18–20, 27,
    46
  and the concept of stimulus nutri-
    ment, 45–46
    see also Stimulus nutriment
  and delay, 47, 94, 159
  and demonstration by therapist,
    see Modeling, technique of
  in development, 18–20
  of nonverbal vs verbal behaviors,
    xv, 16
  of pathological cognitive orienta-
    tions, techniques in
    with aggressive disorders,
      197–201
    with excessive shifts in cognitive
      orientation, 201–204
    with inner orientations, 195–197
    with outer orientations, 192–194
    see also Cognitive control
      therapy programs
  of pathological metaphors, 205–210
    see also Metaphor
  and rehearsing, see Modeling,
    technique of
  and sensori-motor activity, see
    Cognitive control therapy
    programs
  and stimulus complexity, 31, 47
    see also Cognitive control
      therapy, graded tasks, and
      materials used in, Stimulus
      nutriment, concept of
Conflict, 5, 9, 31–33, 71, 77
  see also Cognitive control therapy
    and conflict free information,
    Cognitive coordination,
    pathological

Delay, development of, 36, 47
  see also Cognitive control therapy,
    Cognitive functions addressed

    by programs
Desensitization, see Cognitive control
    therapy, graded tasks in
Developmental deviations, 9, 36
Developmental principles
  and cognition, 7, 9, 34–35, 46
  and cognitive control therapy, xv,
    47, 51–52
    see also Cognitive control
      therapy programs
  and cognitive-behavior therapy, 7–8
  and cognitive controls, 13, 14, 17,
    31–33
Differentiation of behavior, 24
  see also Cognitive differentiation,
    Cognitive structuring
Directed fantasy, technique of, 64,
    65–68, 231–232
  and guided affective imagery
    technique, compared, 231
  see also Cognitive control therapy
    with body ego-tempo regula-
    tion control, with equivalence
    range control, with field ar-
    ticulation control, with focal
    attention control, with leveling-
    sharpening control

Ego ideal, 25, 27, 29–30, 34, 72
  in cognitive control therapy, 47, 54,
    63, 67–68
  in cognitive development, 44, 46
  in development of symbolic func-
    tioning, 44
  in pathological cognitive orienta-
    tion, 35–36
  in the technique of directed fan-
    tasy, 66–67
Emotions, cognitive control of, 40,
    79–80
  see also Cognition and emotions,
    Cognitive controls and
    emotions
Environment, 26
  and cognitive control functioning,
    study in, 213
  coping with, in cognitive control
    therapy, 5

in cognitive-behavioral therapy, 230
definition of, 70
managing in cognitive control
    therapy, 73–75, 78–80, 230
play in child as, 80
play in therapist as, 81
play as means of resolving, 81
see also Cognitive control therapy
    programs, transference and
    resistance
Role-perspective taking, 6
    in cognitive control therapy, see
    Cognitive control therapy
    programs

Schizophrenia, 9
Self-observation in therapy, see
    Observing ego
Self-instruction therapy, 226, 228, 231
Self statements, xiv, 6, 7
    in cognitive behavior therapy, 6, 7
    in cognitive control therapy, xv, 5,
    10, 210
    in cognitive control theory, 16
Standards of behavior, see Ego ideal
Stimulus nutriment, concept of, 45
    and cognitive differentiation, 45–46
    developmental course, abnormal,
    46
    developmental course, normal, 45
    and the need for increasingly
    complex information, 45, 48
    and the technique of graded tasks,
    45, 48
Symbolic functioning, xiv, 10,
    226–227
    in cognitive control therapy, 10, 33,

46–48
    see also Cognitive control
    therapy programs
    cognitive prerequisites for, 44
    definition of, 43
    development of, 41–42, 43–46
    evaluation of, in cognitive control
    therapy, 68–70
    and metaphor construction, com-
    pared with, 22, 43
    preverbal forms, 8, 9, 41–42
    and the process of therapy, xv, 8,
    46, 68–70
    in psychotherapy, xiv
    verbal forms of, 8
Symbols, in psychotherapy, see
    Symbolic functioning

Transference, process of, 40, 65, 70,
    230
    in cognitive-behavior therapy, 230
    in cognitive control therapy, xv,
    71–80, 230
    definition of, 70
    example of, 75–78
    managing, in cognitive control
    therapy, 70–75, 78–80
Type I pathological cognitive orienta-
    tion, see Cognitive coordina-
    tion, pathological
Type II pathological cognitive orien-
    tation, see Cognitive coordina-
    tion, pathological

Unconscious, see Cognition, Cog-
    nitive controls, Cognitive con-
    trol therapy, Metaphor

About the Author

Dr. Sebastiano Santostefano is Director, Department of Child Psychology and Psychoeducation, Hall-Mercer Children's Center of McLean Hospital as well as Associate Professor of Psychology, Department of Psychiatry of the Harvard Medical School. He is also Director of Cognitive Therapy and Diagnostic Service, Wellesley, Massachusetts and a member of the teaching faculty of the Boston Psychoanalytic Institute. In 1957 Dr. Santostefano received the Ph.D. degree in clinical psychology from the Pennsylvania State University and in 1972 was graduated in adult and child psychoanalysis by the Boston Psychoanalytic Institute. He has held faculty positions at the University of Colorado School of Medicine, Clark University, and Boston University School of Medicine. In addition to practicing clinical psychology and psychoanalysis, Dr. Santostefano has been an active investigator in the area of cognition in personality development and adaptation. His essay, "Cognition in Personality and the Treatment Process," published by the *Psychoanalytic Study of the Child* in 1980 was awarded the Felix and Helene Deutsch prize by the Boston Psychoanalytic Society, and the Harold S. Rosenberg Memorial prize by the San Francisco Psychoanalytic Society. Dr. Santostefano is the author of numerous articles and of *A Biodevelopmental Approach to Clinical Child Psychology: Cognitive Controls and Cognitive Control Therapy*, published by Wiley in 1978.

Pergamon Psychology Practitioner Guidebook Series

Editors:
Arnold P. Goldstein, Syracuse University
Leonard Krasner, SUNY at Stony Brook
Sol L. Garfield, Washington University

Edward B. Blanchard & Frank Andrasik – *MANAGEMENT OF CHRONIC HEADACHES: A Psychological Approach*

Philip H. Bornstein & Marcy T. Bornstein – *MARITAL THERAPY: A Behavioral-Communications Approach*

Karen S. Calhoun & Beverly M. Atkeson – *TREATMENT OF VICTIMS OF SEXUAL ASSAULT*

Richard F. Dangel & Richard A. Polster – *TEACHING CHILD MANAGEMENT SKILLS*

Eva L. Feindler & Randolph B. Ecton – *ADOLESCENT ANGER CONTROL: Cognitive-Behavioral Techniques*

Paul Karoly & Mark P. Jensen – *CLINICAL PAIN ASSESSMENT*

Donald Meichenbaum – *STRESS INOCULATION TRAINING*

Michael T. Nietzel & Ronald C. Dillehay – *PSYCHOLOGICAL CONSULTATION IN THE COURTROOM*

Elsie M. Pinkston & Nathan L. Linsk – *CARE OF THE ELDERLY: A Family Approach*

Alice W. Pope, Susan M. McHale & W. Edward Craighead – *SELF-ESTEEM ENHANCEMENT WITH CHILDREN AND ADOLESCENTS*

Raymond G. Romanczyk – *CLINICAL UTILIZATION OF MICRO-COMPUTER TECHNOLOGY*

Sebastiano Santostefano – *COGNITIVE CONTROL THERAPY WITH CHILDREN AND ADOLESCENTS*

Lillie Weiss, Melanie Katzman & Sharlene Wolchik – *TREATING BULIMIA: A Psychoeducational Approach*

Elizabeth Yost, Larry E. Beutler, Anne Corbishley & James Allender – *GROUP COGNITIVE THERAPY: A Treatment Method for the Depressed Elderly*